ADVENTURE G⬤LF™

FROM FAIRWAYS TO FUN DAYS—ATTRACTIONS ON AND OFF THE WORLD'S MOST REMARKABLE GOLF COURSES

pilot guides™
www.pilotguides.com

The Globe Pequot Press

GUILFORD, CONNECTICUT

To buy books in quantity for corporate use
or incentives, call **(800) 962–0973, ext. 4551,**
or e-mail **premiums@GlobePequot.com.**

Text design by Bill Brown

Library of Congress Cataloging-in-Publication Data

Cross, Ian.
    Adventure golf : from fairways to fun days attractions on and off the world's most remarkable golf courses / Ian Cross.— 1st ed.
        p. cm.
    ISBN 0-7627-3790-5
    1. Golf. 2. Golf courses. I. Title.
    GV965.C77 2005
    796.352'06'8—dc22   2005011422

Printed in China
First Edition/First Printing

The prices and rates listed in this guidebook were confirmed at press time. We recommend, however, that you contact establishments before traveling to obtain current information.

CONTENTS

INTRODUCTION iv

SCOTLAND 1
  Royal Dornoch 10
  Gleneagles King's Course 14
  St. Andrews Old Course 18
  Musselburgh Old Course 22
  Lundin Ladies Golf Club 24
  Other Recommended Golf Courses 26
  Between the Rounds Attractions 28

SOUTH AFRICA 35
  Pearl Valley 46
  Soweto Country Club 50
  Gary Player Course, Sun City 54
  Hans Merensky 60
  Other Recommended Golf Courses 66
  Between the Rounds Attractions 70

UNITED ARAB EMIRATES 77
  Nad Al Sheba 86
  Dubai Creek 88
  Emirates Golf Club 92
  Dubai Country Club 98
  Other Recommended Golf Courses 102
  Between the Rounds Attractions 104

JAPAN 111
  Ishioka 122
  Gotemba 124
  Fuji Course, Kawana 128
  Phoenix Seagaia 132
  Other Recommended Golf Courses 136
  Between the Rounds Attractions 138

SOUTHERN CALIFORNIA 147
  Rancho Park 156
  Sandpiper 160
  PGA West, La Quinta 164
  Ranch Course, Alisal 170
  Other Recommended Golf Courses 174
  Between the Rounds Attractions 176

INDEX 182

ABOUT PILOT PRODUCTIONS . . . 184

INTRODUCTION

Golf has been one of the fastest-growing participation sports in the last century. From its supposed origins more than five hundred years ago when a shepherd boy first knocked a stone into a crevasse with his crook, the game of *gowf* in Scotland remained largely unknown until the mid-nineteenth century. The advent of the industrial revolution, the steady growth of world trade, and the gradual increase in wealth and leisure time were the catalysts needed to expand the sport throughout Britain and into North America. Now it is played in the savannahs of Africa, the deserts of Arabia, and the paddy fields of Asia—and the signs are that it is poised to storm central and eastern Europe.

Anyone, professionals included, who has stood on the first tee of a championship course with a driver in hand, an enormous expanse of water, heather, or sand directly ahead, and butterflies in the pit of the stomach, will understand why every single game of golf is an adventure. As international travel becomes cheaper and more accessible, particularly when heading to developing countries, adventure is closer to hand than ever before.

Now there are so many amazing golf holes around the world that provide challenges and adventures for players that it can be difficult to choose between them. Golf television channels

Ian Cross, St. Andrews Old Course, Scotland

and bookstores are awash with programs and books that detail every championship course (and many others) in the world. Information is just a mouse click away as most clubs now have their own Web sites. Paradoxically, the problem for the golfer is data overload: not just establishing where the most interesting and original golf courses are, but whether the locality can offer the traveler as much off the course as on.

The inspiration for producing the *Adventure Golf* television show came from the golfing minibreaks that I take—on my own or with a few friends—to escape from the cut-and-thrust of the urban-executive working week. I'm luckier than most as my day job is managing the team who produces the renowned adventure travel series *Globe Trekker*, so the wonders of the world are on my LCD screen every day. Whenever I can sneak a few days away, I head to northern France, Ireland, or Portugal. Instead of the marathon mantra of *thirty-six holes per day* (that kind of regime is exactly what I am trying to get away from!), I opt for a more leisurely daily round, picking just the most interesting and unusual courses, then I see what other great local attractions I can fit in between the rounds. Did you know St. Andrews, with its royal-endorsed university and ruined castle, is a great place to spend the afternoon? Or that the Phoenix Course in

Miyazaki, Japan, is part of an awesome resort with the biggest indoor water park in the world? Golf for the traveler today should be about much more than just the sport itself. Thus the *Adventure Golf* series was born. Our objective was to have fun playing golf in the greatest places in the world—not just on the greatest courses, but also on some of the most original ones. *Adventure Golf* was originally something of a vanity project to celebrate my favorite sport, but the uptake from viewers and television networks around the world has been phenomenal. Clearly a few golfers out there wanted more from their golfing holidays and shared our philosophy.

So what is an adventure golfer? It is someone who wants to play the best courses imaginable, is not afraid to take on the challenge of playing a menacingly tricky course, and wants to explore the adventures to be had off the greens as well. This person is curious to explore the region in addition to playing golf. An adventure golfer would take an aerial tour of the course in a glider then drive to a nearby vineyard to sample a delicious vintage rather than downing a beer at the nineteenth hole. He (or she) is a golf explorer.

Ten years ago the standard traveling golfer, almost exclusively, was male. As part of a group of eight or more, he would visit only

championship courses in one area, play thirty-six holes per day for a whole week, drink far too much, and sleep very little— then suffer for it. Nowadays the traveling golfer, who is as likely to be a she as a he, may travel and play golf with a partner or friends, or may well bring the kids and combine a golf break with a host of other activities. This is

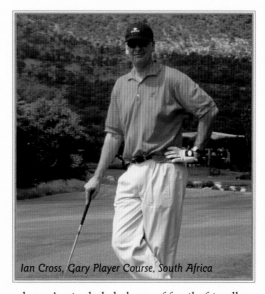
Ian Cross, Gary Player Course, South Africa

why we've included plenty of family-friendly attractions and a seven-day holiday itinerary combining superb golf with superb attractions. Plus we've added an executive break if you can only squeeze in four days or so.

This book details in depth the destinations visited in the first five episodes of American Public Television's *Adventure Golf* series.

We've covered some courses and resorts rich in history, others simply not to be missed, and others plainly bizarre. For each chapter you'll find an introduction to golf in the country, handy travel information, a detailed fact file on the courses featured in the show, tourist attractions, and a list of other great courses in the country. We hope the detailed graphics and photos of the best holes and courses, along with playing tips, will give you a sense of how it feels to be there.

Join us in Scotland, the home of golf, for classic links and historical outings. In South Africa combine golf with an animal safari (and a few stark lessons on apartheid). There is plenty of fun to be had in the desert of the United Arab Emirates, and Japan, with its modern golf technology, has futuristic courses in ancient landscapes. Back in California visit the desert oasis of Palm Springs. I hope this book will be a successful starting point to your new vocation as an adventure golfer.

Ian C

Ian Cross

P.S. I'd like to thank my wife, Atussa, and my children, Louis and Inès, for putting up with my golf obsession!

scotland

About Scotland

Although visitors are drawn to Scotland by the promise of its natural beauty, they are often shocked by just how stunning and varied its landscape actually is. Its forbidding mountain ranges, desolately beautiful moorlands, pastoral sandy beaches, engaging islands, and rolling hills make it a wonderland for those who love the outdoors. Add to that the Gaelic identity that sets the Scots apart from the English and gave rise to centuries of fascinating history of altercation between the nations, and you have more history and culture than you can hope to experience in only one visit.

Activities and Attractions

Hill Walking and Mountain Climbing: Scotland doesn't have Mount Everest, but it does have a 284 munros, named by Sir Hugh Munre in 1891 to classify any mountain 3,000 feet or higher. Climbing a munro means you've bagged it; there are lots of obsessive munro baggers, and some have bagged them all, the record being fifty-one days for the lot. On a leisure trip expect to bag about seven average-size munros a day. Snowcapped Ben Nevis, at approximately 4,500 feet high, is the highest munro, yet it is still a modest climb that can be tackled by the whole family in about eight hours. The best time for walking is late May to mid-September for the mountains, whereas late April to early October is fine for lower climbs.

Lochs and Fishing: Scotland offers great game fishing, coarse angling, and even sea fishing. You'll find salmon, trout, pike, arctic char, and many others to fish for in the streams, rivers, lochs, and firths, with Loch Lomond being the most popular spot. There's no season for coarse fishing or sea angling; check local details for salmon and trout fishing. You don't need a license to fish, but because most land and waters are privately owned, you'll need to buy a permit for about £15 (US$25).

Cycling: Cycling is an increasingly popular pastime in Scotland. Intrepid cyclists will enjoy the more wild and remote areas of northwest Scotland; central and southern Scotland offer beautiful routes through glens, along lochs, and over hills. There are plenty of operators renting bikes in the summer season for between £10 (US$18) for a day to £50 (US$90) for a week's rental.

Castles: Scotland is overflowing with centuries-old romantic castles to visit. The best are Edinburgh's former royal residence, sitting astride an extinct volcano overlooking the city; Blair Castle, an impressive whitewashed, turreted castle that represented baronial Scotland at its best; Stirling Castle, a medieval gem and favored seat of the Stuart kings; and Glamis Castle, where William Shakespeare set his play Macbeth.

History of Golf in Scotland

The true origins of the ancient game of *gowf* (the original British name based on the Gaelic pronunciation) are shrouded in mystery. Numerous theories have been proposed, from a Roman pastime (paganica) to the tale of the bored shepherd boy who knocked a stone into a rabbit hole with his crook.

St. Andrews

scotland

3

Golf has been played in Scotland for at least 500 years. The first official record of the game's existence was in 1457 when James II famously—and unsuccessfully—attempted to ban the game by Act of Parliament because his estate employees were playing golf instead of laboring.

The Royal and Ancient Golf Club (R&A), responsible for the international rules of the game, was formed in St. Andrews in 1754 and still oversees the game (outside of the United States) and runs the Open Championship. The courses of east Scotland are a shrine to centuries of golfing history and a period that laid the foundation for one of the few "gentlemen" games that still exists.

Gleneagles King's Course, third green (left) and seventeenth (above)

4

When to Go and What to Bring

Scotland's high tourism season is from late June to early September, when the rainfall is at its lowest and temperatures peak around a modest 60 degrees Fahrenheit.

The Scottish golfing season is generally regarded to be from April to September, but apart from snow closing some of the Highland courses, golf is playable all year round. Remember that many Scottish courses are located by the sea, so the golf is always likely to be windy. The main championship courses (St. Andrews, Gleneagles, and Carnoustie) host a stream of tournaments from the Open to major Senior and European Tour events throughout the season, so early booking of green fees there is essential to avoid disappointment. Other courses will be pleased to see you at any time of year, and booking long in advance is not necessary.

The Scottish climate will usually deliver gale-force winds, rain, sleet, and glorious warm sunshine all in the time it takes to play one round of golf, so be prepared for anything. Thick sweaters, rain gear, and a flask of whiskey in the bag are all wise precautions.

Costs

Compared with similar courses around the world, green fees are generally reasonable. Championship courses cost approximately £100 (US$180); it's as little as £10 (US$18) to play some of the more remote Highland courses. Average green fees are between £30 (US$50) and £40 (US$70).

Almost all courses will rent clubs to visitors for a modest charge, but apart from the larger resort or championship courses, you probably won't get much in the way of modern club technology. On some of the very old courses you can rent the odd "mashie niblick" (7-iron) and see just how difficult *gowf* was two centuries ago.

Hotels

Accommodation in Scotland is universally expensive, with prices varying substantially. They will often drop outside of high season (May to September). Budget hotels cost around £50 (US$80) per person per night, whereas quality hotels may reach or exceed £100 (US$180). Expect extremes of expense and luxury in the golfing resorts—rooms at Gleneagles are typically £450 (US$900) per night.

Gleneagles Hotel

Travel

Airports: Scotland's main airports are in Edinburgh (EDI), Glasgow (GLA), Dundee (DND), Aberdeen (ABZ), Inverness (INV), and Kirkwall (KOI). All offer direct flights from London and some European cities. Flights from North America fly to Edinburgh or Glasgow, often changing in London. All UK domestic flights and those from Scotland to places in the European Union attract a £10 (US$18) departure tax and £20 (US$35) to other destinations. There are now many no-frills budget airlines that fly from the major European cities to Glasgow and Edinburgh.

Car Rental: Rental is pretty expensive, and it makes sense to find a fly-drive deal in your home country, as small cars start from £150 (US$250) per week. Principal companies include Avis, Europcar, and Budget. Main roads into Scotland from England are busy but quick: Expect to see fewer cars, fewer motorways, and increasingly smaller, winding roads the farther north you go. Travel can be slow going, so don't count on covering distances as if you were using the freeway. Gasoline prices in the United Kingdom (UK) are among the most expensive in Europe and can be up to three times the price in the United States. Don't be deceived by pump prices. They're marked up in liters, not gallons, there being just less than four liters to the U.S. gallon.

Regions and Golfing

Southwest: There are many natural wonders in the little-visited Southwest of Scotland. In the western Galloway Forest Park, the Southern Uplands are at their most dramatic, with craggy peaks higher than 2,000 feet and unforgiving moorland—all perfect for atmospheric walking. Dumfries is the gateway town to the west; past here are the moving remains of Caerlaverock Castle on the Solway Coast. On the Ayrshire coast, a bucolic location with lovely sandy beaches, discover the legacy of Robert Burns in Alloway, the poet's birthplace.

Old hickory clubs

Prestwick is the second home of golf. Other awesome links courses, like Turnberry's Ailsa and Royal Troon, can be found here as well. Many courses are situated along the vast stretches of coastline, where views of the islands and the Atlantic rollers are breathtaking and make a wonderful backdrop for a game. Golfers who prefer to seek off-the-beaten-track courses will find dozens of small villages, even more unsung courses, and a warm welcome from a people who have understood and loved the game for centuries.

Southeast: The natural entrance to the Southeast is through Edinburgh, Scotland's world-class capital city. Sitting atop an extinct volcano, the city is dominated by a fabulous castle that is the centerpiece of its Hogmanay New Year celebrations, as well as its military tattoo during the Edinburgh Festival in August. The city is a cosmopolitan and cultured place with two distinctive parts.

The suggested itinerary is for active 15-hour days. If you prefer a more leisurely trip, pick and choose your favorite activities.

Day 1: Fly from London to Inverness (INV), or drive north from Edinburgh (EDI) or Glasgow (GLA) international airports. From Inverness take the A9 north to Dornoch on the east coast, a one-hour, 43-mile drive around the scenic Moray Firth. Stay the night in the sleepy village of Dornoch.

Day 2: A.M. Play Royal Dornoch. Lunch at the pretty Castle Hotel.
P.M. Drive toward Loch Ness to spot the infamous sea monster. Take the A9 south, and turn off toward Dingwalls onto the A862. Follow the signs to Drumnadrochit and Fort William on the A82, a ninety-minute, 64-mile journey. Enjoy a picnic tea by the loch and watch the sun start to set, or play a round at the Carnegie Club in Skibo Castle, Dornoch. There are few weekday tee times at this super-rich members club—so book in advance.

Begin the three-hour drive south toward Gleneagles, heading down the A82 and A9 toward Perth. Any hotel en route will make a convenient and scenic place to stay, such as in the villages of Newtonmore, Kingussie, and Dalwhinnie by the Grampian Mountains.

Day 3: A.M. Driving south on the A9, stop off en route to tour and buy a few bottles at the Edradour whiskey distiller at Pitlochry. Then it's a one-hour, 40-mile drive to Gleneagles. Turn off on the A823 for Crieff. To fit in two rounds, head straight to Gleneagles.

There are three eighteen-hole courses and one nine-hole course to choose from.
P.M. Play a round at Gleneagles. The King's Course is highly recommended. If you are feeling lavish, spend the night here at one of the most luxurious golf resorts in the world.

Stirling Castle

Day 4: A.M. Enjoy the world-class facilities of Gleneagles: pool, gym, sauna, or—for the adventurous—falconry, clay-pigeon shooting, or four-wheel driving. Or enjoy another game on one of the four courses.
P.M. Drive to St. Andrews, a one-hour, 43-mile drive east. To avoid winding roads take the A9 and A90 to Dundee, then follow the coastline road south. If arriving before 2:00 P.M., enter the ballot to play St. Andrews Old Course; if running late, phone ahead to enter. By late afternoon you'll miss the crowds to tour the sixteenth-century St. Andrews Castle. Alternatively, play one of the six courses at St. Andrews. Spend the night in this quaint and lively historic university town.

Day 5: A.M. If selected in the ballot, play St. Andrews Old Course. Otherwise, play one of the other five courses at St. Andrews, and swing by the Golf Museum. Lunch in St. Andrews.
P.M. Drive west to Stirling along the A91, turning onto the A9 at Causewayhead Roundabout, a one-hour, 50-mile trip. Visit Stirling Castle to discover the history of Braveheart, or play a round at Bruntsfield Links, a parklands course in the suburbs of Edinburgh, a fifty-minute, 38-mile drive from St. Andrews. Spend the night, exploring the medieval winding streets and many cosmopolitan bars and restaurants of Edinburgh's Old Town.

Day 6: Take the day off from traveling and golfing, and explore the historic city of Edinburgh, its superb royal castle, the Royal Yacht *Britannia* in Leith, cathedrals, architecture, and shops. If, however, you're itching for another round, head out to East Lothian—a mecca for golf courses just half an hour's drive east on the A1. Return to Edinburgh and after dinner take a candlelit ghost tour of the city's catacombs.

Day 7: A.M. Drive to East Lothian, and take your pick from numerous world-class links and parklands courses. Spend your last day going golf crazy with one or two games at North Berwick, Musselburgh, or Gullane.
P.M. Head back to Edinburgh airport (EDI).

As an optional extra day, take a day trip by train to the cultural city of Glasgow to explore its superb Rennie Macintosh architecture and museums. Fly home from its international airport (GLA).

FIVE-DAY EXECUTIVE STRESS BUSTER

Day 1: Fly into Inverness (INV) in the north of Scotland. Rent a car, and from Inverness take the A9 north to Dornoch on the east coast, a one-hour, 43-mile drive around the scenic Moray Firth.

Day 2: A.M. Play Royal Dornoch. Lunch at the pretty Castle Hotel.
P.M. Begin the three-hour drive south toward Gleneagles. Driving south on the A9, stop off en route to tour and taste (if you're not the driver) the Edradour whiskey distillery at Pitlochry. Then it's a one-hour, 40-mile drive to Gleneagles. Turn off on the A823 for Crieff. You may get there in time for nine holes on the Wee Course. Spend the night here at one of the most luxurious golf resorts in the world.

Day 3: A.M. Play a round at Gleneagles. The King's Course is highly recommended.
P.M. Enjoy the world-class facilities of Gleneagles—pool, gym, sauna, or—for the adventurous—falconry, clay-pigeon shooting, or four-wheel driving. Or enjoy another game on one of its four courses.

Day 4: A.M. Drive to St. Andrews, a one-hour, 43-mile drive east. To avoid winding roads take the A9 and A90 to Dundee then follow the coastline road south. Phone the day before to enter the ballot to play St. Andrews Old Course. If selected, play St. Andrews Old Course.
P.M. After your game, by late afternoon, you'll miss the crowds to tour the sixteenth-century St. Andrews Castle. Alternatively, play a second round at one of the other five courses at St. Andrews. Spend the night in this quaint and lively historic university town.

Day 5: A.M. Take a 75-mile drive south along minor roads to Gullane in East Lothian to play this classic championship course. Other recommended courses here are North Berwick or Musselburgh.
P.M. It's a fifty-minute, 38-mile drive west on the A1 to Edinburgh. Spend the remains of the day exploring this historic city with its superb royal castle, the Royal Yacht *Britannia* in Leith, cathedrals, architecture, and shops. Head to Edinburgh Airport (EDI) to fly home.

Gleneagles countryside

Royal Dornoch Golf Club

The New Town is laid out along strictly Enlightenment lines. The Old Town is more medieval, with winding alleys and tightly packed streets with hundreds of lively pubs, restaurants, and shops. Southern Scotland is dominated by the beautiful Southern Uplands of hills and dark lochs. There are many delightful old towns in the Scottish Borders, and the Merse Basin has a clutch of grand stately homes, including Floors Castle, Manderston, and Mellerstain House.

Edinburgh is surrounded by sixteen golf courses, all within a few square miles of the city, and one is located in the city center itself. Near the historic Heartlands region, the Southeast boasts a fine variety of renowned historical links and inland and parkland courses, including Musselburgh, Muirfield, and North Berwick. Farther south in the Scottish Borders region, there are more conventional UK courses, including the Roxburghe and Cardrona, two of the most testing parkland and woods courses, both part of luxurious country clubs.

Central Region: Glasgow's reputation languished in the doldrums for decades, but it is now deservedly a growing weekend-break destination. The city has some fantastic museums and galleries, especially the Burrell Collection of art and antiquities. Its architecture is among Britain's most striking, from the restored eighteenth-century warehouses to the art nouveau of architect Rennie Mackintosh. A city championing popular culture, the People's Palace—a social history museum—is a bastion to Glasgow's supposed socialism. The city is a base for exploring the rest of Central Scotland, and from here you can board the West Highlands Railway north to Fort William and Ben Nevis.

As one of the more industrialized areas of Scotland, and with the natural, flatter landscape, golf is less outstanding here. The best-known course is Loch Lomond, a stunning parkland course designed by Tom Weiskopf, and host of the Scottish Open. There are good inland courses clustered in and around Glasgow, although the real gems are to be found in Lanark, and at Muckhart and Grangemouth to the east.

Heartlands: This heavily visited region, falling beneath the Highland Boundary Fault that cuts the country in half, has been the stage for many of Scotland's most significant historical events. There are plenty of vestiges of this past, from well-preserved medieval castles and royal residences to battle sites. Stirling is worth visiting for its imposing castle and Braveheart history, and the fabled Trossach Mountains to the west and north are great for hiking. The kingdom of Fife has many attractions: the famous town of St. Andrews, home of golf and an old university at which the heir to the British throne Prince William studied; ancient Perth, surrounded by stunning scenery; and the town of Scone, the ancient capital.

It is claimed that the ancient game of *gowf* started in the Heartlands. Within this 50-mile radius, you will find the greatest concentration of magnificent links and inland courses in the world, including St. Andrews, Gleneagles, and Carnoustie. There are few trees on these courses, but the natural undulations will make you ponder every shot. Unlike many courses, the bunkers here really *are* hazards, and it is quite common to see professionals and good club golfers playing backward out of them as their only sensible option.

9

Gleneagles King's Course

Highlands and the Northeast: The Northeast and especially the Highlands are the most mysterious, remote, and unexplored areas of Scotland. Beyond the beautiful Grampian Mountains lies Glamis Castle, Balmoral (a favored royal retreat since the 1840s), and the picturesque Angus Glens, which are perfect for hikers and skiers who stay in villages like Blairgowrie and Kirriemuir. The Highlands have Scotland's most spectacular scenery, and it's surprising just how remote many of its mountains, glens, lochs, and rivers actually are. There is a wealth of areas to visit from Inverness (a stepping-stone to the north), such as Glen Coe and the stunning Cairngorm Mountains. In the east Fort William is a good base to explore Ben Nevis and eighteenth-century industrial towns like Ullapool and Wick.

The courses in northern Scotland offer great variety to the traveling golfer, from the best-known links courses in the world like Royal Dornoch, to other course types that provide great tests of golf surrounded by breathtaking mountains, lochs, and moors. The harsh and beautiful weather here can often move from one extreme to another in a matter of minutes, providing an unexpected challenge.

ROYAL DORNOCH

Royal Dornoch, rightly recognized as one of the world's greatest links courses, was described by U.S. Masters winner Tom Watson as "the most fun I've had playing golf in my whole life." This is the world's northernmost golf course for world championship–level golf. Originally constructed in the dunes in 1877 by Old Tom Morris, Dornoch is a beautiful, unspoiled seaside links course outside the pretty lower Highlands town of Dornoch.

The Clubhouse

Food: Traditional golfers' fare, with reasonably priced bacon sandwiches and excellent, wonderful fresh fish and chips. Meals are served 11:00 A.M. to 7:00 P.M., or 9:00 P.M. if you preorder. Alternatively, the nearby Castle Hotel has a superb lawn at the rear for lunch in fair weather.

Changing Rooms: Traditional no-frills locker rooms—bring your own toiletries.

Ladies' Facilities: Dornoch ladies have complete equality, with no restrictions or special privileges. They can request times for ladies-only competitions and usually get them without question.

Pro Shop: Excellent Dornoch memorabilia, including prints and paintings of the course. A good range of wet-weather gear like the traditional Scottish macintosh and golf umbrellas, which are a necessity, given the

cold and unpredictable weather of the Scottish Highlands.

Interior and Exterior: The present clubhouse has been vastly modified since it was built in 1909 in a mock medieval style. Facilities include a large bar serving food.

Background to the Course

Architect: Old Tom Morris laid the first nine proper holes in 1877, when the annual membership was two shillings and six pence (about 50 cents today).

Type: Seaside links.

Landscape: As a result of its location directly on the Dornoch Firth coast, it can get very windy. On a wet day the rain strikes the player horizontally, playing havoc with your game—but the views of the turbulent North Sea coast will leave your imagination breathless.

Historical Facts:

• Dornoch is the third-oldest recorded golf course in Scotland, dated at 1616. Golf was played here long before this date but frowned on by the authorities as being an unwarlike activity.

• Course designer Donald Ross (1872–1948) was once Dornoch's golf pro and green-keeper. Here he learned about simplicity of design, which influenced his best American courses.

• Honorary members include Prince Andrew, Tom Watson and Ben Crenshaw. Celebrity visitors include Greg Norman and Jack Nicholson.

• Nearby Sligo Castle was where the singer Madonna married film director Guy Ritchie. Her baby Rocco was christened at Dornoch Cathedral.

Playing the Holes

Signature Hole: Foxy, the aptly named fourteenth (459 yards, par 4), regularly features in the rankings of the world's best holes as a superb natural hole without artificial hazards. Notable for its total lack of bunkers, the elevated wide but shallow green with its many borrows, some more subtle than others, is a challenge to hit and hold, so a par on the challenging Foxy can be considered an honorable birdie. You will need to strike a good long drive, preferably to the left of the fairway. A shot to the right will leave you with a blind second shot over two large mounds, in which case a good strategy is to lay up short of the green, then use a putter up the slope onto the green to achieve that elusive par.

Best Golf Hole: The ninth (496 yards, par 5) is Dornoch's most rewarding hole. The tee, nestled among remote beachside dunes, is the farthest distance from the clubhouse in a barren landscape with not even one tree to hug. It's a magical setting along the shoreline, with the ever-changing gray-green-blue colors of the sea, the crashing of the waves, and the sight of preying hawks hovering on the wind—all within the whins (gorse bushes) along the right of the fairway. With a following wind the green can be reached in two, but with the wind against, it can seem very far from tee to green. Four bunkers aside the green keep you honest on your approach shot and make for an interesting risk/reward equation.

any short shots to the right into a steeply banked gully, which leaves a third shot over a pot bunker to the flag. A ball played at the left of the green may unwittingly drop down another steep bank and into a deep bunker, which has an almost magnetic attraction for wayward shots.

the wind. If benign, it is one of the most heavenly places on earth, running alongside an isolated sandy beach, redolent with a myriad of wildlife basking in the watery sun of this North Sea coastline. If the wind is blowing from the north or east, it can transform into a golfer's hell. The fairways are narrow and surrounded for the most part by whins. Add to this all the subtle little borrows on these usually quite small putting surfaces, and you have a challenge fit for Tom Watson, or indeed its designer Old Tom Morris, who thoughtfully included eighty-eight of those damned Scottish bunkers.

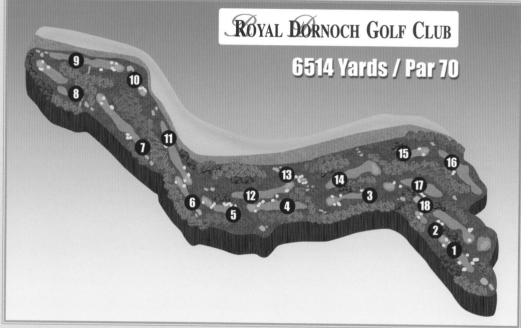

Toughest Hole: The drive from the notoriously tough eleventh (446 yards, par 4) certainly focuses the mind, with the beach and sea only yards off the fairway to the left and a huge bank of gorse bushes to the right. Taking less than a 3-wood off the tee will turn this into a par 5. There's a fairly large landing area for the drive, but the real challenge is the second shot to the green, which is narrow but widens to the rear (a legacy from the days when the course was played the other way round). The fairway contours spill

Playing the Course

Stamina: Royal Dornoch is not strenuous to play; as with most seaside Scottish links, the course is fairly even, although there are larger-than-average hills and mounds. The elements are all important for the enjoyment of playing: On a tranquil day, it is a gorgeous place to be, but when the wind blows, it can turn into a battle against the elements—so don't forget that rain gear.

Skills: The difficulty of Dornoch is critically dependent on the direction and strength of

Links golf has a very definite technique. The greens are usually small and very firm, so any lofted approach shots struggle to hold as, more often than not, there are gullies and hollows containing pot bunkers around the greens. Unless you are very accurate with your approach shot, it is far better to play little chip and runs, a technique locals have perfected over the last 400 years.

The low punch shot under the wind is far more beneficial than any high-lofted approach. The fairways are generally quite narrow, with many mounds and hollows, so blind approach shots are common, and it is advisable to pay out for a stroke saver or caddy.

Score Card

Address: Royal Dornoch Golf Club, Golf Road, Dornoch, Sutherland IV25 3LW, Scotland, UK

Phone: +44 (0)1862 810219

Fax: +44 (0)1862 810792

Web Site: www.royaldornoch.com

Courses and Lengths: Championship: Eighteen holes, par 70, 6,514 yards, 6,229 yards, 5,956 yards (ladies). Struie: Eighteen holes, par 72, 6,276 yards, 6,008 yards, 5,600 yards (ladies).

Tee Times: In high season 7:00 A.M. until dark; in low season from sunrise to sunset.

Handicap: 24 for men and 39 for ladies on the Championship Course.

Green Fees: Range from £69 (US$120) to £90 (US$160) on the Championship course and £15 (US$25) to £40 (US$70) on the Struie Course in high season.

Other Costs: Caddies and bag carriers range from £20 (US$35) to £30 (US$50) and £12 (US$20) to £20 (US$35), respectively. Stroke cards cost £4.00 (US$7.00) each. Trolleys (pull carts) and club rentals are available from the pro shop. Limited buggy (golf cart) rental; medical certificate required.

Facilities: A clubhouse with bar and restaurant, pro shop, and lessons and caddies provided.

Location: The nearest airport is Inverness (INV), from which it is a one-hour drive on the A9 to Dornoch town.

Ian's Opinion

Dornoch offers a wonderful golfing experience. The remote location and stunning scenery is a real draw, particularly on a clear and sunny day. This is a classic links, one of the best in the world to play for vistas and strategic challenges. Every hole has a glorious view of the ocean, but the eighth, ninth, and tenth run parallel to the seashore. The fairways are quite hilly, following the contour of the dunes; they can also be very narrow, sending the wayward shot off the tee, particularly on the signature fourteenth hole. There are plenty of deep, riveted bunkers, which are harsh if you're up against the wall; unless your bunker shots are up to scratch, expect to spend a lot of your game inside them.

GLENEAGLES KING'S COURSE

The three twentieth-century–built courses at Gleneagles are a favorite of the rich and famous. When it first opened in 1924, guests arrived by ocean liner and steam train. Now international flights and no-frills European airlines or four-wheel drives may be the preferred mode of transport, but the appeal of Gleneagles, the "eighth wonder of the (golfing) world" and the "Riviera of the Highlands" as it was once known, has not faded. Gleneagles is one of the world's top and most expensive vacation resorts, with a fabulous hotel, four golf courses, and a growing center for resort activities and family recreation, like shooting, off-road driving, and luxurious relaxation.

The Hotel

Food: Apart from the Michelin-starred Andrew Fairlie restaurant (Scottish chef of the year) serving the finest and freshest Scottish larder food, the stunning Strathearn restaurant offers great views across the grounds, and there are several other bars and eateries. Good-quality golfers' food will

set you back £20 (US$35) per head in the most modest restaurant. The Halfway house is halfway through the King's and Queen's courses, providing sustenance to tired players, and the Juice Buggy brings hot drinks and snacks to those on the PGA course.

Rooms: As befits a luxury hotel, Gleneagles offers the guest everything he or she could wish for a wonderfully comfortable, relaxing stay. You can choose from a selection of 260 richly furnished but tasteful rooms, all of which are replete with queen- or king-size beds, en suite bath and shower, interactive TV, DVD player, and more. Rooms start at £330 (about US$500) per night and rise to £950 (about US$1,800) for some suites. Black-and-white photographs of the hotel and its guests (including Bob Hope, Prince Andrew, and Jack Nicholson) on the walls are a lovely touch.

Facilities: A wonderful art deco dining room and bar, a shopping arcade, and beautifully kept gardens are further features of elegance and excellence. The hotel provides a full range of business facilities, two pools, a gym, a squash court, and a luxury health spa with sauna, sun bed, and massage. There are also a host of concessions from top retailers like Harvey Nichols. The Golf Academy provides lessons with in-depth analysis of your swing and videos for future reference.

Activities

Outdoor activities include falconry, shooting, horse riding, fishing, cycle riding, off-road driving and family activities, all of which can be organized from the hotel. Wimbledon champion Virginia Wade gives an annual tennis clinic every July, costing about £1,400 (US$2,500).

Shooting: In the 1950s Gleneagles was an important fixture in the high-society calendar. After the London season, it was yachting at Cowes and polo at Deauville, followed by golf

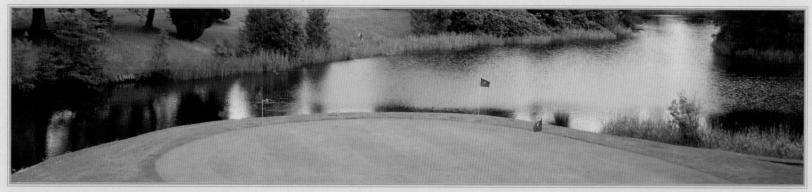

and grouse shooting at Gleneagles. After a round of golf, make sure you try your shot at one of the world's most prestigious shooting schools. There are twelve target disciplines on shooting ranges for sporting clays, skeet shooting, and more. Included in the cost of a lesson are protective clothing, transport, and all sporting clays equipment—including guns.

Costs: Air rifle shooting is suitable for those age eight upward and costs £50 (US$80) for an hour lesson, plus £10 (US$17) as a supplement for guests. Clay pigeon shooting is suitable for those age ten upward and costs £60 (US$100) for one hour with twenty-five cartridges. Each additional box of twenty-five cartridges costs £5.00 (US$8.00).

Off-Road Driving: The most exhilarating activity you can try out at Gleneagles, off-roading excursions take you across courses designed by some of the country's top specialists. Whether you're an experienced driver or a novice looking for thrills, Gleneagles's instructors will guide you through ridges, gullies, steep gradients, ditches, and water splashes through the stunning surrounds of the Scottish countryside. Also worth trying are the scenic safaris, where you'll be taken up through munros, lochs, lochans, and historic landmarks and shown Scotland's diverse wildlife before being treated to a glass of champagne and a gourmet picnic. Bliss!

Costs: Off-roading is suitable for those age twelve upward and costs £110 (US$190) for an hour for up to two people, or £220 (US$300) for a ninety-minute lesson for up to four people. Discover Scotland safari tours cost £600 (US$1,000) a day for three people, plus £120 (US$200) for a guide, with a 30 percent discount for half a day.

Background to the King's Course

Architect: James Braid and Major C. K. Hutchison designed two of the courses in 1914 for a fee of £120 (US$200). The third course, the PGA Centenary designed by Jack Nicklaus in 1993, cost a substantially higher £6 million (US$11 million) to design and build and will host the 2014 Ryder Cup.

Type: Four parkland and moorland courses.

Landscape: Stunning vistas of breathtaking beauty, covered with heather, gorse, and majestic stands of pines, with most holes offering a 180-degree view over the surrounding countryside. Deer in the forest are within sight of the course.

Pro Shop: A great range of clubs and golf bags are available in the golf academy pro shop. The clubhouse has good golf clothing and Gleneagles memorabilia prints of the courses.

Playing the Holes (King's Course)

Signature Hole: Braid's Brawest, the thirteenth hole (448 yards, par 4), is designer James Braid's signature hole. It's difficult to play in all weather conditions, but if the wind is blowing, watch out! It is vital to make good contact off the tee in order to fly the strategically placed bunkers, located from 201 to 297 yards either side of this beautifully undulating fairway. After negotiating these, the second shot is equally challenging: A mid- to long iron or even a fairway wood has to be played into a green that is well guarded by four vicious-looking

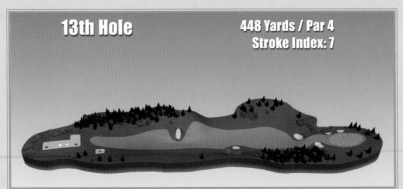

13th Hole

448 Yards / Par 4
Stroke Index: 7

tee shot must be long and straight to have any chance of reaching the green in two and must also be very accurate to avoid the dangerous fairway bunkers. For many golfers the second shot will be more than 200 yards and can be chased toward the hole by playing up the right side of the fairway and letting the contours of the ground bring the ball back in. This green is guarded by a deep bunker to the right, so golfers are advised to play short in two and then get up and down from the fairway.

deep bunkers. On the green, as with most holes here, there are a lot of subtle little breaks and borrows that all add up to making a par on the Brawest quite an achievement.

Best Golf Hole: As a respite to the difficult scoring on Braid's Brawest, look to the fourteenth (260 yards, par 4). With the wind behind, the green is reachable for big hitters, even with an iron. Don't fear the line of five bunkers across the approach to the green—just go for broke, but be warned that putting here can cause golfers to look on in amazement as the ball takes all the subtle breaks of what looks like a reasonably flat green.

Toughest Hole: The fourth hole (466 yards, par 4) is by far the most difficult. Named Broomys Law, this plays more like a par 5 than its rating of par 4, which is rarely achieved here, even by low handicappers. The

Playing the King's Course

Stamina: Although there are some fairly large hills on the King's Course, it is not particularly strenuous to move around. It is rare to find extreme temperatures in this part of Scotland,

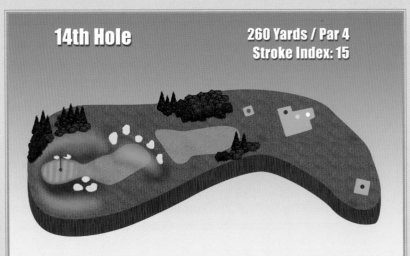

14th Hole

260 Yards / Par 4
Stroke Index: 15

although it is advisable to pack your rain gear in your bag. If you want to travel light, the golf club rents a new set of the very best clubs available. You also get a complimentary bucket of balls at the Gleneagles PGA academy to get that swing going before your round. To make your game easier going, indulge and hire one of the famous Gleneagles caddies.

Skills: The King's Course is an incredibly challenging par 68 of 6,125 yards off the yellow tees with no par 5s at all. Many of the fairways have large mounds and hollows, so the blind approach shot is common. As with many Scottish courses, there are no water hazards, and the main threat comes from the bunkers, which are among the deepest in the world. To score well you have to be a long straight hitter with a good short game.

Score Card

Address: The Gleneagles Hotel, Freepost, Auchterarder, Perthshire PH3 1BR, Scotland, UK

Phone: +44 (0)1764 662231
Fax: +44 (0)1764 662134
Web Site: www.gleneagles.com
Courses and Lengths: King's Course: Eighteen holes, par 68, 6,125 yards, 5,220 yards (ladies). Queen's Course: Eighteen holes, par 68, 5,965 yards, 5,495 yards (ladies). PGA Centenary Course: Eighteen holes, par 72, 7,088 yards, 5,072 yards (ladies). Wee Course: Nine holes, par 27, 1,481 yards.
Tee Times: Vary according to season.
Handicap: None required.
Green Fees: Prices range from £30 (US$50) to £110 (US$200) per round depending on season, time of day, and course, with discounts on tee times booked after 5:00 P.M.
Packages: Golfing vacation and tuition packages are available from the hotel. Prices vary seasonally, starting from about £250 (US$400) a night for one night and a round of golf.
Other Costs: Buggy rental costs up to £30 (US$50) and club rental costs £50 (US$80). It costs up to £5.00 (US$8.00) for trolleys. The PGA Centenary is the only course that allows buggies.
Location: Twenty minutes from Perth along the A9 and one hour, fifteen minutes from Edinburgh along the M90 and A9. The nearest airport is Edinburgh (EDI).

6125 Yards / Par 68

KING'S COURSE

Ian's Opinion

Of Glenagles's three main courses, the King's Course and the PGA are regarded as the most difficult, with the Queen's as the easier option. The King's is a wonderful golfing experience but with major challenges. Its designer, James Braid, was a five-time Open champion and a powerful hitter of the ball, so many of the holes are long, making it difficult to reach the green for the weaker golfer. Stray from the tee and you will be penalized and could end up in the deep bunkers. Holes like the seventh and thirteenth are difficult to score well if, like me, your handicap is 12 or above. It can be an extremely frustrating game, but the course and its views are magnificent, so I would highly recommend the King's if you are game for a physical and mental challenge.

ST. ANDREWS OLD COURSE

St. Andrews is undoubtedly the most famous golf course in the world. It is sacred ground for those who attempt to gain the upper hand in the never-ending battle of man over the elements, the ball, and the card. The Old Course in particular, thought to be the oldest course in the world, has an unassailable place in the history of golf. Home to the Royal and Ancient, without doubt the world's most influential club, St. Andrews is justly named the home of golf. It was here the international standard eighteen holes per course evolved, simply because that is how this piece of links land was most conveniently divided. Millions of the world's great golfers have played here

over the last 600 years, and many have been humbled by the experience.

The Clubhouse

Food: St. Andrews is expensive for everything, including the food. Like the golf, expect the highest standards in traditional British golfing fare using the best local produce, best enjoyed with new and old-world wines.

Changing Rooms: Excellent quality and clean wood decor changing rooms, with spacious overnight lockers, showers, hair dryers, clothes-drying facilities, and overnight facilities for storing and cleaning your clubs and shoes.

Interior and Exterior: St. Andrews has two clubhouses to cater to its many courses. The Links clubhouse near the Old Course caters more for dining, with the Eden clubhouse offering more family facilities.

Pro Shop: The clubhouse has a range of men and women's clothing in St. Andrews Links tartan. Captivating posters and prints are sold in the Golf Museum shop opposite the Royal and Ancient clubhouse.

Background to the Old Course

Architect: The so-called oldest golf course in the world has evolved over time. Those who played a major role in shaping it in the nineteenth and twentieth centuries are Daw Anderson, Old Tom Morris, and Dr. Alister Mackenzie.

Type: A flat links course within sight and sound of the sea.

Landscape: The outward nine expand out to the seafront, and the back nine bring you home. Holes seven to twelve are the most picturesque, located out on the coast peninsular.

Historical Facts:

• St. Andrews is the home of the Royal and Ancient Golf Club, founded in 1754, which administrates the rules of golf around the world (except for the United States) and runs the Open Championship. The R&A oversees the rules of 109 countries and an estimated twenty-six million golfers in Europe, Africa, Asia, and the Americas.

• St. Andrews Links is the largest golf complex in Europe.

• The eleventh hole on the Old Course was made infamous by Bobby Jones. Despite winning all four championships in 1930, Jones cut his teeth at St. Andrews in 1921 and was destroyed by Hill Bunker to the left of the green, which caused him to walk out in disgust.

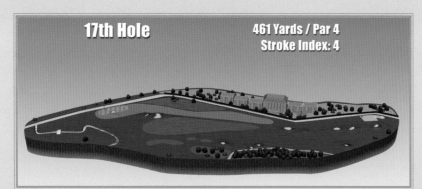

17th Hole 461 Yards / Par 4 Stroke Index: 4

Playing the Holes (Old Course)

Signature Hole: "The most famous hole in golf" is how the seventeenth (461 yards, par 4) is often described. From the tee the drive is blind and has to be played over the old coal sheds that used to be part of the railway buildings but are now a wing of the Old Course Hotel. The fairway is a dogleg to the right, and the ideal line is up the right-hand side, which leaves a second shot into the green, avoiding having to play over the infamous Road Hole Bunker (which has claimed more famous scalps than Sitting Bull!). Anything too far to the right can get you into trouble from the hazards of the road and the boundary wall. Once there, the green provides a test for the most proficient of putters, with its subtle humps and hollows.

Best Golf Hole: The eleventh hole (172 yards, par 3) plays right out to the Eden Estuary. The tee shot has to be pinpoint accurate as the green slopes sharply toward the front with Strathes Bunker to the right (behind which the pin is often placed) and the dreaded Hill Bunker

to the left. Any shot unfortunate enough to finish in the Hill Bunker has to be played out over a 12-foot-high face. If this shot is overhit, the ball can travel across this double green, ending up closer to the seventh pin and leaving up to a 180-foot putt back to the hole.

Trickiest Hole: Standing on the tee of the twelfth (316 yards, par 4), named Heathery In, the golfer might be forgiven in thinking that he or she is being presented with a simple scoring opportunity. Nothing could be further from the truth. Unless you can carry the ball 225 yards over the well-disguised bunkers, the center of the fairway should be avoided at all costs. Forty yards farther on lies a ridge concealing another family of vicious-looking bunkers from whose depths it is almost

impossible to reach the wide and shallow green. The best course of action is to play short, then chip and run up to the pin.

Playing the Old Course

Skills: At first glance the Old Course at St. Andrews can seem fairly benign, but with its hidden hazards and exposure to the elements, it provides an examination of a golfer's accuracy and course management to equal any in the world. Physically it is not a strenuous test, but it will test your mental agility to the max.

Score Card

Address: St. Andrews Links Trust, Pilmour House, St. Andrews, Fife KY16 9SF, Scotland, UK

Phone: +44 (0)1334 466666

Fax: +44 (0)1334 479555

Web Site: www.standrews.org.uk

Courses and Lengths: New Course: Eighteen holes, par 71, 6,604 yards, 5,992 yards (ladies). Old Course: Eighteen holes, par 72, 6,609 yards, 6,032 yards (ladies). Jubilee Course: Eighteen holes, par 72, 6,742 yards, 6,043 yards (ladies). Eden Course: Eighteen holes, par 70, 6,195 yards, 5,455 yards (ladies). Strathtyrum Course: Nine holes, par 69 (eighteen holes), 5,620 yards, 4,705 yards (ladies). Balgove Course: Nine holes, par 69 (eighteen holes), 1,520 yards.

Tee Times: Vary; high season 6:30 A.M. to 8:30 P.M.

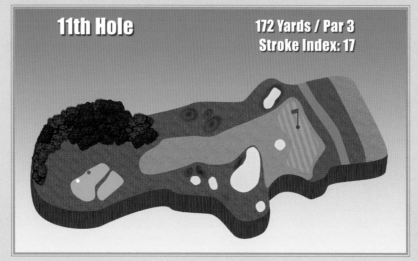

11th Hole 172 Yards / Par 3 Stroke Index: 17

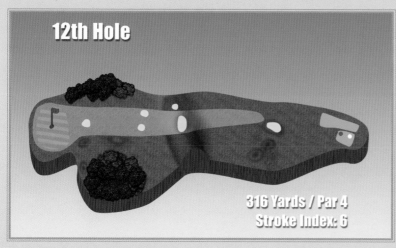

12th Hole

316 Yards / Par 4
Stroke Index: 6

Handicap: 24 for men and 36 for ladies at the Old Course.

Green Fees: High season runs from April to October. Fees are £110 (US$200) for the Old Course, dropping to as little as £10 (US$18) for the nine-hole Balgove. Prices drop in low season (November to March).

Packages: Available on all courses bar the Old Course. You can purchase three-, seven-, and fourteen-day tickets for unlimited play on all other courses at a rate of £120 (US$200), £240 (US$380), and £430 (US$700), respectively, during high season.

Other Costs: Caddies cost £35 (US$60) and trainee caddies £25 (US$45). Trolleys are £3.00 (US$5.00) per round, allowed on all courses except the Old Course. There are a small number of two-person electric buggies for rent on the New and Strathtyrum Courses. They can be rented by senior citizens for £18 (US$30) and medical certificate holders for £12 (US$20). Balls cost £2.70 (US$4.00) for fifty.

Facilities: From the Eden and Links clubhouses, you can rent sets of new Titleist 762 irons, 980 fairway woods, 983K drivers, and Scotty Cameron putters in a Titleist stand bag, along with Footjoy golf shoes (with a complimentary pair of socks). Get your swing going at the Golf Practice Centre.

Location: On the edge of the university town of St. Andrews, the courses can be accessed by car from Edinburgh along the M90 and A915 and from Perth on the M90 and A91.

OLD COURSE
ST ANDREWS LINKS

6609 Yards / Par 72

Ian's Opinion

The Old Course was an adequate flat links, flowing into the landscape of the dunes, with riveted bunkers as the number-one hazard. Some are incredibly deep and steep; it can be impossible to escape from some positions without penalty. The bunker on the twelfth (Bobby Jones) and the Road Hole bunker on the seventeenth are especially irksome. Playing the first off the tee and then the eighteenth coming home into the town are often-photographed moments in a golfer's traveling life and will leave you with wonderful memories. Where else in the world does a golf course begin and end in the center of a town? Make sure you arrive before 2:00 P.M. the previous day to enter the ballot, which draws 50 percent of the tee times on the Old Course.

MUSSELBURGH OLD COURSE

This charming, wee nine-hole links is a hidden gem of the East Lothian region. It is thought to be the one of the oldest courses in the world with 500 rich years of history, from the beheading of Mary Queen of Scots and the sixteenth-century ban of golf to producing five nineteenth-century Open champions and the standardization of the 4¼-inch hole. The course has changed very little over the last five centuries, although since 1816 it shares its ground with the Musselburgh racecourse. Why not hire a pair of hickory clubs and discover how difficult this game was once to play?

Background to the Course

Type: Nine-hole links, with plans to expand to a full-size eighteen.

Landscape: Views of the stunning western coastal front are in parts cloaked by trees. The incredibly flat, wind-formed course offers easy going golfing activity within a racecourse.

Historical Facts:

• Mary Queen of Scots played on the Old Course in 1567 before her beheading at the command of her cousin Queen Elizabeth I. Other royal visitors include James VI in 1603, and the not-so-royal Oliver Cromwell set up camp on Musselburgh course in 1650.

• King James IV of Scotland, the first royal golfer, lifted his grandfather's ban of golf (he claimed it kept his subjects from their archery

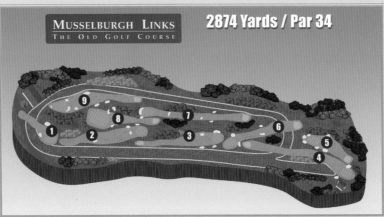

MUSSELBURGH LINKS
THE OLD GOLF COURSE

2874 Yards / Par 34

practice) in 1502, although golf was still frowned upon. Legend has it that the second hole was used as a burial ground for soldiers killed at the Battle of Pinkie in 1547 to deter locals from playing.

• On New Year's Day 1811, Musselburgh hosted the first-ever Women's Golf Competition. Participants were mainly local fishermen's wives competing for a new creel and skull (fish baskets).

• The 4¼-inch-diameter hole standard originated from here, as this was the width of

the cutting tool used. In 1893 the R&A made the size mandatory for all golf courses.

• Mrs. Foreman's Inn at the fourth green is a Musselburgh institution. There was once a hatch to pass through refreshments to thirsty golfers, and today they still serve a fine pint of warmed ale.

• Six of the first-ever Open Championships were played here between 1874 and 1891, and five of the first twelve Open winners were Musselburgh men.

• The Rhind Stone, a golfing scene carved in stone by artist John Rhind, a member of the former club Edinburgh Burgess, once occupied the exterior wall of the 1891-built clubhouse, where the current Five Open Champions carving (depicting the faces of the five champions from Musselburgh) now sits.

Score Card

Address: Musselburgh Links, The Old Golf Course, Balcarres Road, Musselburgh, East Lothian EH21 7SD, Scotland, UK

Phone: +44 (0)1316 655438

Web Site: www.musselburgholdlinks.co.uk

Course and Length: The Old Course: Nine holes, par 70 (eighteen holes), 2,874 yards, 2,665 yards (ladies).

Tee Times: 8:00 A.M. to 8:00 P.M. summertime. In winter 8:00 A.M. till dusk.

Handicap: None.

*Lionel Freeman,
Club Secretary of
Musselburgh*

Green Fees: £8.50 (US$17) on weekdays, £9 (US$16) on weekends throughout the year.
Other Costs: Hickory clubs £24 (US$40), modern £15 (US$25). Trolleys £4.00 (US$7.00) per round.

Facilities: The clubhouse has a bar with snacks available. The starters hut provides both modern and historic hickory clubs and trolleys.
Location: In East Lothian on the eastern outskirts of Edinburgh, which is served by an international airport (EDI). If traveling by car, Musselburgh is well signed from the A1 and the A720 Edinburgh bypass. Local rail stations are Musselburgh or Wallyford.

LUNDIN LADIES GOLF CLUB

Lundin Ladies is a nine-hole course surrounded by fields on the outskirts of the village of Lundin, a convenient twenty minutes from St. Andrews. It is famed as the oldest free-standing ladies golf course in the world, and although gentlemen visitors are welcome to use the course, they may feel intimidated, as

Landscape: Situated on what was originally meadowland, the course covers a stretch of Fife farmland and is formed on the sandy soil of Massney braes between a railway line and higher-rise ground. The bulk of Largo Law can be seen to the east, and the centuries-old Lundin Tower is also visible.

women rule the roost here. This is one of the few courses where the gents' tees are in front of the ladies', and men are not allowed to enter the clubhouse. Bronze Age standing stones on the second fairway make for an interesting hazard.

Background to the Course
Architect: Designed by James Braid in 1910, who lived in Elie, just 4 miles away, this course became the envy of many gentlemen's clubs. Braid won his fifth Open title the same year he designed this course.
Type: Parklands.

Historical facts:
• Lundin Ladies historic turf has been played by Scotland's most famous lady: Mary Queen of Scots.
• Constituted in 1891, the ladies were ousted to the Standing Stones Park in 1908 from the overcrowded Leven/Lundin Gentlemen's Course.
• The first ladies captain, Miss Maud Gilmour, was appointed in 1904.
• Although only a petit nine holes, the size yo-yoed to fifteen holes in its early years until resettling at Nine holes in 1903.
• An attempt to transform into an eighteen-

hole course was aborted by the advent of World War I in 1914. During World War II sheep and lambs grazed on the course, parts of which were set aside for essential food production for the war effort. After the war the future of the course was in jeopardy, but its loyal members held fetes and raffles to pay the greenkeeper's wages.

• The Standing Stones are a Bronze Age monument dating from twentieth century B.C. They are thought to be a prehistoric ritual site of Danish chiefs, as a stone-lined grave was discovered in 1844. The three impressive red sandstone pillars may have once formed the circumference of a complete circle.

• Strict religious rules have affected play: Sunday play on the course was not permitted until the 1950s, and play before 1:00 P.M. was only introduced in 1965.

Score Card

Address: Lundin Ladies Golf Club, Woodielea Road, Lundin Links, Fife KY8 6AR, Scotland, UK

· PRIVATE ·
CLUB HOUSE
FOR
LADY PLAYERS
ONLY

Phone: +44 (0)1333 32083 (secretary) or +44 (0)1333 320022 (starter)
Web Site: www.lundinladies.co.uk
Course and Length: One nine-hole, par-68 (for eighteen holes) course of 2,365 yards for ladies only.
Tee Times: Dawn until dusk.
Handicap: None.
Green Fees: Ranges from £5.00 (US$8.00) to £18.75 (US$30.00) for two rounds of the course. There's an annual ticket of £125 (US$200).
Facilities: You can eat at the Lundin Links Hotel across the road from the course, which can be arranged through the club or directly. Pre-golf soups, bacon rolls, and hot drinks or post-golf two-course (£9/US$16) or three-course (£11/US$19) meals are available. The clubhouse is modest with no pro shop or showers, although trolleys can be rented.
Location: Lundin is twenty minutes from St. Andrews along the A915. From Dunfermline take the A92, and from Edinburgh take the M90 north, at junction 3 take the A92, and then the A915.

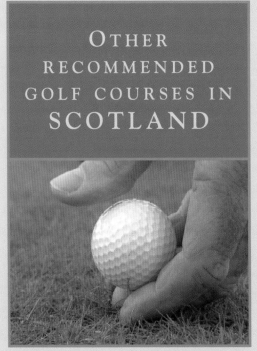

OTHER RECOMMENDED GOLF COURSES IN SCOTLAND

1. BALLATER GOLF COURSE
Address: Victoria Road, Ballater
Aberdeenshire AB35 5QX, Scotland, UK
Phone: +44 (0)1339 755567 (secretary) or
+44 (0)1339 755658 (professional)
Web Site: www.ballatergolfclub.co.uk
A beautiful and easygoing eighteen-hole, par-67 heathland course just a few miles from Balmoral Castle (the Queen's summer residence) on the banks of the River Dee. Ballater is an ideal destination for the tourist golfer, with seasonal fishing and shooting available.

2. BELLEISLE GOLF COURSE
Address: Belleisle Park, Doonfoot Road, Ayr
Ayrshire KA7 4DU, Scotland, UK
Phone: +44 (0)1292 616255 (reservations) or
+44 (0)1292 441314 (professional)
Web Site: www.golfsouthayrshire.com
Close to Royal Troon, Turnberry, and Prestwick, this par-71 course is an undiscovered pearl in the shadow of its mighty neighbors. At a fraction of the cost, it is still a challenging eighteen-hole course with lots of character.

3. GOLF HOUSE CLUB ELIE
Address: Elie, Leven, Fife KY9 1AS, Scotland, UK
Phone: +44 (0)1333 330301 (reservations) or
+44 (0)1333 330955 (professional)
Only 10 miles from St. Andrews, Elie is a typical links course with many bump-and-run and blind shots. The eighteen-hole, par-71 course is a must for golf enthusiasts with its stunning views and an old submarine periscope on the first to see if the coast is clear—which can only be described as fun.

4. NORTH BERWICK GOLF CLUB
Address: New Club House, Beach Road
North Berwick, East Lothian EH39 4BB
Scotland, UK
Phone: +44 (0)1620 895040 (reservations) or
+44 (0)1620 893233 (professional)
Web Site: www.north-berwick.co.uk
Internationally renowned, eighteen-hole, par-71 North Berwick is the classic links course on the east coast. It is best known for its unbelievably difficult fifteenth: a par-3 hole named Redan, which is said to be the golf hole most copied around the world.

5. BLAIRGOWRIE GOLF CLUB
Address: Rosemount, Blairgowrie PH10 6LG
Scotland, UK
Phone: +44 (0)1250 872622 (reservations) or
+44 (0)1250 873116 (professional)
Web Site: www.theblairgowriegolfclub.co.uk
Redesigned by James Braid of Gleneagles fame, eighteen-hole Blairgowrie is one of the most beautiful inland courses in Britain. The heather, a feature of the par-72 course, is beautiful in the autumn, and the traditional Scottish fare served in the clubhouse is to die for.

6. CARNOUSTIE GOLF LINKS
Address: Links Parade, Carnoustie
Angus DD7 7JE, Scotland, UK
Phone: +44 (0)1241 853789 (reservations) or
+44 (0)1241 411986 (professional)
Web Site: www.carnoustiegolflinks.co.uk
Eighteen-hole, par-72 Carnoustie is regarded as one of the world's most difficult courses. Its notoriety has been enhanced by several high-profile defeats: most famously Jean Van de Veldem in 1999, who narrowly failed to secure the first Open Championship for France.

7. BRUNTSFIELD LINKS GOLFING SOCIETY
Address: 32 Bamton Avenue
Edinburgh EH4 6JH, Scotland, UK
Phone: +44 (0)1313 361479 (secretary) or
+44 (0)1313 364050 (professional)
Almost 250 years old and once just a six-holer, eighteen-hole, par-71 Bruntsfield Links is actually a parkland course. The greens are small. Watch out for the trees—they come into play more often than you'd expect. Great food is served here.

8. BOAT OF GARTEN GOLF CLUB
Address: Nethybridge Road, Boat of Garten
Inverness-shire PH24 3BQ, Scotland, UK
Phone: +44 (0)1479 831282 (reservations)
Web Site: www.boatgolf.com
Although this remote eighteen-hole, par-70 heathland course is fairly short, it is a challenge to play. Its setting in the Highlands among snowcapped mountains and close to the Aviemore Ski Center makes it ideal for the energetic vacationer.

9. THE WESTIN TURNBERRY RESORT GOLF COURSES
Address: Turnberry (Ailsa)
Ayrshire KA26 9LT, Scotland, UK
Phone: +44 (0)1655 331000 (reservations) or
+44 (0)1655 334032 (professional)
Web Site: www.turnberry.co.uk
With views toward Ireland and the famous Ailsa Rock and Mull of Kintyre, Turnberry is a class act. Although very expensive, the eighteen-hole, par-70 Ailsa Course is a classic links championship course that must be played if you are near the Ayrshire coast.

10. ROYAL ABERDEEN GOLF COURSE
Address: Balgownie, Links Road, Bridge of Don
Aberdeen AB23 8AT, Scotland, UK
Phone: +44 (0)1224 702571 (reservations) or
+44 (0)1224 702221 (professional)
Web Site: www.royalaberdeengolf.com
Truly a hidden jewel with centuries-old history, this was the first golf club in the world to adopt the five-minute lost-ball rule. Although sometimes hard to tell where the fairways start and finish, the eighteen-hole, par-70 course has one of the best first nine holes anywhere in the UK.

11. THE ROXBURGHE GOLF COURSE

Address: The Roxburghe Hotel, Kelso
Roxburghshire TD5 8JZ, Scotland, UK
Phone: +44 (0)1573 450331 (reservations) or
+44 (0)1573 450333 (professional)
Web Site: www.roxburghe.net
Although not known for its golf courses, the Borders region does have this magnificent hotel and eighteen-hole, par-72 parkland course owned by the Duke of Roxburghe. This fine tourist golfer's destination combines a great golf challenge with a castle, fishing, shooting, and riding, all on the estate.

12. HAGGS CASTLE GOLF CLUB

Address: 70 Dumbreck Road
Glasgow G41 4SN, Scotland, UK
Phone: +44 (0)1414 271157 (reservations) or
+44 (0)1414 273355 (professional)
Haggs Castle is a pretty yet unconventional eighteen-hole, par-72 parkland course on the outskirts of Glasgow. Although not a long course, many holes are deceptively hard to reach, and accurate pitching is important.

13. CRUDEN BAY GOLF CLUB

Address: Aulton Road, Cruden Bay
Peterhead AB42 0NN, Scotland, UK
Phone: +44 (0)1779 812285 (reservations) or
+44 (0)1779 812414 (professional)
Web Site: www.crudenbaygolfclub.co.uk
Originating in the late eighteenth century, Cruden Bay features all the early links classic traits: large dunes, blind tee shots, hanging lies—everything that golf should be. North of Aberdeen, the eighteen-hole, par-70 course is often subject to severe weather and imposing roughs, making for a daunting challenge.

14. DOWNFIELD GOLF COURSE

Address: Turnberry Avenue
Dundee DD2 3QP, Scotland, UK
Phone: +44 (0)1382 825595 (secretary) or
+44 (0)1382 889246 (professional)
Web Site: www.downfieldgolf.co.uk
Situated halfway between St. Andrews and Carnoustie, and with green fees at just one-third of its illustrious neighbors, eighteen-hole, par-73 Downfield was described by five times Open champion Peter Thomson as "one of the finest inland courses I have played in the world."

15. THE CARNEGIE CLUB

Address: Skibo Castle, Dornoch
Sutherland IV25 3RQ, Scotland, UK
Phone: +44 (0)1862 894600 (reservations) or
+44 (0)1862 894600 (professional)
Web Site: www.carnegieclub.co.uk
Once the home of Andrew Carnegie, Skibo Castle (where Madonna married) is now a private members club for the seriously wealthy and famous. However, there are a few weekday tee times at this superb eighteen-hole, par-72 links course that can be booked by prior arrangement.

16. SOUTHERNESS GOLF CLUB

Address: Clubhouse, Southerness
Dumfries DG2 8AZ, Scotland, UK
Phone: +44 (0)1387 880677 (reservations) or
+44 (0)1333 450960 (professional)
Web Site: www.southernessgolfclub.com
Located between Troon and Turnberry, Southerness is yet another beautiful eighteen-hole links course, built in the 1940s. With enormous beaches and views across to Ireland in one direction and the Lake District in the other, this par-73 course is not to be missed.

17. CRAIL GOLFING SOCIETY

Address: Balcomie Clubhouse
Fife Ness, Crail KY10 3XN, Scotland, UK
Phone: +44 (0)1333 450686 (reservations) or
+44 (0)1387 880677 (professional)
Web Site: www.crailgolfingsociety.co.uk
Only a few miles from St. Andrews, Crail's standard scratch of 69 on its Balcomie Course belies its difficulty, particularly against the wind. Short holes combined with small greens makes for a difficult eighteen-hole, par-69 course that is known and loved the world over.

18. ROYAL TROON

Address: Craigend Road, Troon
Ayrshire KA10 6EP, Scotland, UK
Phone: +44 (0)1292 311555 (reservations) or
+44 (0)1292 313281 (professional)
Web Site: www.royaltroon.co.uk
The scene of numerous British Open championships, eighteen-hole, par-73 Royal Troon is a classic Scottish links course, well worth its green fees, which are among the highest in Scotland. The only course to be patronized by Queen Elizabeth II, Troon is famous for its par-3 eighth hole, the "postage stamp," which can be impossible to hit in the ever-present winds.

19. GULLANE GOLF CLUB

Address: West Links Road, Gullane
East Lothian EH31 2BB, Scotland, UK
Phone: +44 (0)1620 842255 (reservations)
Web Site: www.gullanegolfclub.com
Golf has been played on Gullane No. 1, the physically demanding eighteen-hole, par-71 championship course overlooking the Firth of Forth, for more than 350 years. Regardless of weather or time of year, this course is a classic that must be experienced. The fifteenth hole alone makes a trip worthwhile, with a double dogleg, tall rough, deep bunkers, and a green of which nightmares are made.

20. MUIRFIELD GOLF CLUB

Address: The Honourable Company of Edinburgh
Golfers, Muirfield, Gullane
East Lothian EH31 2EG, Scotland, UK
Phone: +44 (0)1620 842123 (reservations)
E-mail: hceg@muirfield.org.uk
Muirfield, an eighteen-hole, par-70 course, is the home of the Honourable Company of Edinburgh Golfers. It is widely considered to be the oldest golf club in the world, whose members drew up the first rules of the game ten years before the Royal and Ancient Club was founded. Unfortunately for visitors, however, the club's officials are less than enthusiastic in welcoming strangers, and unless you know a member or are super rich or famous, you may find it difficult to personally experience this wonderful championship course.

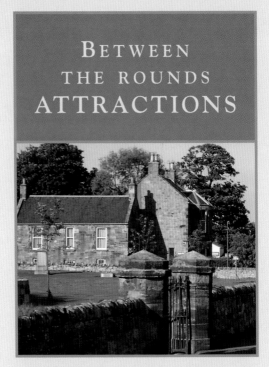

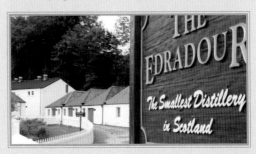

BETWEEN THE ROUNDS ATTRACTIONS

Attractions near Gleneagles

Edradour Distillery: Edradour is the smallest legal distillery of Scotch whiskey in the world. It can only legally be defined as whiskey once matured for three years in an oak cask. Established in 1825, it still uses traditional wooden tools to make one of Scotland's favorite whiskeys. Its output in one year (50,000 bottles) is equivalent to the production of a major distillery's production in just one week, yet it receives two visitors for every bottle produced. Housed in delightful white stonewashed buildings, the distillery, just north of Perth, is situated in Scotland's temperate belt, where conditions are perfect for whiskey distillation. The process is managed by just three men. On the free tour you can learn all about the history of the distillery, the old ways of making whiskey, and the importance of what casks are used to store the liquor. You can also buy whiskey at the on-site shop.

Edradour certainly has a colorful history since its inception two hundred years ago; most of its output ended up in America during prohibition, where it allegedly fell into the hands of the mafia. Indeed, a significant proportion of the content of the 264,000 bottles of Scotch whiskey in the hold of the shipwrecked SS *Politician*, upon which best-selling 1946 novel *Whisky Galore* was based, contained Edradour-produced whiskey. Certainly something to mull over during the free tasting session.

Address: Edradour Distillery, Pitlochry PH16 5JP, Scotland, UK
Phone: +44 (0)1796 472095
Fax: +44 (0)1796 472002
Web Site: www.edradour.co.uk
Hours: Beginning of March to end of October, Monday through Saturday 9:30 A.M. to 5:00 P.M. and Sunday Noon to 5:00 P.M. November to mid-December, Monday through Saturday 10:00 A.M. to 4:00 P.M.

Scone Palace: The family-owned stately home of Scone Palace is the site of countless auspicious historical events. The sixteenth-century abbey once here was where all Scottish kings until James I were crowned. The grounds were home to Moot Hill's Coronation Stone of Destiny, a legendary tablet used in Scottish coronations, fulfilling an ancient prophecy that "the Scots in place must reign where they this stone shall find." The two-story building is packed with priceless antiques and furnishings befitting its grand past, consisting of a restored sixteenth-century core surrounded by earlier buildings. The Long Gallery is the oldest part, which has been walked by many Scottish legends, including Charles II on his way to his coronation on the Moot Hill in 1651 and Bonnie Prince Charlie, who visited during the 1745 Jacobite Rebellion. Don't miss the stunning State Dining Room or Marie Antoinette's writing desk. You can't fail to notice the vast stuffed brown bears in Inner Hall, shot by the family's ancestor Sir Lancelot Carnegie.

Address: Scone Palace, Perth PH2 6BD, Scotland, UK
Phone: +44 (0)1738 552300
Fax: +44 (0)1738 552588
Web Site: www.scone-palace.net
Hours: From late March or early April

through October daily 9:30 A.M. to 5:30 P.M. Last admission 5:00 P.M. Grounds close at 6:00 P.M. Evening and winter tours by arrangement.

Attractions in Glasgow

Mackintosh House: In the years following Glasgow's 1990 nomination as European City of Culture, the once-maligned second city of Scotland has undergone a renaissance in vibrancy, reputation, and heritage. Charles

Rennie Mackintosh, one of its most prolific artists, has been reclaimed from his ignominious death in 1928, and his works are now a centerpiece tourist attraction. Born in 1868, Mackintosh trained as an architect and studied art and design at the Glasgow School of Art, where he met his wife and collaborator Margaret Macdonald, with whom he designed furniture, metalwork, and illustration. It took a while for his fusion of Scottish traditions, art nouveau, and simple Japanese-style lines to gain a following in Britain, where he was deemed a little too "continental." Finally, in the mid-1890s, he attracted several patrons and underwent an intense twenty-year period of creativity, during which he created the designs for House for an Art Lover (built sixty years posthumously in 1988). You can visit these and other showpieces of his style across the city, including the Willow Tea Rooms and the painstakingly recreated Mackintosh House in the Hunterian Art Gallery. The interiors of the end terrace house Mackintosh and his wife lived in from 1906 to 1914 convey their ability to reproportion buildings and imbue them with lots of light and space, and showcase their personally designed furniture and bric-a-brac.
Address: The Mackintosh House, Hunterian Art Gallery, University of Glasgow, Hillhead Street, Glasgow G12 8QQ, Scotland, UK
Phone: +44 (0)1413 305431
Web Site: www.hunterian.gla.ac.uk
Hours: Monday through Saturday, 9:30 A.M. to 5:00 P.M. (closed noon to 1:30 P.M.)
Admission: £2.50 (US$4.00) except Wednesday afternoon after 2:00 P.M., when admission is free.

Glasgow College of Piping: Bagpipes and kilts are synonymous with Scotland. Scottish bagpipes are thought to have evolved in the fifteenth century, and the tradition has continued to the present day. The Piping Centre, housed in a historic nineteenth-century building, is a national and international center of excellence for the instrument and its music. The center offers individual and group lessons as well as a degree in several varieties from the Highland pipe to Scottish smallpipes, uilleann pipes, fiddle, accordian, and drumming. Visit the college for lessons and a fine museum showcasing the complex folklore that's developed over

centuries with the help of the bagpipe.
Address: The Piping Centre, 30-34 McPhater Street, Cowcaddens, Glasgow G4 0HW, Scotland, UK
Phone: +44 (0)1413 530220
Fax: +44 (0)1413 531570
Web Site: www.thepipingcentre.co.uk
Hours: Contact the museum in advance to arrange a visit.

Attractions in and near Edinburgh

Edinburgh Festival: Edinburgh's world-renowned arts festival comprises the International, Fringe, Film, Jazz, Book, and Television festivals. It was first staged in August 1947 by an Austrian seeking to promote the spirit of European reconciliation and combat the austerity of postwar life and featured musicians from Central Europe. Eight Scottish and English theater troupes turned up uninvited to perform ad hoc in local venues, simultaneously launching Edinburgh's Fringe. In the following decades the resolutely highbrow International festival, alongside the wonderfully egalitarian Fringe event, have

both grown in stature and reputation, and Edinburgh's buzz rises octaves during this annual interlude. The Military Tattoo, a separate event but very much part of the festival experience, is held on the regal Castle Esplanade. It's an atmospheric event, especially at the close of proceedings, which is marked by a lone piper on the battlements.
Web Site: www.eif.co.uk
Phone: +44 (0)1314 732001 (info line)
Hours: Annually for three weeks, in late August to September.

Stirling Castle: Historically, Stirling has been a strategic location for both clan warfare and battles between the Scots and the English foe. It was here that Scotland's national hero, William Wallace, defeated the English in 1297 (iconicized in the Mel Gibson movie *Braveheart*) and where the coronation of a young Mary, later to become Queen of Scots, took place in 1543. There has been a fortress on this site as far back as the Iron Age, but the present building

dates from Stirling's golden age in the fifteenth and sixteenth centuries, when it was a residence for the Stuart dynasty. The Great Hall with its vast fireplaces is a stunning piece of medieval architecture, and the kitchens recreate the preparations made by Mary for a supremely indulgent banquet for the baptism of the future James IV. From the Douglas Gardens you can view the small window from which the Earl of Douglas, suspected of treason, was thrown by James II in 1452.
Address: Castle Wynd, Stirling FK8 1EJ, Scotland, UK
Phone: +44 (0)1786 450000
Web Site: www.stirlingcastle.com
Hours: Throughout the year: April to September: 9:30 A.M. to 6:00 P.M.; October to March: 9:30 A.M. to 5:00 P.M. Closed Christmas Day and Boxing Day (December 26).

Royal Yacht *Britannia*: Continuing an unbroken 300-year tradition in the British royal family for owning yachts, the Royal Yacht *Britannia* was launched in 1953. After clocking a million miles, it was decommissioned in 1997 in Portsmouth after a public outcry over royal spending. It's now an award-winning tourist attraction in Edinburgh's historic port of Leith.
Address: *Britannia* is berthed at Ocean Terminal, Leith, Edinburgh's new waterfront retail and leisure development.
Phone: +44 (0)1315 555566
Web Site: www.royalyachtbritannia.co.uk
Hours: Winter, October to March, 10:00 A.M. to 3:30 P.M. (closes 5:00 P.M.) daily. Summer, April to September, 9:30 A.M. to 4:30 P.M. (closes 6:00 P.M.) daily.

The Heritage of Golf Exhibition: The charismatic ex-vet Archie Baird began collecting golf memorabilia more than thirty years ago and has since built up a formidable private collection that he opens to the public upon request. He has an unbounded passion for the game and is arguably Scotland's foremost golf historian. His exhibition runs from the early Dutch origins of golf to the feathery ball era of the pre-1850s, to the "gutta percha" ball of the late nineteenth century, which allowed for a massive expansion of the game. An absolute must for golf lovers everywhere.
Address: Next to Pro's Shop, Gullane, East Lothian EH31 2BB, Scotland, UK
Phone: +44 (0)1875 870277, ask for Archie Baird.
Hours: By appointment.

Attractions in and near Royal Dornoch

Loch Ness: Long, narrow, and ruggedly scenic, Britain's biggest lake, Loch Ness, is primarily known for its legendary inhabitant, the Loch Ness monster—affectionately known as Nessie—whose unproven existence guarantees a steady stream of visitors to the loch every year.

The first sighting of Nessie supposedly occurred in sixth century A.D., when St. Columba reported an encounter with a sea serpent. In 1933 the mystery deepened. An

unconfirmed story goes that a great monster crawled on land from the water and killed three onlookers. There are

several competing theories about Nessie's true identity. Some claim it's a giant sturgeon or

catfish; others think it comes through a time tunnel from the past; some think Nessie's a modern day plesiosaur dinosaur born from eggs frozen beneath the earth's crust that thawed during shifts in the tectonic plates.

This mystery will run and run since it's hard to get any sort of sighting in the peat-filled loch waters, where visibility only extends a few feet down. The closest you're likely to come to the monster is the cut-out variety at

the lake, but a visit is still worthwhile for the stunning scenery.
Address: Situated between Inverness and Fort Augustus in the Highlands.
Web Site: www.lochness.co.uk

Mey Castle: Way up in the farthest northeast of the Highlands is Mey Castle, a place that the late Queen Elizabeth (the Queen Mother) fell in love with, bought, and renovated. It's not hard to see why: It's a perfectly proportioned sixteenth-century abode, sitting 400 yards from the sea with great views across to the Orkney Islands. It was opened to the public in 2003, a year following her death at the age of 101, and it paints an intimate

portrait of its owner and her tastes. Beginning in the entrance hall and taking you through the library, bedrooms, drawing room, dining room, and kitchen, you can see everything from her Wellington boots and raincoat and the corgis' dog bowls to opulent furnishings and paintings by fellow family members.
Address: Mey Castle, Thurso, Caithness, Highlands KW14 8XH, Scotland, UK
Phone: +44 (0)1847 851473
Fax: +44 (0)1847 851475
Web Site: www.castleofmey.org.uk
Hours: From May Day through September; closed ten days in late July to early August. The Castle and Gardens are open 10:30 A.M. to 4:00 P.M. Subject to change.

Attractions in and near St. Andrews

St. Andrews Castle: The ruined St. Andrews Castle stands on the rocky coastline on the east side of the town, its walls dropping down on three sides into the sea and rearing up on the fourth behind a deep moat. It was founded in the thirteenth century and over the centuries was the castle of Scotland's bishops and archbishops. It witnessed grim events during the sixteenth century reformation, including the murder of Cardinal Beaton in 1545 in revenge for the execution of Protestant reformers by their fellows, who then threw his body into the chilling bottle-shaped dungeon you can still view today. They spent the following year besieged in the castle, digging the siege tunnel complex you can still climb through; it is said to be the best surviving example of such engineering in Europe. Plan

your trip first thing in the morning or later in the day, when the castle can be almost deserted.
Address: Historic Scotland, St. Andrews Castle, North Street, St. Andrews, Fife KY16 9QL, Scotland, UK

Phone: +44 (0)1334 477196
Web Site: www.visit-standrews.co.uk
Hours: All year, 9:00 A.M. to 6:30 P.M. daily.

Jim Farmer's Golf Shop: Jim Farmer's is one of the top—if not *the* top—pro shops in Scotland. Jim stocks a huge range of quality brand-name sports clothing and merchandise featuring the St. Andrews logo.
Address: Jim Farmer's Golf Shop, 1 St. Mary's Place, Market Street, St. Andrews KY16 9UY, Scotland, UK
Phone: +44 (0)1334 476796
Web Site: www.standrewshopro.com

British Golf Museum: If you're golfing in St. Andrews, a trip to this museum is worthwhile. It takes you on a neatly chronological tour of golf's history through the prism of the town of St. Andrews, the home of golf. Its galleries trace its history using a mixture of text, memorabilia, and touch screens, simultaneously teaching you all about golf's heritage and testing your knowledge.
Address: British Golf Museum, Bruce Embankment, St. Andrews, Fife KY16 9AB, Scotland, UK
Phone: +44 (0)1334 460046
Fax: +44 (0)1334 460064
Web Site: www.britishgolfmuseum.co.uk
Hours: Vary according to day and time of year.

Troywood Bunker: If you end up spending too much of your golfing holiday within the sandy variety, why not visit a more unusual

kind of bunker? The Troywood Bunker, a quite remarkable vestige from the recent Cold War, is now open for the world to see the precautions the British government took to prevent meltdown in the face of a nuclear attack by the USSR. From the outside of what looks like an innocent farmhouse, you walk down a 500-foot tunnel to a secret bunker 130 feet below the ground to where, in the case of a nuclear emergency, senior ministers from Edinburgh would be evacuated to live, along with their key 300 civil servants.

Address: Crown Buildings, Troywood (near St. Andrews), Fife KY16 8QH, Scotland, UK

Phone: +44 (0)1333 310301

Fax: +44 (0)1333 312040

Web Site: www.secretbunker.co.uk

Hours: Late March through early October, 10:00 A.M. to 6:00 P.M. daily.

Cross-Regional Attractions

Highland Games: The Highland Games are celebrated throughout mainland Scotland and its isles from May to September annually. The most famous are the Clanloddoch Games and Gathering in Strathdon and the Braemar Gathering at Ballater.

The games were originally used as a test of skill and strength when recruiting clan warriors.

This isn't a games for the meek and mild. Activities include putting the stone, similar to the shot put in the Olympics but using a larger, heavy stone ball; throwing the hammer, a variation using a sledgehammer with a ball on the end; and tossing the caber, running and throwing a tree trunk cut to about 20 feet and weighing around 150 pounds. Stand well back!

The games started centuries ago as a gathering between Scottish clans. It was revived in 1821. For those less mighty, piping and dance competitions and a group tug-o-war are another feature of the day, as well as more modern track and field athletics, traditional crafts, and even sheep-shearing competitions. Activities vary, but it usually costs a few pounds to get in. You're guaranteed a traditional, fun day out for all the family.

Address: Braemar Royal Highland Society, Coilacriech, Ballater AB35 5UH, Scotland, UK

Phone: +44 (0)1339 755377

Web Site: www.braemargathering.org

Admission: Less than £5.00 (US$8.00)

West Highland Railway: Billed as one of the world's most spectacular rail journeys and unlikely to disappoint, the trip along the West Highland Railway features particularly dramatic sections across Rannoch Moor and from Fort William to Mallaig. Along the way you'll be faced with romantic sights ranging from picturesque villages to rolling moors, towering mountains, and historic glens. After the departure from Glasgow and the initial climb upward around Beinn Odhar (a breathtaking engineering feat of a horseshoe loop of viaducts), the line crosses Rannoch Moor, where the track had to be laid on tree roots, brushwood, and tons upon tons of earth and ashes. Passing along the side of Loch Ossian and Ben Nevis, the train enters Fort William from the northeast. If that's only whetted your appetite, take the train along the Mallaig extension to the horseshoe-shaped Glenfinnan Viaduct. The viaduct was a radical experiment by "Concrete Bob" McAlpine, but apparently during 1900 a horse and cart fell through planks onto one of the hollow piers, where the horse's ghost remains to this day among the impossibly beautiful mountains.

Address: Scotrail, Caledonian Chambers, 87 Union Street, Glasgow G1 3TA, Scotland, UK

Phone: +44 (0)8456 057021 (info service)

Web Site: www.scotrail.co.uk

south africa

Once you have experienced Africa, you cannot help being touched by the wonder of this vast land and its inhabitants. You will soon appreciate that many of the nations within the borders of this beautiful, but hostile, continent are incredibly poor. There are hundreds of thousands of square miles of bush and desert, baking under an unrelenting sun, in a land where many people are underfed and even starving.

South African winelands landscape (left)
Lost City Course (above)

It is one of the last places on earth where you would expect to find a golfer's paradise, but if you head far enough south, you will find that paradise in South Africa.

Not only are there numerous championship standard courses around Johannesburg and Cape Town and along the south coast—such as Gary Player's oasis resort Sun City and the Durban Country Club—but South Africa also offers the ultimate package for the adventure golfer: golf and safari. You can find world-class game reserves full of elephant, rhino, giraffe, and other wild animals adjacent to first-class golf courses; in the case of the Hans Merensky Course, you will find yourself sharing the course with free-roaming wildlife. An unusual hazard!

Another aspect of South Africa's appeal is that, by western standards, the cost of playing championship courses and staying in reasonable hotels is ridiculously inexpensive—sometimes less than 25 percent of what you would expect to pay back home. First-class golfing facilities combined with inspirational backdrops—like Table Mountain or Kruger National Park—and sunshine year-round make South Africa the perfect location for the perfect game.

Venda Tribe children (above)

Farm ostrich, Oudtshoorn (below)

About South Africa

The Rainbow Nation has awesome scenery, from icy mountain peaks to subtropical beaches to fertile wine valleys. Its people are as diverse and welcoming as its landscapes. Now that the days of racial segregation are over, South Africa, the wealthiest nation in mainland sub-Saharan Africa, is establishing itself as a center for tourism. It's not without its problems, such as rising crime and HIV infection rates, but sticking to safe areas and using a little prudence should ensure a problem-free trip. Like the skies, your options are endless: Tour battlegrounds of tribal and colonial history in Zululand, track lions in the great grasslands of Kruger National Park, trek the awe-inspiring Rift Valley or the dramatic Drakensberg Mountains, or drive along the Riviera-style Garden Route with its sunshine beaches.

Activities and Attractions

Wildlife: South Africa's national parks and nature reserves, easily the country's biggest attractions, are home to 300 species of mammal alone, including antelope, baboon, buffalo, cheetah, hippo, crocodile, elephant, giraffe, leopard, lion, rhino, springbok, wildebeest, and zebra. National parks are a good value, well maintained, and easily accessible—particularly with your own vehicle. The best one to visit is Kruger National

Park to see the "big five" game animals (lion, rhino, buffalo, elephant, and leopard). Private reserves let you get closer to the animals for a higher entrance fee.

Beaches: With its endless sunshine South Africa has some of the best and least-crowded beaches for surfing in the world, particularly in Durban and Cape Town. The waves are big and fast, so you'll need a decent-sized board. You can buy them in the big surfing towns. The subtropical KwaZulu-Natal and Western Cape coastlines have lots of resort towns with diving schools and opportunities to dive with great white sharks. The beaches are often long and wide, particularly along the South Coast Garden Route, and they are great for horse riding and walking. The beaches are not only warm but clean; eight in Western Cape and KwaZulu-Natal have the Blue Flag award for superb environmental standards.

Hiking and Outdoors: The most accessible hiking is in the Table Mountain National Park in Cape Town. Farther afield, walks along the Garden Route and the Drakensberg Mountains offer spectacular mountain scenery. There are so many different terrains to explore in this vast land: desert, forest, coast, mountain, and *fynbos* (600 indigenous varieties of heath). You can stay in luxury guesthouses on the Wild Coast or Dolphin Trail, or sleep in a tent or cave in the designated wilderness areas of Cedarberg or Drakensberg. Mountain biking has become popular, with many outfitters renting bikes; bike trails are marked in the national parks. There are numerous crazy sports for the adventurous like abseiling (rappeling), gliding, snowboarding, bungee jumping, hot-air ballooning, sky diving, and kayaking.

Wine lands (above)
Sunset (below)

History of Golf in South Africa

Golf in South Africa dates back to 1885, just eight years before the second-oldest open championship in the world, the South African Open, first took place. Since then, this beautiful country has produced a succession of South African–born Open champions and world number-one ranked golfers, from Bobby Locke and Gary Player to Retief Goosen and the "Big Easy," Ernie Els. Surprisingly, the game did not gain widespread popularity until the apartheid regime was abolished in the 1990s, when the new republic was formed and tourism blossomed. Subsequently, magnificent courses have been built, and the number of golf tourists increases each year. Inevitably, albeit to a lesser extent than before, the black/white divide is still as evident in golf as it is in society. There are stark contrasts in the quality and maintenance of courses, with South Africa's growing population of black and colored golfers typically playing cheap but poorly maintained courses.

Caddies, Gary Player Course

When to Go and What to Bring

For temperature and humidity, there are no bad golfing seasons, as it rarely gets cold—even in the winter. In the south there may be a little winter rain, but it becomes increasingly drier if you move farther inland. Some parts of the bush have no rain for several months, and there are many courses to play. October to March (spring to fall) offers the most pleasant weather. If you are heading north or east in the spring or summer, malaria tablets and mosquito repellent are a wise investment. Playing conditions are magnificent, with lots of sunshine and high temperatures; sunscreen, shorts, and bottles of water are the order of the day for much of the year. Remember that this is a nation with a long golfing history: On the top golf courses, correct dress and etiquette are very important.

Costs

Compared with equivalent Western courses, South Africa courses are very, very cheap. You can play most championship courses for less than $75 per round and afterward enjoy the luxurious splendor of the clubhouse and other facilities for a fraction of the usual price. Many courses offer attractive discounts of up to half-price green fees during the low, winter season (May to October). In fact South Africa is one of the few golfing countries where everything is a fantastic value for the money.

Hotels

Accommodation, from numerous B&Bs to luxury resorts, is plentiful and a good value. High season (summer) and school holidays (Christmas and Easter) can triple prices, and one-week minimum stays can apply to popular hotels. A good five-star hotel costs upward of $200 for a double, and a chain like Holiday Inn in Cape Town can cost up to $500 a night in high season. For $100 a night, you can usually secure a nice room in a luxury three-star hotel.

Travel

Airports: Thirty airlines fly to South Africa. The main entry point is Johannesburg International (JNB), with an increasing number of flights to Cape Town (CPT) and some to Durban (DUR). Within the country flying is a good option, as internal flights are the most comprehensive in all of Africa. South Africa

Airways is the main domestic carrier. Be aware that internal airfares, like those to the country, can be very expensive, although booking within the country a month in advance gives you a 50 percent discount.

Car Rental and Other Transport: South Africa has the best road network in all of Africa, so it's great for driving, and the astonishingly scenic and little trafficked coastal roads like the Garden Route are what driving was made for. Avoid driving in Jo'burg, where carjacking is a problem, and discuss your route with the rental company to avoid any potential danger zones. Car theft is another problem, so make sure your insurance covers all inevitabilities. Drive on the left side, and be prudent, as many people drive fast and dangerously. There's also a reasonably extensive network of buses, trains, minitaxis, and the backpackers Baz Bus network. Avoid public transport in the major cities—you can become a target for criminals. The famous Blue Train running from Pretoria to Cape Town is a twenty-five-hour journey of sheer luxury, which can be done in sections.

Regions and Golfing

Essentially, the courses in the north of the country are nearer the equator and therefore hotter and drier than courses in the south. Courses near the west coast attract the cooler sea breezes from the Atlantic Ocean, but farther east toward the Indian Ocean, they become more and more subtropical.

Metro Arch Hotel foyer (top)
Highway at night (above)

Accordingly, there are more desert, sandy courses in the north and the west and lush-green, water-feature courses in the south and the east. There are exceptions everywhere as entrepreneurs have carved magnificent water features out of arid deserts and bushlands: Gary Player's Sun City in North West Province is a classic example.

Western Cape: This southwest province is the most-visited region with its amazing flora, sea life, wine lands, and mountain scenery.

Described by Sir Francis Drake as "the fairest Cape in all the circumference of the World," the Cape of Good Hope, with its crashing waves and floral blooms, has been widely traversed by daring seafarers. At the foot of the awesome Table Mountain, Cape Town is charming and relaxing with great diving, climbing, history, and unique Cape Malay Muslim culture. The wine lands region around Stellenbosch and Paarl is loved for its quaint fishing villages, Cape Dutch architecture, and chances to sample New World wine vintages. Namaqualand, a semidesert area, is spectacular in the spring (August/September) when it bursts to life with a vibrant floral display. East of Cape Town head out along the Riviera-style Garden Route, full of luxury resorts, golden beaches, lush forest

Lost City Hotel dome (above)
Vrede en Luste Winery (top right)
Wine lands (bottom right)

and lakes, a rugged coast fringed with towering mountains, and great golf courses. You can even saddle up and ride (and later eat) an ostrich in Oudtshoorn.

The diversity of landscapes—mountains, arid plains, sandy beaches, and enormous wetlands—provides the golfer with almost every imaginable challenge. The courses are as varied as the stunning scenery, with a huge variety of types: mountain, desert, parkland, and links. The numbers and contrasts of the courses have made Western Cape a mecca for golfers.

Eastern Cape and Lesotho: Eastern Cape is a province with a rich history of battles between the Xhosa, British, and Afrikaans. There are plenty of famous beaches and resorts along the Sunshine Coast and the Wild Coast, with world-class surfing in Jeffreys Bay near the major hub of Port Elizabeth, "the Friendly City." Inland you'll find the forested Amatola Mountains—great for trout fishing and hiking—and the Karoo Desert. The parks here are specialized: The Mountain Zebra and the Addo Elephant National Parks contain many unique subspecies like the Cape elephants. Many of the best golf courses are in sight and sound of the Indian Ocean's seemingly incessant white rollers, and the whales, which are a regular sight from the shore, can distract your game.

Lesotho, the "Kingdom of the Sky," is a small enclave country inside South Africa. Enjoy good hiking or pony treks and spectacular views from challenging climbs at Thaba-Bosiu (mountain at night).

Northern Cape and Free State: In contrast to the southern coastal regions, the remote Northern Cape and Free State, covering one-third of South Africa, are dry with few forests and mountains, and more plains and deserts. Relatively few golfers stray from the main tourist areas to visit this remote region, although you will find a few parkland courses scattered around.

The westerly Northern Cape is a rugged space ideal for those in search of tranquillity, where only Kimberley, the "City of Diamonds," counts as urban development. The province includes part of the Kalahari Desert, which is home to Gemsbok antelope, springbok, black-maned Kalahari lion, and Sishen Golf Course, home of the Kalahari Open.

Besotho Tribe member (above)
Venda Tribe members (left)

Pick and choose your favorite golf or leisure activities. Two activities plus travel gives you fifteen-hour, adventure-packed days.

Day 1: A.M. After arriving in Cape Town Airport (CPT) the previous night, take a tour with an ex-political prisoner of Robben Island, a high-security jail made notorious during the apartheid. Or play a round and spot birds at Clovelly Country Club just south of town. **P.M.** Play Royal Cape Golf Club on the outskirts of town. Hang out in Bo Kaap, and take an evening walking tour of this historic Muslim quarter.

Day 2: A.M. Ascend the cable car to explore the spectacular Atlantic Ocean views from Table Mountain. Alternatively, enjoy fantastic views of Table Mountain while playing a game at Milnerton Golf Club. **P.M.** Rent a car and hit the road. Head to Pearl Valley in Franschhoek, about 50 miles east of Cape Town, for a round, and stay on the lovely estate. Alternatively, taste a glass or two of divine wine at the Vrede en Lust winery, a ten-minute drive from Franschhoek.

Day 3: A.M. Head 30 miles south to play Arabella Golf Club in Kleinmond by the Kogelberg Mountains. **P.M.** Head back to Cape Town for a little more sightseeing or nine holes at Clovelly Country Club or Milnerton Golf Club. Take a flight to Johannesburg International (JNB) in the central-north. Stay here for two nights—the Metro Arch Hotel is superb.

Day 4: A.M. Visit the Apartheid Museum in Jo'burg to learn the stark history of racial segregation in South Africa. Or play a round for just $45 at championship course Glendower in the east suburbs of Jo'burg.

Gary Player Course

P.M. Head for a round at Soweto Golf Club, possibly the most underdeveloped golf course in Africa. With a reputable guide, take a night tour of the shanty town and *shebeens* (drinking joints) in Soweto, where they know how to party and the nightlife is buzzing. Stay the night back in Jo'burg.

Day 5: A.M. Rent a car and drive to Cullinan for a tour of the most famous diamond mine in the world. Take the N1 north, then just after Pretoria follow the east signs in Cullinan, a journey taking about an hour. Alternatively, play the championship Houghton Golf Club in Jo'burg before heading northwest by road or air to Rustenburg Airport, 25 miles from Sun City.

P.M. Drive west from Pretoria some 60 miles along B roads to Sun City resort in the North West Province, a journey taking an hour and a half. Play the Gary Player Course, then dine in the spectacular Palace of the Lost City, the most opulent hotel in Africa (and stay there, too, if you can afford it!).

Day 6: A.M. Enjoy another round at one of the six other Sun City courses. The championship Lost City Course is recommended. **P.M.** The final leg of your journey is a trip, half on B-roads and half on the N1 motorway, some 500 miles northwest to Phalabarwa in the North West Province. You may want to take a few days to do the trip or investigate charter tourist flights to the airport here. Stay the night at the Hans Merensky Estate.

Day 7: A.M. Play the Hans Merensky Course. Avoid the animals along the fairways! Or head a few miles east to the greatest nature reserve in the world—Kruger National Park—to spot wild game. **P.M.** Wind your way back to Jo'burg International Airport (JNB) by heading 150 miles west on B roads, then 200 miles south on the N1. You should be able to get an internal flight from either Phalabarwa or Hoedspruit in the park directly to Jo'burg.

You could extend your trip by next visiting the fantastic courses in and near Durban: the Durban Country Club, Zimabli Country Club, and Prince's Grant Golf Club. The weather's great for surfing and diving, too.

FIVE-DAY EXECUTIVE STRESS BUSTER

Day 1: **P.M.** Fly to Johannesburg International (JNB), and transfer to Rustenburg Airport, 25 miles from Sun City. Dine in the spectacular Palace of the Lost City, the most opulent hotel in Africa (and stay there, too, if you can afford it!).

Day 2: **A.M.** Play the Gary Player Course. You may also have time for either nine holes on the Lost City Course or a splash around Water World.
P.M. Take a charter flight 500 miles northwest to Phalabarwa in the North West Province. Stay the night in the Hans Merensky Estate, and go game spotting at sunset.

Day 3: **A.M.** Play the Hans Merensky Course. Avoid the animals ambling along the fairways!
P.M. Take a flight back to Jo'burg. The Metro Arch Hotel is superb.

Day 4: **A.M.** Play a round for just $45 at championship course Glendower in the east suburbs of Jo'burg.
P.M. Head for a round at Soweto Golf Club, possibly the most underdeveloped golf course in Africa.
   With a reputable guide, take a night tour of the shanty town and *shebeens* (drinking joints) in Soweto, where they know how to

party and the nightlife is buzzing. Stay the night back in Jo'burg.

Day 5: **A.M.** Visit the Apartheid Museum in Jo'burg to learn the stark history of racial segregation in South Africa. Or play the championship Houghton Golf Club in the city.
P.M. Take your flight home from Jo'burg International (JNB).

Lost City Course

Free State, in the heart of the country, has a prairie feel, with plenty of wide-open space interspersed with windmills and farmlands that offer hospitable homestays. There are several resorts along the Vaal River near its two large dams. The Eastern Highlands offer opportunities for hiking and bird-watching in the sandstone formations of the Golden Gate National Park or the vulture sanctuary of the adjoining Qwaqwa National Park. Meet the South Sotho people at the Basotho Cultural Village in Witsieshoek.

Northwest and Gauteng: The agricultural North West Province is famed for its art, from ancient bushman rock paintings to the fine arts and curios of its nineteenth-century settlers, the Batswana people. Sun City resort is the principal tourist draw, containing the most extravagant hotel in Africa, the Palace of the Lost City, and its nearby excellent Pilanesberg National Park—not to mention its seven superb golf courses. There are plenty of resorts, game lodges, guesthouses, and reserves, including Madjkwe by the Botswana border and a rhino reserve near Christiana. Get a taste of the wild northwest in the Vryburg region, with its cattle farms and game ranches reminiscent of Texas, or tour working mines on the Diamond Route.

Gauteng, "the heartbeat of Africa," is the commercial center of the country, containing the urban cities of Pretoria, Johannesburg, and the ghetto township of Soweto. Explore the province's legacy of apartheid and diamond trading. Outside the notoriously dangerous urban sprawl, head out to Gauteng's numerous game farms, bird and nature reserves, dam lakes, and rivers for fishing, hiking, and the outdoors.

Venda Tribe children (above)
Cape Town Township (below)

Gauteng and the east side of North West Province are the most heavily populated areas for golf. There are dozens of first-class facilities, mostly parkland courses, within a stone's throw of Johannesburg and the capital, Pretoria. Perhaps this explains why many golf tourists don't risk the well-publicized (but often unfairly exaggerated) security dangers of traveling away from the main tourist areas. There are far too many courses to recommend, but try Gary Player Country Club (part of Sun City), Glendower, and Houghton for starters.

Limpopo and Mpumalanga: These northernmost provinces are nearest to the equator and the hottest. The region is attracting an increasing number of golfers who want to experience the true African safari—and play a few rounds as well. Limpopo (formerly Northern Province) in the far north is much visited for the exceptional Kruger National Park, probably the best safari park in the world. The southern region has many hot springs dotted among red-rock cliffs, wetlands, rolling hills, and mountains. The Makapan Valley, near the vibrant gold-mining capital of Pietersburg, was the site of the earliest human fossils. In the northwest the Limpopo River Valley encompasses Iron Age history with bushman cave paintings and hilltop fortifications. The west is a bushveld full of haunting old baobab trees. Meet the fascinating tribes of north Sotho, such as the Venda people in the northeast, who perform rituals like the python dance to ward off evil spirits: Teenage girls perform a slow, rhythmic dance to the beat of drums.

Mpumalanga is a superb region for sportsmen with gliding, hiking, trout fishing, water sports, and many golfing opportunities in scenic locations. Hike the dramatic, steep escarpment facing down to Kruger National Park; traverse the giant red sandstone gorges of the Blyde River Canyon, the third-largest canyon in the world; or meander through the Botanical Reserve with its mountain peaks, river rapids, and indigenous forest. Discover the history of the late-nineteenth-century gold rush on the Long Tom Route and in the open-air museum of Pilgrim's Rest Village.

KwaZulu-Natal: Although small, KwaZulu-Natal has many attractions. Visit tribal villages in Zululand, and stay in a beehive-shaped hut. Lovers of colonial history can explore the major Anglo-Zulu and Anglo-Boer battlefield sites, many near Pietermaritzburg, known as "the last outpost of the British Empire." There are some significant game reserves like Hluhluwe-Umfolozi, where the white rhino was saved from extinction, and the coral reefs of St. Lucia. The Drakensberg Mountains are idyllic for hiking, mountaineering, and seeing bushman cave art, and the midlands region is superb for family vacations with its fishing, rafting, crafts, and country hotels. The province's subtropical climate make it a focal point for beach vacations and water sports, particularly in Durban, with a "golden mile" of hotels and fine opportunities to take in the surf.

KwaZulu-Natal probably has the country's best golfing climate. Even South Africans vacation here! There are several magnificent courses, not least the Durban Country Club, which is considered by many to be the top national course and is a regular host to the South African Open. The coastal regions are subtropical, and the roar of the surf is a constant feature on its numerous links courses like Selborne and Beachwood.

Derelict power station
cooling tower, Soweto

THE GOLF COURSES

PEARL VALLEY

6085 Metres / Par 72

PEARL VALLEY
SIGNATURE GOLF ESTATE & SPA

The Clubhouse

At the time of this publication (2005), despite the club opening two years ago, the clubhouse has yet to be built! The Malaysian owner is a perfectionist who aspires to create the perfect environment for his members. If it is constructed in keeping with the rest of Pearl Valley, the finished article will be stunning.

Food: Because of the lack of a clubhouse with full kitchen, the club is limited as to what it can provide; however, the food is standard golfers' fare superbly prepared and presented.

Changing Rooms: Until the main clubhouse has been completed, facilities will remain limited; however, the changing rooms are well presented, with complimentary Molton Brown products.

Ladies' Facilities: Exactly the same as for men.

Pro Shop: Well run and extremely efficient with no long lines and friendly and helpful staff. If you require club rental, a cart, or a caddie, they will be organized in an instant.

Background to the Golf Course

Architect: Jack Nicklaus designed the course, which opened in 2003 at a cost of $60 million. Pearl Valley is one of the few to which he has given his signature, which means that he oversaw the entire project.

Type: Parkland.

Landscape: Surrounded by the stunning Cape vineyards, Pearl Valley offers some of the most breathtaking scenery in South Africa. Its design has been thoughtfully realized so that the course blends into its environment. Like other premier golf estates, there are manicured stylish residential areas (though

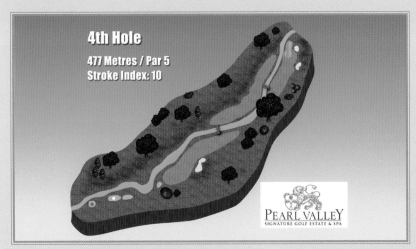

4th Hole

477 Metres / Par 5
Stroke Index: 10

PEARL VALLEY
SIGNATURE GOLF ESTATE & SPA

fewer than most), and secure access points and boundaries. Nicklaus's signature golf course has set the superior tone for the entire estate. In fact everything about Pearl Valley is of signature standard.

Course Facts:

• *Paarl* is Afrikaans for pearl, so called because when it rained, an area of the mountain would glisten like a pearl.

• Pearl Valley was conceived in 1997 but remained on Nicklaus's drawing board during a period when a number of new golf courses made an appearance on the South African landscape. The interval between planning and execution enabled "the Golden Bear," together with the local professional team, to monitor these developments, take note of international trends, and refine the original master plan in subtle yet significant ways.

• Its most famous resident is Francois Pienaar, a 6-handicap golfer who was captain of South Africa's World Cup–winning rugby team. The rugby trophy was handed to him by newly elected President Nelson Mandela in 1995.

• The course was christened by a match play event between designer Jack Nicklaus and former sparring partner Gary Player. Observers watched the match in awe as the two senior players competed as eagerly then as they had always done. Nicklaus, trailing by three holes going into the back nine, decided to focus. He managed to pull it back, and the match finished all square.

Playing the Course

Pearl Valley is a design masterpiece. For example, all the par 5s and par 3s are played in different directions, so no advantage will be gained by prevailing wind directions. Although there are many bunkers on the fairways and surrounding the beautifully manicured greens, as with most Nicklaus designs, these are generally big and shallow but not overly daunting, with an emphasis on hazard rather than penalty. There are nine cleverly designed lakes, like on the fourth (par 5), where you have to cross the same water three times to reach the green.

Ian's Opinion

This top-of-the-line Jack Nicklaus signature course is one of the numerous new resort courses in the wine lands region near Cape Town. Like all Nicklaus courses, it's exciting and challenging to play, and you'll need to spend time contemplating every shot, yet it still gives a midhandicap golfer a chance to do relatively well. If you stray, it will test your bunker game. A very enjoyable golfing experience.

Temperatures in the Western Cape region are pleasant as there is invariably a sea breeze. With a tempting and well-stocked refreshment hut halfway around and some shady trees on the course, it is not as tiring to play as some other courses in South Africa.

Score Card
Address: Pearl Valley Signature Golf Estate and Spa, Franschhoek, Western Cape, South Africa
Phone: +27 21 867 0761
Fax: +27 21 867 0769
Web Site: www.pearlvalley.co.za
Course and Length: One eighteen-hole course, 6,085 meters (6,655 yards), par 72.
Dress Code: Smart/casual golfing attire. No sneakers or above-the-knee shorts.

Tee Times: In ten-minute slots from dawn to dusk.
Handicap: No certificate required.
Green Fees: Rand (R)300 (US$50) for nine holes, R500 (US$85) for eighteen holes.
Other Costs: R180 (US$31) for a golf cart (no caddies allowed). Club rental R200 (US$34) per set. Driving range balls are R15 (US$2.50) for a basket of fifty-five balls.
Facilities: When the clubhouse construction is completed in spring 2006, it will have a spa and swimming pool.
Location: A five-minute drive from the towns of Franschhoek and Paarl. Take exit 59 off the N1, just south of Paarl, which is very close to Cape Town Airport.

SOWETO COUNTRY CLUB

Opened in the 1970s, Soweto Country Club occupies an area with a rich history. The sixth green overlooks Freedom Square, where Nelson Mandela and other members of the Africa National Congress (ANC) wrote the most radical and forward-thinking constitution in South Africa's history.

Today the site, set in an area of tranquillity in the heart of bustling Soweto, remains virtually unchanged. Soweto Country Club has always struggled to provide adequate golfing facilities. The committee manages with

meager funds, and there is a constant battle with the local council, who are seemingly incapable of maintaining the course. There are no facilities as such, only a common room.

Playing the Course

A round at the Soweto Country Club course is a humbling experience. The tees are semi-derelict, marked by a rough lump of concrete. Shots hit onto the fairway grass, long and rough, are often lost. The fairways are more demanding than the rough areas of most

championship golf courses elsewhere in South Africa, so much so that the fairway drive requires "placement" before the next shot can be taken. Many of the bumpy and unpredictable greens are diseased and in desperate need of some TLC. Holes like the thirteenth are a challenge to play: This one contains the only water hazard on the course—that is, when the committee can afford to fill it with water. Soweto Country Club once had the longest golf hole in Africa on the ninth, but it has now been shortened to a mere 629 meters (688 yards) off the back tees.

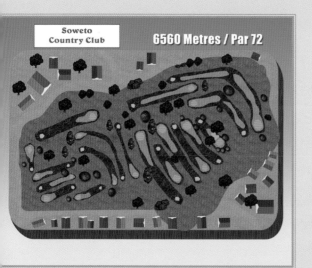

Soweto Country Club — 6560 Metres / Par 72

Paul Obeda, Soweto Country Club manager (left)
Barrels used as fairway markers (far left)
Derelict tractor (below)

Score Card

Address: Soweto Country Club, Soweto, Johannesburg, Gauteng Province, South Africa
Phone: +27 11 938 5934
Fax: +27 11 933 2029
Course and Length: One eighteen hole course, 6,560 meters (7,174 yards), par 72.
Dress Code: Shorts allowed with socks above the ankle. Players must have a collared shirt.
Tee Times: 6:00 A.M. to 4:00 P.M.
Handicap: Certificate required.
Green Fees: R14 (US$2.00).
Other Costs: Caddies R75 (US$13), no buggies (golf carts).
Location: A twenty-minute drive southwest of Johannesburg. Take a cab recommended by your hotel.

Ian's Opinion

This is a must for any traveling golfer. The links and green are in poor condition, and the club, financed in part by the council and in part by subscriptions, is continually broke. At less than two dollars a round, funds are very scarce. The club is short of the most basic facilities, including tractor equipment and mowers to keep the fairways in a playable condition. It can take six or seven hours to play a round, mainly because you can spend a lot of time looking for your ball in the fairways. What makes a round so enjoyable, and makes you want to come back, is the sheer enthusiasm of its multicultural 400-strong membership. The members are inventive—they even fashion their own golf clubs from metal coat hangers and trash bags. There are emerging numbers of young black players who, with some support, could become the next Tiger Woods.

GARY PLAYER COURSE, SUN CITY

The Resort

Hotels: The Sun City Resort has four separate hotels. The undeniable jewel in the crown is the Palace of the Lost City, which is both opulent and expensive. The icon of Sun City, the Palace offers guests complete luxury, and it is regarded as the greatest hotel in all of Africa. Fabled to be the royal residence of an

ancient king, the Palace lavishes its guests with five-star service and is luxurious in every facet of its fabulous architecture and decor. The Palace has 338 rooms, inclusive of 4 deluxe suites. This is the ideal location for access to the Lost City Golf Course. It's worth a visit, simply to marvel at the audacity and humor of the architects and to dine in its elegant restaurant. It is overly grand, but surprisingly not tacky.

The three other hotels all offer suites and luxury rooms. The Cascades, the epiphany of elegance, has tropical birds and water features. Many rooms at the subtropical Sun City Hotel, overlooking the Gary Player Course and Water World, face onto the hanging gardens. This is the liveliest hotel, and it houses the famous casino. Sun City Cabanas is considered to be the most relaxing of Sun City's hotels, and it is popular with families with young children. Designed to blend into the foot of the mountain, it is surrounded by gardens that are great for walks.

Facilities: Besides its golf and hotel facilities, Sun City offers a variety of leisure activities: a famous casino, water sports, cinemas, varieté shows, a wide range of sporting facilities, and a vast choice of restaurants. The resort lies adjacent to the Pilanesberg National Park and Game Reserve, where the "big five" game reside in abundance.

Activities: The large lake of Water World runs along the sixteenth and seventeenth holes of the Gary Player Country Club. It offers waterskiing, paragliding, and rental of wave runners (Jet Skis). For the kids there are bananas and donuts—inflatable white-knuckle rides. For a more sedate trip on the beautiful lake, you can glide on a pedal boat or take a cruise. Adrenaline junkies can sail the highest zipline (parasail) in the world, which overlooks the entire Sun City complex and reaches speeds of up to 50 mph soaring above the tree line. For other water adventures, the Cascades Hotel has its own beach and swimming pool, which provide a tranquil spot to take time out and relax. For a more energetic day, head to the Valley of the Waves, Sun City's own water park with rides and pools that offer plenty of thrills and soaking spills.

Background to the Gary Player Course

Architect: Gary Player.
Type: Bushveld.
Landscape: The kikuyu-grass fairways and bent-grass greens contrast with the thorn-scrub and aloe-covered hillsides and untamed bushveld bordering the fairways.
Pro Shop: The Pro Shop is well stocked with Gary Player Country Club merchandise. Take

away a polo shirt or cap to remind you of the day you lost a thousand balls on the course!

Course Facts:

• In the late 1970s legendary entrepreneur Sol Kerzner bought an area of land on the site of an ancient volcano. Kerzner planned to build a leisure complex that would welcome the finest entertainers in the world, be home to the best sporting facilities in the country, and attract tourists who would gamble to their hearts content in an era when it was banned in the rest of South Africa. The story goes that when Kerzner escorted Gary Player to the proposed site of the new golf course, the helicopter landed and the two men got out and walked around. Player asked where the water sources were, to which Kerzner replied, "There aren't any." An irrigation system was introduced, and the results are splendid.

• Gary Player Country Club is considered to be the best golf course in South Africa. Its reputation is upheld at the Nedbank Challenge tournament, held every December. The competition, with a prize of $2 million, is only open to the top twelve golfers in the world.

Playing the Holes (Gary Player Course)

Signature Hole: The ninth hole (465 meters [509 yards], par 5) is a challenge for even the most experienced player. If you manage to hit

5962 Metres / Par 72

a good drive, avoiding the bunkers on the right and the many trees on the left, the big decision is whether to go for the green in two or to lay up. The green is surrounded by a lake containing rocks; any balls that end up in it tend not to get fished out. As befits a top championship course, the greens will hold a pitching ball well, so laying up is a good option.

Best Golf Hole:

This course is very unforgiving when it comes to wayward shots. If golfers have not realized this by the thirteenth hole, they soon will. Fiendishly obtrusive fairway bunkers on the left mean players tend to steer away from them a little too much and end

up in the bunkers, or rough, on the right of the fairway. With approximately 180 meters (195 yards) to the green, from here you can say goodbye to a low score on this hole.

Toughest Hole: Many players consider the eighteenth hole (459 meters [502 yards], par 4) to be the toughest on this course. Both the water on the left and the bunkers on the right of the fairway are in range from the tee. A second shot, played across water, has to carry 200 meters (219 yards) to reach the small irregular-shaped green, with large bunkers guarding it front-left and front-right.

Playing the Gary Player Course

Gary Player Country Club has consistently been voted the top course in South Africa. It is one of the longest courses in the country

9th Hole
465 Metres / Par 5
Stroke Index: 5

and perhaps the most difficult. Kikuyu grass is used on the semirough, tees, and fairways. At semirough length, it is very difficult to play out of, as the ball nestles down deep within it, so any attempt to play a ball out results in the club head being pulled down by the grass.

Although the course is fairly flat, the lack of gradient is made up for by cunningly situated bunkers, pins cruelly placed on kidney-shaped greens, and numerous water hazards. To score well, your approach shots to the greens have to be spot on for accuracy and also length.

The caddies at Gary Player are world renowned for their golfing knowledge, which is a great help when playing this challenging course. Having a caddy to carry your golf bag may seem like a luxury, but on this course, it is a must. By the time you reach the eighteenth, though, your bag will probably be lighter by the weight of several golf balls.

Score Card

Address: Sun City Resort, P.O. Box 2, Sun City 0316, North West Province, South Africa

Phone: +27 14 557 1245
Fax: +27 14 557 3426
Web Site: www.suninternational.co.za
Course and Length: At 5,962 meters (6,520 yards), the championship Gary Player Country Club (eighteen holes, par 72) is one of the longest courses in the world.
Other Courses: Six courses, all par 72, eighteen holes: the Lost City Golf Club (Championship Course), Zimbali, Royal Swazi Spa Country Club, Wild Coast Sun Country Club, Flamingo Casino Golf, and Riverfish.

Ian's Opinion

The Gary Player is challenging and in immaculate condition, with beautiful fairways and small, strategically placed greens. The Sun City caddies are legendary. Unless you're a pro, you'll find they're better at the game than you are as they're close to being scratch golfers. They're entertaining company, and their local knowledge of the course proved invaluable to my game. The Lost City Course, with its spectacular Fred Flintstone–style clubhouse looking down to the valley over the links, also comes highly recommended.

Dress Code: Shorts allowed with socks above the ankle. Players must have a collared shirt.
Tee Times: 6:50 A.M. (summer) and 7:30 A.M. (winter) until 6:00 P.M. The Gary Player Course is closed on Monday.
Handicap: Required for tournaments only.
Green Fees: R350 (US$60) for hotel residents, R400 (US$70) for nonresidents.
Other Costs: Caddies are compulsory, with a minimum payment of R75 (US$13). No buggies are allowed, as the aim is to walk the course and appreciate its beauty and design. Rent Cleveland Classics clubs for R200 (US$35) for nine holes or R350 (US$60) for eighteen holes.
Facilities: Four world-class hotels, a casino, car parking, multiple swimming pools, and restaurants to suit all tastes. Try golf lessons at Gary Player for R450 (US$78). Its clubhouse serves great fruit smoothies, a full English breakfast, and snacks.
Location: Sun City is located 95 miles (a two-and-a-half-hour drive) northwest of Johannesburg. Take the N4 west of Pretoria.

THE GOLF RESORTS

HANS MERENSKY

The Resort

Set in the Valley of the Olifants and bordering Kruger National Park, the Hans Merensky Estate in Limpopo Province is an oasis of both adventure and elegance. Its cool ambience is created by beautifully landscaped gardens, large trees, traditional thatching, and gorgeous water features. The estate is home to the world's largest thatched property, which is designed in keeping with the original bushveld theme. There are strict ecoguidelines to prevent introduction of alien plants and to ensure that the lodges blend aesthetically into their surroundings.

The estate offers a wonderful range of accommodation to complete your wildlife experience. There are fifteen rooms in the main hotel, all facing the pool, and twenty delightfully designed garden rooms, also close to the main hotel. Around the first tee and eighteenth hole are the chalets—large rooms with luxury facilities designed purposefully to blend into their environment and complement the landscape. If you want to experience real luxury, stay in one of the Estate Lodges, beautiful and opulent thatched properties with up to four

en suite bedrooms, kitchen, huge lounge, and a private pool and deck—perfect for an evening *braii* (barbecue).

You can also stay at Olifants River Bush Lodge, the estate's private game lodge, about twenty to thirty minutes from the estate by jeep. On the edge of the Olifants River, the lodge offers five private huts for two guests. The huts are well designed, but there is no television, and you won't get a signal on your cell phone. This is tranquillity personified—a beautiful spot to watch the sunset with the sound and smell of a traditional Afrikaans

braii crackling in the background. Meals are prepared on an open fire in a traditional *boma* (enclosure). The raised deck overlooking the river is the ideal place to have your sundown drinks while watching the sunset and crowds of wild animals quenching their thirst. On a good evening you can see any number of the "big five," as well as a host of other smaller inquisitive animals. Your guide is Greg Austin, a fantastic character who has a vast knowledge of the bush and many fascinating stories.

Background to the Course

Architect: Bob Grimsdell, who designed the course in 1967.
Type: Bushveld.
Landscape: Covers a vast area of indigenous bush interspersed with tranquil pools and velvet greens.

Clubhouse: The nineteenth hole at Hans Merensky is more treehouse than clubhouse, and it's all built in wood. It's a great spot for lunch or a cocktail or two.
Pro Shop: When you get to the Pro Shop, ask for Sean Pappas, the director of golf. He is a wealth of knowledge and will help you with any of your golfing needs. The shop is well stocked with all the latest gear.
Course Facts:
• Originally established by the Phalaborwa Mining Company, this "safari" course has the lure of bumping into any of the "big five" right on the golf course. Fortunately, your chances of running into a lion, rhino, buffalo, elephant, or leopard are slim, as the experienced rangers check the golf course every morning to ensure that the more dangerous visitors have slipped quietly back to their sanctuary in the Kruger National Park. Of course,

there is a good chance that certain water-loving mammals will observe your approach to Hippo Hollow on the seventeenth. The course is also home to an abundance of more timid

6164 Metres / Par 72

wildlife, such as giraffe, zebra, impala, warthog, monkey, baboon, alpaca, and a wide variety of birds, which can be seen on the edge of the fairways.
• The club has been dominated by one family for the last three decades. The Pappas are

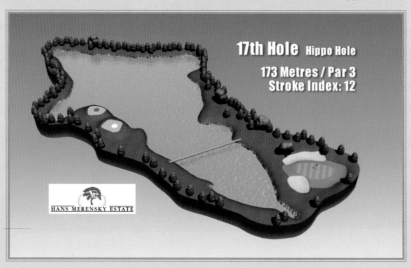

17th Hole Hippo Hole

173 Metres / Par 3
Stroke Index: 12

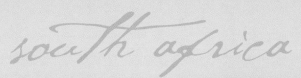

all exceptional golfers, especially Merensky's director of golf, Sean Pappas, a former US PGA Tour player. His two brothers still compete on the PGA tour. Sean became known as "Mr. 59" following an astounding round in Kentucky in 1989. His father, Leon, who ran the club before him, is also a talented golfer and legendary raconteur who has hundreds of stories and photographs of encounters with the animals at Hans Merensky.

Playing the Holes
Signature Hole: The signature hole is the seventeenth (173 meters [189 yards], par 3),

named Hippo Hollow. As the name suggests you have to play over a large water hazard, which is home to hippos and crocodiles. But there are more hazards to come. The green is surrounded by bunkers and a large tree

guarding the left, which tends to grab any tee shots that have a left-to-right shape.
Best Golf Hole: Another hole to look out for is the second (144 meters [157 yards], par 3), a tricky shot over water. Although short, it is a difficult tee shot to take so early in the round, which tests your accuracy as well as your nerve.
Toughest Hole: The toughest hole is the sixth (402 meters [440 yards], par 4), which quite accurately has a stroke index of one. There is a right-hand dogleg 250 meters (273 yards) down the narrow fairway, so unless a drive is well hit, the second shot will be

blocked out by the trees on the right. The green is small with some vicious bunkers, front-left and front-right, guarding it.

Playing the Course
Hans Merensky offers the adventure golfer a unique experience, with the emphasis on adventure. There's some pretty wild things in residence on the course. There are water hazards full of crocodiles and hippos that you really should not try to fish your ball from and bush that you should think twice about before venturing into to find any wayward balls.

At 6,164 meters (6,741 yards), this is a championship course to test the accuracy and course management skills of any golfer.

Currently rated eighteenth in South Africa, this course was built with conservation in mind, using the existing topography and bush growth. This results in ten holes having a dogleg shape to varying degrees.

There are uphill and downhill holes, but none have a particularly steep gradient. Apart from playing in the searing midday heat, the only danger of expending too much energy here is running away (not recommended by the rangers) from any wild animals that may take umbrage to a hooked shot entering their hangout within this beautiful course.

Score Card

Address: Hans Merensky Estate and Golf Club, Club Road, Phalaborwa, 1390, Limpopo Province, South Africa
Phone: +27 15 781 3931
Web Site: www.hansmerensky.com
Course and Length: One eighteen-hole course (6,164 meters [6,741 yards], par 72 from the championship tees).
Dress Code: Shorts allowed with socks above the ankle. Players must have a collared shirt.
Tee Times: 6:00 A.M. to 4:00 P.M.
Handicap: Certificate required.
Green Fees: Nine holes: R200 (US$35), eighteen holes R350 (US$61).

Other Costs: Caddies are R50 (US$9.00) for nine holes, R85 (US$15.00) for eighteen holes. Buggies are R100 (US$17) for nine holes, R180 (US$31) for eighteen holes.
Facilities: There's plenty of car parking around the hotel, and lodges have their own driveways and garages. There is a main hotel swimming pool and bar. Larger lodges have their own swimming pools. The Leadwood Restaurant, open for breakfast and dinner, serves excellent food.
Location: By road, the estate is well signed from Phalaborwa Airport 2 miles away, which offers daily flights to Johannesburg International Airport with SA Airlink. The estate offers complimentary transfers for up to seven guests. It will take at least five hours for the more scenic road option driving from Jo'burg. Drive north on Route 1 from Jo'burg to Polokwane. From there head east to Phalaborwa.

Ian's Opinion

There are purposely built holes in the fence of Kruger National Park to allow animals to explore the course, although the fence surrounding the course prohibits elephants from getting in and the three resident giraffes from getting out. Cheetah Kill, the fifteenth, is so named as once a golfer was preparing to tee off when he noticed blood dripping down his shirt. He looked up to see a cheetah eating a deer. There's only ever been one fatality on the course: On the fifteenth green, a German lady was trampled by an elephant. This is a quality course in excellent condition, and there are A-1 facilities in the villas and hotel complex. The resort makes for a fantastic holiday for the family. Try an early-morning or late-afternoon park tour to the nearby river to watch game, or a longer trek over a day or two into Kruger.

OTHER RECOMMENDED GOLF COURSES IN SOUTH AFRICA

We've listed many so you can take advantage of South Africa's numerous opportunities for playing championship courses at a fraction of the cost of anywhere else in the world.

1. MILNERTON GOLF CLUB
Address: Bridge Road, Milnerton, Cape Town, 7441, Western Cape, South Africa
Phone: +27 21 552 1047
Web Site: www.milnertongolfclub.co.za
A par-72 links course of classic design, Milnerton has fantastic views of Table Mountain from almost every hole. This eighteen-hole championship course is home to numerous PGA events. With slick greens and lots of sand, it's well worth a visit, but do book early.

2. ROYAL CAPE GOLF CLUB
Address: 174 Ottery Road, Wynberg, 7800, Western Cape, South Africa
Phone: +27 21 761 6551
Web Site: www.royalcapegolf.co.za
Established in 1885 and gaining its Royal Charter in 1910, the par-72 Royal Cape, conveniently located on the outskirts of Cape Town, claims to be the oldest golf club in South Africa. As it has been an eighteen-hole championship course for nearly a century, Royal Cape knows all about golf and how to present its course. New U.S. PGA greens, laid in the late 1990s, are still in magnificent condition. Take advantage of unbelievably cheap green fees of $35 between May and October.

3. CLOVELLY COUNTRY CLUB
Address: Clovelly Drive, Clovelly, Cape Town, 7974, Western Cape, South Africa
Phone: +27 21 782 1118
Web Site: www.clovelly.co.za
The eighteen-hole, par-72 Clovelly—with rolling fairways, sand dunes, and high-quality greens—is a real treat. Its location, in a valley on the Cape Peninsular away from railways and roads, sustains an abundance of bird life not seen inland.

4. ERINVALE GOLF CLUB
Address: Lourensford Road, Somerset West, Cape Town, 7130, Western Cape, South Africa
Phone: +27 21 847 1906
Web Site: www.erinvale.co.za
Having come to prominence with the hosting of the South African Open in 2003 and 2004, Erinvale (part of the Erinvale Hotel complex) is a relatively short, but very testing, parkland course that is not for the fainthearted. The eighteen-hole, par-72 course features some enormous bunkers and water just about everywhere.

5. ARABELLA GOLF CLUB
Address: R44, Kleinmond, 7195, Western Cape, South Africa
Phone: +27 28 284 9383
Web Site: www.arabella.co.za
A newly built parkland course, Arabella has consistently been rated in the top-ten courses in the country almost since it opened in 1999. Located within a nature reserve beside the largest lagoon in Western Cape and against a backdrop of the Kogelberg Mountains, the eighteen-hole, par-72 course has fantastic views. Water is the major hazard, and the greens are as fast as lightning. The weather around Cape Town is idyllic for golf year-round and, like so many others locally, the course is always in superb condition.

6. FANCOURT HOTEL AND COUNTRY CLUB ESTATE
Address: Montagu Street, Blanco, George, 6530, Western Cape, South Africa
Phone: +27 44 804 0185
Web Site: www.fancourt.co.za
Open to hotel guests only, Fancourt has three eighteen-hole, par-72 courses, two of which (the Montagu and Outeniqua) are consistently voted in the top ten in South Africa, and the third (the Links, yet another Gary Player–designed inland links course) is so good that it hosted the Presidents Cup in 2003. The downside is the $125 green fee, which, by South African standards, is outrageously high.

7. EAST LONDON GOLF CLUB
Address: 22 Gleneagles Road, Bunkers Hill, East London, 5201, Eastern Cape, South Africa
Phone: +27 43 735 1356
One of the oldest courses in South Africa, East London is the leading club in the Border region of the Eastern Cape—possibly the windiest part of the country. The eighteen-hole, par-72 course is built high on the coast overlooking the Indian Ocean and its magnificent beaches. Large undulations on the fairways and steep climbs to some tees make it as much a test of fitness as golf, although golf carts are available.

8. FISH RIVER SUN HOTEL AND COUNTRY CLUB

Address: P.O. Box 232, Port Alfred, 6170, Eastern Cape, South Africa
Phone: +27 40 676 1002
Web Site: www.sunint.co.za

A Sun International–owned resort, the eighteen-hole Fish River Course is part of a complex where you can enjoy a complete range of sporting and leisure activities, from bowls to deep-sea fishing. The par-72 course is well maintained and has some great golf holes that are made much harder by the seemingly incessant winds that are a feature of the Eastern Cape coastline. This is where the colonists first landed on African soil and sparked the Cape Frontier Wars in the 1800s.

9. HUMEWOOD GOLF CLUB

Address: Marine Drive, Summerstrand, Port Elizabeth, 6001, Eastern Cape, South Africa
Phone: +27 41 583 2137
Web Site: www.humewoodgolf.co.za

You will find the eighteen-hole Humewood Golf Club almost halfway between Cape Town and Durban. This is a true championship links course in every sense of the word, which has hosted the South African Open many times. Quite apart from the par-72 course's difficult design, the wind variations make accurate club selection almost impossible, so to score well here you have to be both skilled and lucky.

10. DURBAN COUNTRY CLUB

Address: Walter Gilbert Road, Durban, 4001 KwaZulu-Natal, South Africa
Phone: +27 31 313 1777
Web Site: www.dcclub.co.za

One of South Africa's oldest clubs, Durban Country Club proudly exudes the colonial grandeur of its history. Not an easy course, it features some unbelievable fairway undulations and a par 3 that in 1924 the Prince of Wales supposedly took seventeen shots to conquer! Don't even consider playing the eighteen-hole, par-72 course without a caddie—they are worth every bit of the $15 they cost. An absolute must for anyone visiting the Cape.

11. ZIMBALI COUNTRY CLUB

Address: Off M4, Ballito, 4390, KwaZulu-Natal,
South Africa
Phone: +27 32 538 1041
Web Site: www.zimbali.org
You will find this Tom Weiskopf–designed course
on the lush, windy coast 25 miles north of Durban.
Opened in 1998, the eighteen-hole, par-72 course
is a small part of an enormous hotel and leisure
development. Golf and accommodation costs are
very reasonable. Although not of championship
standard, it is still an excellent course that provides
fantastic views of the Indian Ocean coastline from
its elevated position.

12. PRINCE'S GRANT GOLF CLUB

Address: The Lodge, 1 Babu Bodasing, Stanger,
4450, KwaZulu-Natal, South Africa
Phone: +27 32 482 0005
Web Site: www.princesgrantlodge.co.za
Part of a large estate, the eighteen-hole, par-72
Prince's Grant effectively combines parkland and
links features, which in combination offer a testing
challenge for all levels of golfer. It's even trickier
when the coastal wind blows, which it does often.
Situated north of Durban, the development is
within easy driving distance of the Hluhluwe
Game Reserve, where you can see elephants, black
rhinos, white rhinos, and other big game up close.
This is also traditional Zululand and not far from
Rourkes Drift, where the British and Zulu tribes famously clashed in 1879.

13. SELBORNE HOTEL, SPA, AND GOLF ESTATE

Address: Old Main Road, Richards Bay, 4184,
KwaZulu-Natal, South Africa
Phone: +27 39 688 1800
Web Site: www.selborne.com
Created in 1985, Selborne was South Africa's first
golf estate. The eighteen-hole, par-72 course was
based on the famous Augusta Estate in America,
combining gracious living with golf. Set in a
coastal forest on the windy northeast shoreline,
with lots of water and trees, very tight fairways,
and daunting par 3s, Selbourne is an unforgettable
experience.

14. KIMBERLEY GOLF CLUB

Address: Transvaal Road, Kamjersdam, Kimberley, 8301, Northern Cape, South Africa
Phone: +27 53 841 0127
Established in the 1890s, eighteen-hole, par-71 Kimberley Golf Club has been close to some epic historic events. Be sure to visit the Kimberley Museum to explore the diamond rush history of the 1880s, which saw a large hill in Kimberley excavated into the largest man-made hole in the world—about a mile across and 700 feet deep. With green fees of about $10 a round don't expect too much, but you will get a warm welcome, great value for your money, and plenty to explore nearby.

15. SISHEN GOLF CLUB

Address: Kathu, Northern Cape, South Africa
Phone: +27 53 723 3288
Situated on the outskirts of the Kalahari Desert, the huge semidesert region that extends across much of Southern Africa, eighteen-hole Sishen must be one of the most remote golf courses in the world. It comes as a surprise that it has lush fairways and serious water hazards on three holes, and is ranked in the top twenty in South Africa. Less surprisingly, the par-72 course is home to the Kalahari Open.

16. GLENDOWER GOLF CLUB

Address: 20 Marais Road, Dowerglen Extension 2, Bedfordview, 2008, Gauteng, South Africa
Phone: +27 11 453 1013
Web Site: www.glendower.co.za
Situated near Johannesburg and a past host of the South African Open, Glendower was originally built in the 1930s, but it has been substantially changed over the years to raise it to its current championship standard. Top green fees of $45 make this eighteen-hole, par-72 course a good value, and with many water hazards and nearly one hundred bunkers, quite a challenge.

17. HOUGHTON GOLF CLUB

Address: Second Avenue, Lower Houghton, Johannesburg, 2041, Gauteng, South Africa
Phone: +27 11 728 7337
Web Site: www.houghton.co.za
Houghton has hosted the Alfred Dunhill Championship, the southern hemisphere's Ryder Cup, and South Africa Open Championships, all on numerous occasions. Located on the outskirts of Jo'burg, the eighteen-hole, par-72 course has been subject to continual change and improvement over recent years to provide the golfer with the ultimate challenge and every conceivable obstacle to a good score.

18. LEOPARD CREEK GOLF CLUB

Address: Malelane Gate, Malelane, Mpumalanga, South Africa
Phone: +27 13 791 2000
Web Site: www.leopardcreek.co.za
Adjacent to the Kruger National Park and Crocodile River, eighteen-hole Leopard Creek is another classic Sun International resort course and offers magnificent golf facilities against a backdrop of everything you expect to see in South Africa. No number of superlatives can adequately describe the quality of the fairways and greens, the stunning views, and sheer opulence. Only hotel guests can play this very exclusive par-72 course; if you need to ask how much it costs, don't go there.

19. PIETERSBURG GOLF CLUB

Address: Voortrekker Street, Polokwane, 0700, Limpopo, South Africa
Phone: +27 15 295 4118
Web Site: www.ptbgolf.co.za
Pietersburg is in the far north of South Africa, and the surrounding areas are fairly dry. The eighteen-hole, par-72 club is a surprisingly green parkland course, which has hosted some big tournaments in the past. Its main claim to fame is that a former professional of the club, Retief Goosen, was playing there when he was seventeen years old and got struck by lightning—melting his watch to his arm.

20. BLOEMFONTEIN GOLF CLUB

Address: Mazelspoort Road, Bloemfontein, 9300, Free State, South Africa
Phone: +27 51 447 0906
Although Free State, with its rolling prairies, is usually bypassed by tourist traffic traveling between the major cities, Bloemfontein town and its golf course have much to offer—including a warm welcome. Designed by Scottish Railway workers more than a century ago, the eighteen-hole, par-72 course has hosted amateur championships in the past and is a surprisingly good value at $20 per round. If you plan to drive there, make sure you have done your sums: It's a long way from anywhere, and there aren't many gas stations nearby.

BETWEEN
THE ROUNDS
ATTRACTIONS

In and Around Cape Town

Robben Island: The offshore maximum security prison of Robben Island, a mile from the commercial waterfront area, was a key site in the struggle to oppose apartheid and end the regime of racial segregation. It attracted international attention as Nelson Mandela, the first black postapartheid president of South Africa, was held here for eighteen of the twenty-eight years he served in prison. From his cell in Robben Island, Mandela went on to become the single greatest figure of freedom and resistance in the twentieth century. Members of Mandela's ANC party, freedom fighters for equal rights for all races, were kept in solitary single cells as they were considered the most dangerous people in South Africa. During the apartheid era (1948 to 1990), the prison became notorious for brutal treatment and human rights abuses. When apartheid collapsed, the prison became a symbol of liberation and the triumph of the human spirit over oppression.

For four centuries the island was an offshore prison for social outcasts and political prisoners, and during the 1930s and 1940s, it became a dumping ground for leprosy victims and a World War II defense station. Today the prison is a museum, and the island became a World Heritage site in 1999. The preserved site offers opportunities to watch birds, like the jackass penguin and guinea fowl, and see veld flowers in the spring. The boat trip from Cape Town allows great viewing of Cape fur seals, southern right whales, and dusky and Heaviside's dolphins. You can tour the prison with an ex-political prisoner as your guide. They provide this service as part of the belief that apartheid should be forgiven but never forgotten.
Phone: +27 21 405 4500 (Cape Town tourism office)
Web Site: www.robben-island.org.za
Hours: Tours leave on the hour from 9:00 A.M. to 3:00 P.M. Tours last three-and-a-half hours.
Admission: R150 (US$24) adults, R75 (US$12) children (ages 4 to 17), with discounts from May to September.

Bo-Kaap: Located on the slopes of Signal Hill, this is one of Cape Town's oldest areas, with examples of brightly colored nineteenth-century Dutch and Georgian terraces, winding alleyways, *kramats* (Islamic shrines), and mosques. Bo-Kaap is the center of South Africa's Malay Muslim community descendants of those enslaved by the Dutch and brought here from Southeast Asia. The Cape Malay suffered some of the worst abuses of the apartheid regime. Visit the small Bo-Kaap Museum on Wale Street (open Monday through Saturday 9:30 A.M. to 4:30 P.M., entry 5R (US$6.00) for a look into nineteenth-century life for a rich Cape Malay. Be sure to try a curry in Bo-Kaap; the Cape Malay curry, containing rich spices and fruits, is world renowned. The best and safest way to explore the quarter is on a walking tour; try to find one run by local residents.

Table Mountain National Park: Ascending Table Mountain is an essential activity—the views across Table Bay and the Atlantic are spectacular. The popular and easy option is to ascend in a state-of-the-art cable car, which offers a rotating 360-degree panoramic view. The cable car leaves from Tafelberg Road from 7:30 A.M. to 10:00 P.M. (shorter hours operate during summer) leaving every ten to twenty minutes and costing R68 (US$11) return May to October, or R85 (US$14) return November to April. The "table cloth" effect comes into force in the summer (December to February) when wind crossing the bay hits the cooler air of the mountain and condenses to form thick, white clouds, at which time ascending the mountain is best avoided.

For the adventurous you can of course hike to the summit, which is three to four hours round-trip and involves some steep and rocky sections. When you get to the top, try an adrenaline-fueled abseil (rappel) down a 3,000-foot vertical cliff face. The Table Mountain National Park (www.tmnp.co.za)

has many great hiking trails, the best being Hoerikwaggo Trail, a five-day and six-night hike covering the full length of the peninsula and designed to protect the environment and bring economic benefits to the six communities within the park. Get up close to fun-loving monkeys on a family-friendly three-hour Baboon Matters tour (Phone: +27 21 783 3882), or try horse riding.

Western Cape

Cape Bays and Beaches: The Atlantic Coast around the Cape has scenery that will leave you breathless. Cape Town's beaches are hot spots for sunbathers in Clifton and Hout Bay, divers in Agulhas and Benguela, and surfers in Kommetjie, with great breaks from Bloubergstrand through to Cape Hope. From August to November, southern right, humpback, and bride whales come to the warm waters of False Bay to calf. Some 40 miles outside of the city, the Cape of Good Hope is a notorious projection of rocks combined with wind swells where many fifteenth-century Portuguese sailors met their death. There are several wrecks to explore, two of which you can walk to, and the view from the nineteenth-century Old Lighthouse is world famous. Cape Point is part of a small nature reserve featuring a rocky landscape that contains more plant species than in the whole of Britain. It's amazing to visit during the spring bloom. Indigenous species include the ancestors of garden favorites: geraniums, gladioli, lilies, and irises.

Garden Route: The Garden Route covers the coast from Heidelberg in the west to just

beyond the vast Plettenberg Bay in the east. Packed tourist buses and trains serve the route, but it's most magnificent to drive along. This Riviera-style region has a Mediterranean climate with warm summers and wet, mild winters. Its fashionable coastal villages and seaside resorts attract jet setters and inspire writers from around the world. There are plenty of activities like scuba diving, abseiling, fishing, and golf. Hike-friendly mountains tower over the golden beaches and bays, bordered by colorful wildflowers, lakes, and forests.

The gateway town of George is set against lush greenery. Nearby stay in the manor of the 350-acre historic Fancourt Hotel and Country Club Estate, with its Gary Player–designed links course. Take a ride on the Outenigua Choo-Choo, one of South Africa's last remaining steam trains. It's the most stylish way to make the three-hour journey from George to Knysna. At Oudtshoorn, a semiarid valley where ostriches are farmed, you can try either riding or eating one, or visit a nineteenth-century Feather Palace. The nearby Cango Caves are limestone caverns and chambers with halls and tunnels formed from twenty million years of rainwater erosion. Nature lovers can visit Tsitsikamma National Park, a 50-mile-long nature reserve of rugged coastline, tall cliffs, evergreen forests, and heath, with many opportunities for spotting sea and woodland birds like the Knysna loerie. The Lakes Area National Park comprises the Wilderness National Park, with tranquil rivers, fens, and estuaries full of kingfishers, and the Knysna National Lake Area, home to the endangered Knysna seahorse, whales, and

dolphins. At the end of the route just north of Plettenburg Bay, the Monkeyland Primate Sanctuary (Phone: +27 44 534 8906, www.monkeyland.co.za) is a charming wander among free-roaming primates, mainly the small and cute varieties like lemurs, marmosets, and squirrel monkeys.

Vrede en Lust Winery: For the perfect wine-tasting experience in a stunning location, visit Vrede en Lust. This is not just another tourist attraction; the winery seeks to encourage

smaller groups of visitors, thus enhancing the intimacy of the tasting experience. Located just a ten-minute drive from the center of Franshhoek, this winery offers a warm welcome, good food, and above all, great wines. Do taste their superb selection of rosé wines and cheeses.

Vrede en Lust is a modern wine farm that has built on its three-centuries old foundation. It aspires to become one of South Africa's best-loved wineries without becoming a mass producer. The vineyard's philosophy is based

on respect for the environment and a total commitment to quality. Their approach to winemaking is simply to make the highest-quality wines possible. The team believes that red blends are capable of producing wines of greater complexity, so they do not produce single cultivar reds.

Address: Vrede en Lust Winery, Intersection R45 and Klapmuts Road, Simondium, Western Cape, South Africa
Phone: +27 21 874 1611
Web Site: www.vnl.co.za
Hours: Every day, 10:00 A.M. to 4:00 P.M.

KwaZulu-Natal

Zululand Battlefields: From Durban it's a five-hour drive into the heart of Zululand. Its rolling hills and rock formations saw many battles between the Zulu and the British, then later the Boer (white Afrikaan settlers from the south). The region is littered with battle-fields, monuments, museums, historic towns, and military headquarters covering numerous wars and bloodshed between 1818 and 1906. In the early nineteenth century, the Zulu were a powerful and fearless tribe who conquered most of the KwaZulu-Natal region with their own modern-technology weaponry: full body shields and stabbing spears. They prolonged

the inevitable capture of land by their white-skinned invaders using sheer force of numbers and bravery over guns and modern weaponry.

The Battlefields Route Association (www.battlefields.kzn.org.za) has developed six self-drive routes to explore the region. Isandlwana is a fascinating tour that is easy to visit from Dundee, a large coal-mining town in the Thukela region. The Battle of Isandlwana saw the biggest slaughter of the British witnessed in South Africa. On January 22, 1879, a soldier from one of the five British battalions peered over a ridge to see 15,000 Zulu warriors ready to attack. The Zulu adopted their battle formation of two horns on the flanks and a main force in the center. After defeating the British, the warriors then moved onto Rorke's Drift, where fewer than a hundred British soldiers defended their position against four thousand Zulu warriors. This was immortalized in the film *Zulu* starring Michael Caine (who uttered the immortal line, "Stop throwing those bloody spears at me!").

Drakensburg Mountains: Drakensburg, a World Heritage site, is a 130-mile-long mountain range on the border between KwaZulu-Natal and Lesotho. Drakensburg translates as "dragon mountains" after a Boer man reported seeing a giant-winged lizard flying over the peaks. Its Zulu name, Quathlamba, means "battlement of spears," which accurately describes its jagged escarpment. Summer (November to February) is the best time to visit the mountains to avoid frosts, though it can be wet then. There are many places to stay, from private resorts to B&Bs to caves.

There are thousands of marked trails traversing indigenous fern forests with opportunities for horse treks, abseiling, and trout fishing. Thirty-five thousand bushman rock-art paintings are testimony to a million years of human habitation since the Stone Age, particularly condensed in the Ndedema dome region. For more than a casual afternoon's hike, you will need to pay a fee and complete the Mountain Rescue Register.

The Royal Natal National Park is the most visited area, with its 2.5-mile natural amphitheater of sheer basalt cliffs and Thukela Falls, the second highest waterfall in the world at 3,110 feet. Here, you will need prior mountaineering experience and suitable equipment, including ropes, to tackle the many freestanding peaks like Devil's Tooth, the Pyramid, and the Column. If you're very lucky the world-renowned Drakensburg Boys Choir may be putting on a mountaintop choral show in the Champagne Valley. The southern part of the mountain range is an adventure playground filled with golf courses in stunning surroundings, fly fishing, mountain biking, bird-watching, and polo.

Surfing and Diving with the Great Whites in Durban: Durban has a renowned surfing culture. South Beach and Addington are the best for beginners,

whereas the Bay of Plenty and Snake Park have perfect breaks for the more experienced surfer. The best and least-crowded surfing beaches are Balito Bay, Tekweni, and

Zinkwazi north of the city. South of Durban the Bluff is one of the country's most famous spots. Waves are big, so check the currents before heading out into the swells.

During July North Beach in the city hosts the Gunston 500, a popular festival that includes night surfing, music, beer tents,

beauty contests, and fashion shows. If sharks are your thing, Durban has become a hot spot for cage diving with great whites. Sharks are a constant presence off the coast, particularly in the area known as Shark Alley, between the fishing village of Gansbaai and Dyer Island toward the west coast. The cages generally hold two people and are incredibly safe. For qualified divers the opportunity to come face to face with a great white is an experience of a lifetime, but be aware that environmentalists believe the dives are harmful to the feeding patterns and breeding of the sharks.

Kruger National Park

Kruger National Park, established in 1898, is the most famous wildlife reserve in the world and the biggest, covering an area the size of Wales. The park was expanded across the border into Mozambique in 2002. Almost a million visitors a year flock to see the vast variety of animals on show: Antelope, zebra, giraffe, cheetah, hippo, monkey, and crocodile augment the "big five."

The abundance of people means that although the park is not as "wild" as many

others, animals are used to humans and let you drive very close. With a road network of 1,300 miles, it's easy to get around; avoid crowds by heading down gravel roads. Unlike other African parks, the excess of elephants in Kruger is a serious issue, and elephants are culled every year. Relocating elephants is starting to take place, however, and elephant contraception is under discussion.

The wilderness trails offer walks with an expert armed guide. There are several trails to choose from, and you don't have to be superfit to enjoy them. Hikes usually last two nights and three days and cost around $12 per person, however, they are popular, so book well in advance with the National Parks Board. On the Bushman Trail you are taken to see ancient rock art, and on the popular Olifants Trail, you stay near the river and get a chance to observe hippos and crocodile at close range. There are dozens of safari choices, from student options of staying in tents to honeymoon safaris with luxury lodge accommodations. Bring comfortable clothes, sunblock, walking shoes, and a camera.

Phone: +27 12 343 1991 (National Parks Board for Accommodation)

Web Site: www.krugerpark.co.za

Admission: R27 (US$4.00) for adults, R14 (US$2.00) for children, and R34 (US$5.00) for a car. No bikes permitted.

Hours: Gates open at 4:30 A.M. in summer and at 6:30 A.M. in winter. Daily numbers are restricted, so arrive early during the holidays. If staying in a camp, you must book in

advance and arrive by the designated hour or face a fine.

Around Johannesburg

Cullinan Mine Diamond Tour: Diamonds are synonymous with South Africa, and the Cullinan Mine, about 25 miles east of Pretoria, is at its epicenter. Cullinan, founded in 1902, currently mines around one-and-a-half million carats of diamonds every year. It has produced three of the biggest diamonds ever found, the biggest of which—the Cullinan, or Star of Africa—was presented to King Edward VII of England and now forms part of the Crown Jewels housed in the Tower of London.

You can take a guided tour of the mine from companies operating from Pretoria; it costs about R68 (US$10). It is possible to buy diamonds here, although it is just as economical to buy them in shops throughout the rest of the world. It is illegal in South Africa to sell diamonds to individuals or companies other

than the De Beers Consolidated Mines Company or buy black-market diamonds. Also, you are likely to end up with a *slenter*— a fake made from lead crystal and practically impossible to detect. The safest bet is to buy from a regulated De Beers Diamond Trader.

Soweto Township Tour: For the majority of Jo'burg inhabitants, home continues to be black townships surrounding the city, and most likely it's Soweto, the twenty-one South Western Townships. Soweto was created in the 1930s, and many blacks were relocated there from Jo'burg during the apartheid regime, when people were segregated into communities based on their skin color, with the blacks and Muslims at the bottom of the chain with no rights to vote, little state education, and bleak prospects. Throughout the 1970s and 1980s, the townships, home of political campaigners like Nelson Mandela's ANC party, played a crucial role in the struggle against apartheid.

The two million Sowetans are streetwise detribalized urbanites who have their own style and lingo. Native Sowetans look down on the new rural immigrants, calling them *moegoes*. "Influx control" theoretically prevents people from coming to Soweto, "the city of gold," in search of work, and many new arrivals end up in squat camps, which have few amenities and are horribly dangerous and unhygienic.

But even within Soweto there is much segregation. Diepkloof, with its four-room "matchbox houses," contrasts with the opulent Diepkloof Extension of the emerging black middle classes. In Orlando you can see the exterior of the modest former home of Nelson Mandela, whereas across the neighborhood you can see his ex-wife Winnie Mandela's flashy pad, along with Archbishop Desmond Tutu's house. Here the Ubuntu Kraal Park has one of South Africa's only statues of Mandela, and the Hector Pieterson Memorial Museum in this township tells the history of the 1976 Soweto uprising. The Regina Mundi church on the Old Potchefstroom Road holds tales of political residence as it was the base for many antiapartheid groups. In Freedom Square, Kliptown, the Freedom Charter was signed as the guiding document of Mandela's ANC party, which went on to govern South Africa after the collapse of apartheid.

If you want to visit Soweto, you should join a tour, ideally given by locals. There are numerous operators; three-hour day tours or four-hour night tours are popular. Some specialize in jazz, drinking, visiting artists, local

churches, or homestays with local families. Be prepared to stand out and to see some pretty extreme levels of poverty in the shanty towns and *shebeens* (drinking joints), where you're often encouraged to give money or buy local craftwork. Despite the living conditions, the nightlife in Soweto is fantastic with lots of clubs. The most popular with tourists is the restaurant-cum-lounge bar Wandie's Place.

The Apartheid Museum: If you only have time to visit one attraction in Johannesburg, make it the Apartheid Museum. This incredibly powerful exhibition, thoughtfully and skillfully put together, illustrates the rise and fall of apartheid, the racially prejudiced

system that blighted much of South Africa's progress from 1948 to 1994. The museum is a beacon of hope, showing the world how the nation is coming to terms with the past and working toward a future that all South Africans can call their own.

The museum, built on a seven-hectare (seventeen-acre) site, has been assembled and organized by a multidisciplinary team of architects, curators, filmmakers, historians, and designers. The exhibits, divided into twenty-two individual areas, comprise film footage, photographs, text panels, and artifacts illustrating the principal events and human stories. Entering the museum you are given a randomly printed ticket and have to explore apartheid society by entering from a door marked "whites" or "nonwhites."
Address: The Apartheid Museum, Northern Parkway and Gold Reef Road, Ormonde, Johannesburg, South Africa
Web Site: www.apartheidmuseum.org
Hours: Tuesday through Sunday, 10:00 A.M. to 5:00 P.M.
Admission: Adults R25 (US$4.00), children R12 (US$1.75).

united arab emirates

Golf in the United Arab Emirates (UAE) is a marvel of invention and ingenuity unrivaled in the world. What other nation would ever consider building a golf course in a land that has only a few days of rain each year, daytime temperatures shooting to 120 degrees Fahrenheit, humidity swelling to 80 percent, and few endemic blades of grass within the 50,000 square miles of its borders?

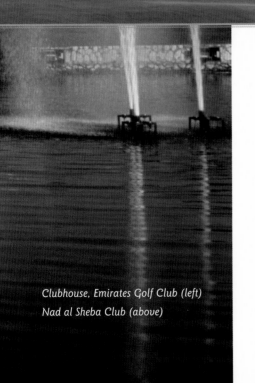

Clubhouse, Emirates Golf Club (left)
Nad al Sheba Club (above)

Despite these natural inconveniences, there is not just one golf course in the region but more than a dozen courses within a flourishing golf industry, mainly focused in Dubai. As with so many other new buildings and construction projects in the UAE, the clubhouses and golf courses have won awards for their innovative designs, including the dhow sail–shaped clubhouse of the Dubai Creek Golf and Yacht Club and the 58,000-square-foot green and 360-degree teeing ground on one of the par 3s at The Montgomerie.

Many of the clubs boast magnificent championship courses designed by some of the world's best golfers and most renowned course designers, such as Jack Nicklaus, Colin Montgomerie, and Ian Baker-Finch. What is even more remarkable is the variety of course types that you will find: lush green parklands with water features, all-sand courses where you carry your own piece of Astroturf and putt on "browns" instead of greens, and fully floodlit courses for play into the cooler nights to avoid the sweltering summer heat. It's a truly unbelievable golfing experience—in the middle of a desert!

United Arab Emirates flag (above)

Architecture (right)

Shopping mall (opposite)

About Emirates

With amazing blue-sea beaches, top-quality scuba diving, and airlines targeting Dubai for stopover tax-free shopping trips, the United Arab Emirates is putting itself on the map as a serious vacation destination. Sheikh Mohammed's rapid transformation and investment in his empire has known no bounds: The boldest architecture, the richest horse race, the most luxurious hotel, and the greatest retail spaces on earth have transformed his sovereign states from desert and fishing villages to modern city metropolises in just fifty years. The cities entice guest workers from across Asia and Europe with competitive, tax-free salaries. With modern skyscrapers and numerous shopping malls, it's sometimes hard to believe you're in the Middle East, but hear the call to prayer or experience the pious fasting of Ramadan and the Eastern qualities of the UAE come into focus.

Activities and Attractions

Shopping: The twentieth-century renaissance of the UAE has positioned it once more as a center for trade. As an open port with low import duties, the country has become a mecca for shoppers who come to snap up brand-name bargains, sometimes cheaper than in their country of origin. The main hubs are Dubai and Abu Dhabi, particularly during their twice-annual shopping festivals. There are more malls than your credit card company wants you to know about, often with space-age or tacky decor, sitting alongside traditional souks (open-air markets) where you can haggle down the price of local goods like leather, spices, perfumes, carpets, and electronics. Shops tend to open at 1:00 P.M., malls at about 10:00 A.M., with both staying open until around 10:00 P.M. and later on Friday. If you're flying out of Dubai, allow time to visit Dubai Duty Free, one of the largest in the world.

Architecture: The Emirate cities are full of contrasts: traditional mosques, *al-housh* houses built around courtyards, and wind towers between giant blue-glass skyscrapers and colorful Indian silk markets. The architecture is extravagant, powerful, and cosmopolitan—the sky's the limit for height, design, and budget. Buildings often have an Arabian twist (in Abu Dhabi it's a prerequisite that all buildings have Islamic features like archways), from the dhow boat sails design of the distinctive Dubai Creek Golf Club to a similar motif in the ultraopulent Burj al Arab hotel. Across the country you'll see ruined forts and watchtowers as relics from an era of tribal wars, piracy, and pearls.

Water Activities: The Arab Gulf waters are deliciously warm and prove excellent for all kinds of water sports: sailing, surfing, scuba diving, sailboarding, jet skiing, and water skiing. It's a great place to learn to dive; visibility ranges from 16 to 65 feet, with water temperatures ranging from 65 degrees in winter to 90 degrees in summer. The best dive sites are on the east coast between Khor Fakkan and Dibba. Marine life includes tuna, moray eels, black lionfish, catfish, lobsters, rays, barracuda, and soft corals. Many water sports and beaches are tied to a big hotel or private club where nonguest day fees can be up to 200 Arab Emirates Dirham (AED) (US$55). For man-made watery fun, check out the Wild Wadi Waterpark in Dubai, a water theme park of twenty-four rides, including the highest and fastest free-fall waterslide outside of America.

Dubai Country Club (above)

Desert (below)

History of Golf in the United Arab Emirates

Emirates golf history began in recent decades; the first nine-hole all-sand course was opened in 1971. Since then the sport has taken off, and many of the region's golf courses and facilities are second to none. Golf has become such a major tourist attraction that several larger hotels have built nine-hole courses.

When to Go and What to Bring

Only during the winter, from December to February, is the temperature and humidity comfortable for daytime golf. Between May and September temperatures are likely to be higher than 100 degrees during the day. Unless you are seriously into sun worship, the floodlit night courses (or play during the very early morning or late afternoon) are strongly recommended. The region's major tournament, the Dubai Desert Classic, is held in March at the Emirates Golf Club; before and during the tournament, the club is closed to tourists. Standard golf attire is mandatory on all courses, and only soft spikes or rubber-soled shoes are permitted. Bring your certificate as maximum handicaps are strictly enforced.

Costs

Green fees on the major courses vary from 250 AED (US$68) to 600 AED (US$163), with an average of more than $100. Costs are comparable to similar-quality courses in Europe and North America. Lesser-known courses can cost a fraction of this, and all courses give generous discounts in the hot summer months. Book time slots well in advance.

Hotels

Hotels are plentiful and relatively cheap across the country, with reasonable hotels starting from around 150 AED (US$40) a night. Expect Western-style decor and food with Arab hospitality. Luxury is at hand with a bountiful supply of five-star accommodations starting from 800 AED (US$217).

Travel

Airports: The UAE's main international airports are Dubai International (DXB), which serves sixty-five airlines, and Abu Dhabi (AUH). Travelers from North America usually enter from a connecting flight from Europe. The state airline, Emirates, flies to most major cities worldwide. Two- or three-day stopovers en route from Europe to Australia, the Far East, or India are increasingly popular. There are smaller airports in Al Ain, Sharjah, Ras-al-Khaimah, and Fujairah.

Burj al Arab Hotel foyer

Car Rental: The UAE has a very modern road system, making travel by car hassle free. If you're on a stopover, contact your airline for deals. Car rental is reasonably priced, starting from just $20 a day. Make sure you have insurance to cover *diyah* (bad accidents); if you are responsible for a fatality, you're obliged to maintain the family of the deceased. Carry plenty of water, a cell phone, and an emergency kit in case you break down in the desert.

Taxis: Taxis are plentiful; some are unmetered, so check the rate before you make the journey. Costs start from 7 AED (US$2.00); a fifteen-minute journey will cost around 15 AED (US$4.00),

The suggested itinerary is for active days of around 14 hours. If you prefer a more leisurely trip, pick and choose your favorite activities.

Day 1: Fly into Dubai International Airport (DXB), and check into your hotel—perhaps the ultraluxurious seven-star Burj al Arab. If you've time for a late nine holes, play the Jebel Ali Golf Resort and Spa by the Arabian Gulf.

Day 2: A.M. Get up early before the sun strikes, and play the Dubai Creek Golf and Yacht Club on the Al-Garhoud Road. Take lunch in the clubhouse, with its distinctive boat-sail architecture.
P.M. Take a round-trip from Al-Makhtoum to Deira down the Dubai Creek on an abra sailboat. Visit the Dhow Building Yard, 1 mile south of Al-Garhoud Bridge in Jaddaf, to see how these traditional boats are made.

If you want to play thirty-six per day, don't miss a round at the Montgomerie, which has the largest single green in the world.

Take a taxi twenty minutes out of town, down the Oud Metha Road near the World Trade Center, to Nad al Sheba. If it's a race night (Thursday), let thoroughbred horse racing be your entertainment.

Day 3: A.M. Take a short taxi ride to Interchange 5 on the Sheikh Zayed Road in Safa to play the Majlis Course at Emirates—the "desert miracle."
P.M. Check out the numerous shopping malls and souks around Deira, in particular the aromatic spice souk and dazzling gold souk. If

it's hot, the shops stay open into the evening. Head back to Nad al Sheba for a round of relaxing night golf (unless it's race night!).

Alternatively, play the watery delights of the Robert Trent Jones II–designed Al Badia Golf Resort in Deira, Dubai's newest course.

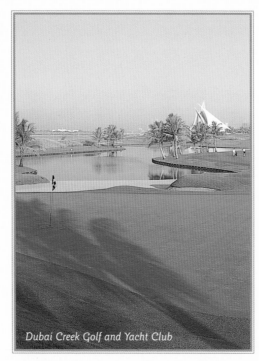

Dubai Creek Golf and Yacht Club

Day 4: A.M. Get up early, to avoid the noonday sun, and drive a couple of minutes from the city center to Dubai Country Club on the Ras al-Khor Road for an early-morning round of desert golf. Carry your own fairway!
P.M. Explore Dubai's architecture, from space-age skyscrapers to traditional mosques, such as Jumeirah and the Old Mosque in Bur Dubai. See the old wind towers in Bastakia, a nineteenth-century form of air-conditioning.

Or, if you've developed a taste for desert golf, play a round at the Arabian Ranches on

Emirates Road, although you may want to wait until late afternoon when it cools down a little.

Drive 85 miles west along the coastal road to the city of Abu Dhabi.

Day 5: A.M. Play the Abu Dhabi Airport Golf Club, the best opportunity for desert golf in the world.
P.M. Go dune bashing, a four-wheel-drive motor sport, in the "Empty Quarter" in the west of Abu Dhabi province. Or, for more golf, play a relaxing nine holes at the Abu Dhabi Golf and Equestrian Club.

Spend the night in stylish and cosmopolitan Abu Dhabi. Shops and souks are open until late.

Day 6: A.M. Play one of the two par-72 grass courses of Abu Dhabi Golf Club in the Umm Al Nar district.
P.M. Visit the Presidential Palace and the fort of Al Hosn, or play the other course at Abu Dhabi Golf Club.

Drive 85 miles inland to the oasis of Al Ain by the Oman border. Stay at the Hilton International, which has its own nine-hole, par-3 golf course.

Day 7: A.M. After an early round and a meander around the ancient oasis of Al Ain, drive 40 miles north (through Oman) to Hatta, a mountainside retreat with relaxing waterfalls and carved rock pools.

Or, if diving is your passion, there are some great spots about 50 miles north of here between Khor Fakkan and Dibba on the east coast.
P.M. Drive back 60 miles northeast to Dubai International to fly home.

FIVE-DAY EXECUTIVE STRESS BUSTER

Day 1: **P.M.** Fly into Dubai International Airport (DXB) and check into your hotel—perhaps the ultraluxurious seven-star Burj al Arab.

Day 2: **A.M.** Get up early before the sun strikes, and play the Dubai Creek Golf and Yacht Club on the Al-Garhoud Road. Take lunch in the clubhouse, with its distinctive boat-sail architecture.
P.M. Take a round-trip from Al-Makhtoum to Deira down the Dubai Creek on an abra sailboat. Visit the Dhow Building Yard, 1 mile south of Al-Garhoud Bridge in Jaddaf, to see how these traditional boats are made.

Or, if you want to play for the full thirty-six per day, don't miss a round at the Montgomerie, which has the largest single green in the world.

At night dine at a restaurant by the Dubai Creek.

Day 3: **A.M.** Take a short taxi ride to Interchange 5 on the Sheikh Zayed Road in Safa to play the Majlis Course at Emirates, the "desert miracle."
P.M. Lounge around and get a tan at the Jumeirah Beach Resort (by the Burj al Arab hotel). While you're there, play nine holes at the Jebel Ali Golf Resort and Spa by the Arabian Gulf.

Day 4: **A.M.** Get up early, before the oppressive noonday sun, and drive a couple of minutes from the city center to Dubai Country Club on the Ras al-Khor Road for an early-morning round of desert golf. Carry your own fairway!
P.M. Explore Dubai's impressive architecture, from space-age skyscrapers to traditional mosques, like Jumeirah and the Old Mosque

in Bur Dubai. See the old wind towers in Bastakia, a nineteenth-century form of air-conditioning.

In the cooler evening, head to Nad Al Sheba for a round of night golf.

Day 5: If time allows, play the watery delights of the Robert Trent Jones II–designed Al Badia Golf Resort in Deira, Dubai's newest course.

Otherwise, go shopping in Dubai's many malls or the gold souk before taking in the massive Duty Free at Dubai International Airport (DXB) when you fly home.

Dubai Country Club

and long-distance trips are also a good value. Many smaller roads in the cities have no names, but cab drivers will know the major hotels and landmarks. There are no trains in the UAE, but there are long-distance buses and well-signed city bus routes. Walking is unheard of by Westerners even in cities, which have very dusty roads and no sidewalks, and taxis will swoop by if they see you walking.

Regions and Golfing

If you're golfing, it's likely you won't be straying outside of Dubai, but as the UAE is tiny—a mere 300 miles wide and 240 miles long at its furthest points—there's no excuse not to explore its varied sights. The seven highly individual emirates that make up the UAE are cut haphazardly along tribal lines, some enclaves within other emirates territories, and several comprise two separated regions. They were linked in 1971 after the British withdrawal from the Gulf. More than 80 percent of the region is desert, with enormous dunes contrasted by the rocky Hajar Mountains along the east coast. Inevitably most courses have been built around the natural oases and in the populated fertile plains. There are no distinct golfing regions.

Dubai: Dubai is the commercial center for the Middle East. For centuries it has been on a major

Nad Al Sheba Club

trading route, and today you can still find traditional souks with spices, gold, and regional crafts

brought in by dhow boat interspaced with towering glass skyscrapers, ultramodern architecture, and shopping malls. Thanks to its tax-free status, it's the best place in the world to spend, spend, spend. Stay in the Burj al Arab, the world's only seven-star hotel, or take a relaxing boat cruise down the Dubai Creek.

Abu Dhabi: A fishing village as recently as fifty years ago, Abu Dhabi City has transformed into a modern metropolis with a neon high-rise skyline and the nation's capital and administrative quarters.

To explore the region's history, visit the Presidential Palace, the fort of Al Hosn, or the island of Umm an-Nar with its 5,000-year-old tomb excavations. Inland, Al Ain, a desert oasis with an ancient history, is popular during the humid summer. Abu Dhabi is the largest emirate, but it is mostly desert and restricted oil fields. The west area, known as "the Empty Quarter," is a popular spot for desert sports.

North and Eastern Emirates: The remaining emirates of Sharjah, Ras Al Khaimah, Fujairah, Ajman, and Umm Al Quwain cover the north and east coast, and each contains a principal city of the same name. Sharjah has great architecture, traditional fishing, and souks to rival Dubai. Ras Al Khaimah in the far north is a stark contrast, as irrigation has led to greenery on the edge of the mountains and desert. It's popular with weekend visitors from Dubai and Scandinavia, as the city is a great base to explore the outdoors. Visit Digdagga, 6 miles south of here, for water sports or the camel races, which take place on Friday mornings throughout winter. Hot springs are within an easy drive, as are ancient sites like Shimal (the Queen of Sheba's palace dating from the thirteenth century), the ruined fort of Dhayah, and watchtowers in Rams.

On the east coast by the Gulf of Oman, top sites are Fujairah with its ruined fort and bullfighting; the nearby T-shape site in Bithna, a burial chamber dating from 1350 B.C.; the resort town of Khor Fakkan, with great water sports; the oldest mosque in the UAE in Badiyah; and the fishing village of Dibba, site of a great battle in A.D. 633 when Muslims reconquered Arabia. A thrilling road trip is to take a four-wheel-drive vehicle across the Hajar Mountains from Ras Al Khaimah to Dibba via the Wadi Bih, following an old trade route.

Emirates Golf Club clubhouse (top)
Dubai Country Club (above)

THE GOLF COURSES
NAD AL SHEBA

The Clubhouse

Food: On race nights choose from a fixed-price buffet, three-course meal, or all-you-can-eat deals starting from 130 AED (US$35). At the club the Links Terrace offers al fresco dining with fantastic views of the golf and racecourse, Spikes Bar serves a great cooked breakfast every morning, and the Dubai Restaurant is at its best for its Family Friday Roast.

Changing Rooms: Quality separate changing rooms for both sexes.

Pro Shop: Stocked with the latest brands, including "try-before-you-buy" Callaway Clubs, Cutter and Buck clothing for both ladies and gents, and shoes by Footjoy, Oakley, and Etonic.

Interior and Exterior: Stylish, lavish, and modern with superb banqueting and conference facilities, a gallery, and fantastic views of the racecourse and night golf.

Background to the Course

Architect: Designed to championship standards in association with renowned modern architect Karl Litten.

Type: Traditional links style.

Landscape: The course, which draws similarities with St. Andrews in Scotland, is built around eight lakes with double greens, deep pot bunkers, and water hazards on both nines.

Course Facts:

• It's the home of the $6 million, richest horse race in the world—the Dubai World Cup—which is held annually at the end of March.

• There are seven special race events during the year; six for thoroughbreds and one for purebred Arabians.

• This oasis in the desert is a result of one million liters (263,900 gallons) of water per night hydrating the course after play finishes.

Playing the Course

The best option is to play a round of night golf in Dubai during the summer months. Possibly the biggest challenge, apart from the testing water hazards, is finding your ball after you have hit it. Although following the direction is not difficult with the powerful floodlights, the distance it travels can be very deceptive. It's a good idea to bring Day-Glo balls with you.

Score Card

Address: Nad Al Sheba Club, P.O. Box 52872, Dubai, UAE

Phone: +971 4 3363666

Fax: +971 4 3363717

Web Site: www.nadalshebaclub.com

Course and Length: One par-71, eighteen-hole course, 6,503 yards from the back tees and 5,619 yards from the front.

Dress Code: Collar shirts, long trousers and shoes in the clubhouse; rubber but no metal-spiked shoes in any area of the club. On the course shirts with collars and sleeves are required, and no jeans.

Tee Times: From 7:30 A.M. to 10:00 P.M. The

course closes at midnight. The driving range is open 7:00 A.M. to 10:00 P.M.

Handicap: Presentation of certificate may be required. Nonhandicap golfers may use the driving range.

Green Fees: Day rate: eighteen holes 220 AED (US$60), nine holes 110 AED (US$30). Night rate: eighteen holes 295 AED (US$80), nine holes 150 AED (US$40).

Other Costs: Driving range: 20 AED for fifty balls (US$5.50). Carts are 50 AED (US$14.00) for a full round, and pull trolleys (pull carts) 10 AED (US$3.00).

Facilities: A golf academy run by four British PGA golf professionals offers instruction for all abilities, a thrice-annual training week for eight- to ten-year-olds, and "learn golf in a week" courses taught in small groups. Individual lessons start from 135 AED (US$37). At the racecourse enjoy a stable tour of the world's best thoroughbred training facilities. The race season runs from November 6 until April 15. There's free access to most of the races which usually take place on Thursdays and Saturdays, when golf is not in play. The course benefits from ample free parking.

Location: A twenty-minute drive or taxi from the center of Dubai or a ten-minute drive from the Dubai World Trade Center and the Emirates Towers. Head down Oud Metha Road towards Al-Ain, then follow the signs.

Ian's Opinion

The eighteen holes of floodlit golf are not only a novelty but very enjoyable to play on this compact and fairly straightforward course, set in and around the Nad Al Sheba horse racetrack. It's a test of accuracy rather than length. It takes a while to get used to the light, and you can often lose sight of the ball. Nad Al Sheba offers possibly the best night golf in the world, with a fully floodlit course offering respite from the desert heat and allowing you to enjoy playing into the long, cool Arabian nights.

DUBAI CREEK

The Clubhouse

Food: Six food options leave you spoiled for choice: The aQuarium seafood and steak restaurant has fabulous views of the creek and a tropical indoor floor-to-ceiling aquarium; international snacks are offered all day and night at the Boardwalk and Lakeview; enjoy a pizza, shisha, or puff on a hubbly bubbly at QDs; try Black Angus steaks nightly at Legends; or sample modern international cuisine in the Academy cafe.

Changing Rooms: Large changing facilities for gents and ladies, both equipped with a steam room.

Ladies' Facilities: Ladies enjoy the same playing privileges as men.

Pro Shop: Stocks a wide range of logo clothing depicting the iconic "sail" design of the clubhouse, golf accessories, and souvenirs. The Academy shop has a similar stock, plus the latest golf clubs, including demonstration sets and club-fitting systems.

Interior and Exterior: The distinctive contemporary sail design, which depicts a traditional Arab dhow, makes Dubai Creek the Sydney Opera House of the golf world. Designed by UK architect Brian Johnson in 1993, it won Best Clubhouse in *Golf World's* "Best of the Best" awards. The interior is a cabin of western luxury.

Background to the Course

Architect: Karl Litten (who also designed Emirates Golf Club) designed the original Dubai Creek, which opened in 1993. The course was redesigned in 2004 by European Golf Design in association with Thomas Bjorn. There are big changes planned for the Dubai Creek Golf and Yacht Club in 2005, with the addition of a large hotel, necessitating the redesign of some of the course.

Type: Resort-style riverside course.

Landscape: Its rolling green fairways sit on the edge of Dubai Creek, the saltwater inlet running through the heart of the city, which comes into play on four holes

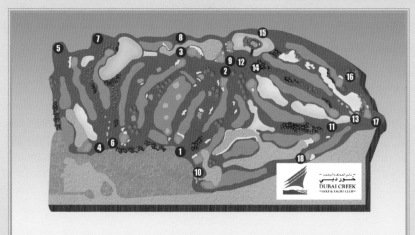

17th Hole
363 Yards / Par 4
Stroke Index: 11

All along the right of the fairway there are vast bunkers waiting to gather any wayward drives or second shots, followed by a third shot onto an island green which is completely surrounded by water. At 363 yards the signature seventeenth hole is not a long par 4, but playing your tee shot over an inlet with Dubai Creek on your left, trees and bunkers to the right, and traffic from the freeway roaring past just yards behind you is a real knee shaker.

located alongside it. Numerous water features and tropical palm foliage create an atmosphere of seclusion in the heart of Dubai.

Playing the Course

This 6,950-yard, par-72 course is set on a small piece of land so close to a busy road that when you play off some of the back tees it feels like you are standing on the hard shoulder. The thirteenth hole, a 545-yard par 5, has a stroke index of 3, which is a warning of its difficulty.

Score Card

Address: Dubai Creek Golf and Yacht Club, Garhoud Area, P.O. Box 6302, Dubai, UAE

Phone: +971 4 2956000

Fax: +971 4 2956044

Web Site: www.dubaigolf.com

Course and Length: An eighteen-hole, par-72, 6,857-yard championship course from the back tees, and a nine-hole, par-3, 774-yard floodlit course from the gents' tees.

Dress Code: Rubber but no metal spikes allowed. Shirt with collars and sleeves. No denim, beachwear, or otherwise inappropriate attire.

Tee Times: Open during daylight hours with tee times at ten-minute intervals. During most weekends shot-gun starts operate for

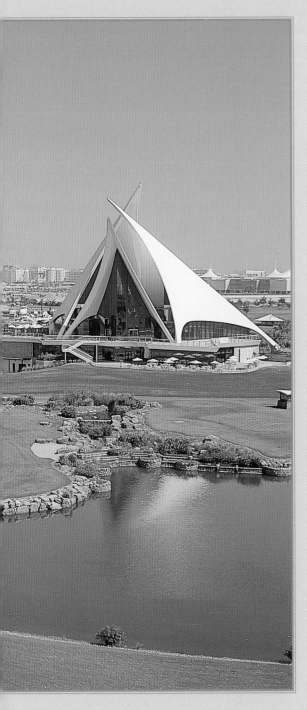

corporate and society groups, which means that everyone starts and finishes at one time, usually early in the morning and lunchtime.

Handicap: Certificate required; 28 for men and 45 for ladies. No handicap required for the nine-hole course.

Green Fees: The eighteen-hole course costs 395 AED (US$108) Sunday to Wednesday, and 475 AED (US$130) Thursday to Saturday and public holidays. The nine-hole floodlit course is a modest 50 AED (US$14).

Other Costs: Carts cost 50 AED (US$14) per person, and Ping club rental is 120 AED per set (US$33), with 20 AED (US$5.50) for practice balls.

Facilities: Flood lighting allows golfers to play through the darkness until 10:00 P.M. Dubai's first-created golf academy offers tuition to all ages and abilities using V1—the latest in swing

Ian's Opinion

This small, tight course has plenty of water, which severely punishes any stray shots. It is a beautifully designed course with a lot of water hazards and some massive bunkers. It's an exceptionally high-quality course in downtown Dubai, which has been the location of several past championships, such as the PGA Dubai Desert Classic in 1999 and 2000.

analysis technology. Three floodlit practice holes, a marine and yacht club, a swimming pool with a swim-up bar, and a Health Club Gym 2000 with personal trainers keep the active occupied day and night. The superbly facilitated club has hosted concerts by major talents, such as Rod Stewart and Elton John.

Location: A few minutes' drive from Dubai International Airport on the Al-Garhoud Road just across the Al-Garhoud Bridge, opposite the City Center Shopping Complex.

THE GOLF COURSES
EMIRATES GOLF CLUB

The Clubhouse

Food: Plenty to tempt your taste buds here: Choose fine-dining lunches and dinners combining Arabian and modern styles at Le Classique restaurant; enjoy live sports on plasma screens with drinks, snacks, and light meals at Spike Bar or the Sports Bar from breakfast to late, try al fresco continental food at the Terrace Bar; enjoy a morning coffee at the Library Lounge or a business lunch at the Conservatory; or sample healthy salads and tropical cocktails at the Pool Bar.

Changing Rooms: Large locker rooms for gents and ladies, each with its own steam room. Lockers are free.

Ladies' Facilities: Ladies have the same playing privileges as men.

Pro Shop: Numerous international brands, including clubs, apparel, merchandise, and golfing equipment. The club is the exclusive distributor of Dubai Desert Classic logo merchandise.

Interior and Exterior: The club house is highly unusual and modern, taking the form of a series of buildings designed to look like giant Arabic tents. The interior is ultraplush and chic, with sumptuous fittings and wood paneling.

Background to the Course

Architect: Florida-based architect Karl Litten, who also designed the Nad al Sheba

course, created the Majlis Course in 1988 and later created the Wadi Course with Jeremy Pern in 1995.

Type: Dunes.

Landscape: Constructed into the dunes on the edge of Dubai and maintained, according to the instructions of Sheikh Mohammed, in its natural state with undulating fairways and dry, sandy, desert floor. The Wadi tempts the average golfer with its space and large greens, which are cleverly protected by fourteen lakes and numerous bunkers.

Course Facts:

• Emirates is known as the "Desert Miracle," as it was the Gulf region's first all-grass championship course. It was the brainchild of Sheikh Mohammed, who donated the site to create an attraction to entice tourists and the corporate sector to Dubai.

• Within a month of opening, the Pan-Arab, the most important regional golf tournament, took place on the Majlis Course.

• In 1995 the club was voted Favorite of the Year by players of the European Tour.

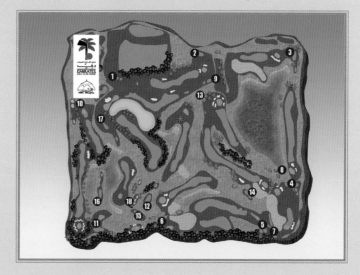

• The Majlis Course takes its name from the Arabic for "meeting place." One of the most prominent features on the course is the Majlis building, positioned between the eighth and ninth holes.

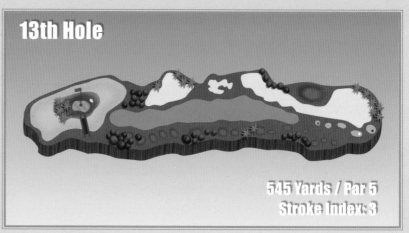

13th Hole

**545 Yards / Par 5
Stroke Index: 3**

Playing the Holes

Signature Hole: The signature hole is the thirteenth (545 yards, par 5) with a left-hand dogleg. If you can hit a ball 250 yards, you can carry the trees on the left and dramatically shorten the hole; however, it is prudent to resist this temptation, as there are vast areas of desert waste to the right and large groups of trees to the left. If you do clear the trees, your next dilemma is whether to try for the green in two or be cautious of the large lake lurking just to the right of it. As with all the par 5s on this course, it's a tricky risk/reward equation, so you need to be courageous to lower your score.

Best Golf Hole: The eighteenth (547 yards, par 5) is a left-hand dogleg. If you can carry 250 yards over the trees, you will cut off the corner and save yourself about 100 yards. This sets up a possible second shot onto the green—if you can clear the lake in front of it. Be warned: This is the hole where Ian Woosnam successfully chipped into the lake after laying up and subsequently lost the $2 million Dubai Desert Classic by one stroke.

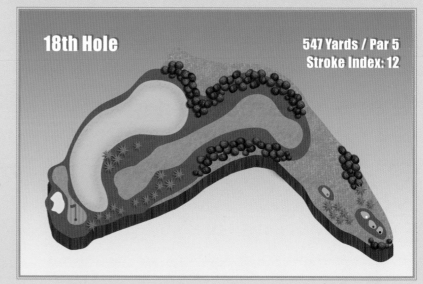

18th Hole

**547 Yards / Par 5
Stroke Index: 12**

Toughest Hole: A tough hole, which surprisingly only has a stroke index of 10, is the tenth (549 yards, par 5). Your tee shot has to carry 200 yards over desert waste before reaching the narrow fairway. With bunkers left and trees and bushes right, this drive has to be accurate. The second is played up the fairway to an area that narrows to about 10 yards. The third shot is played onto a green completely surrounded by bunkers.

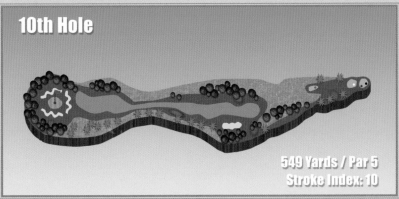

10th Hole

549 Yards / Par 5
Stroke Index: 10

Playing the Course

The Majlis Course is widely regarded as the best in Dubai. With fast greens and large, awkward bunkers, this is a true championship course and home to the world-renowned $2 million Dubai Desert Classic. It's a tight course with vast tracts of desert waste, numerous trees, and many water hazards. Any wayward shots are severely punished. To score well you need to play an accurate game and be able to hit the ball a long distance. With lush fairways, shady spots, and lots of water on the course, it is possible to play this world-class course in the hottest of temperatures without too much discomfort—but do take a buggy (golf cart). Take a rest at the very welcome, halfway refreshment hut.

Score Card

Address: Emirates Golf Club, P.O. Box 24040, Dubai, UAE
Phone: +971 4 3801999
Fax: +971 4 3801752
Web Site: www.dubaigolf.com
Courses and Lengths: Two eighteen-hole courses: Majlis Course, a par-72, 7,211-yard championship course, and the Wadi Course, a par-72, 7,114-yard course.

Dress Code: Soft spiked shoes only. Usual golf attire required.
Tee Times: During daylight hours, with a floodlit driving range for after dark.
Handicap: Certificate required: men 28, ladies 36.
Green Fees: Majlis Course costs $144; the Wadi Course between $103 and $116.
Other Costs: Carts, $14.00; club rental, $33.00; bucket of fifty practice balls, $5.00.
Facilities: At Emirates Academy of Golf, learn with Peter Cowen, one of the world's top teachers, and benefit from a climate-controlled environment, swing analysis, and its own three-hole course. There are two driving ranges, one fully floodlit. There's much for sports fans and families alike: a fully equipped gym with personal trainers, squash courts, a luxury swimming pool with swim classes, a tennis academy, a soccer academy for children aged five to sixteen, and relaxation sports like power yoga, reflexology, Reiki therapy, and Balinese massage.

Ian's Opinion

Emirates has been home to the Dubai Desert Classic since 1989, which attracts such golf stars as Tiger Woods and Ernie Els, not to mention millions of TV viewers. The Majlis Course is beautifully maintained and very tight; if you stray off the fairway, you hit the desert. The facilities are extraordinary, and the clubhouse is wonderful, with a great restaurant, large terrace, stacked clubhouse, and a cooling pool. The views over the skyline to the nearby beach resorts are stunning. A fantastic golf experience.

Location: Interchange 5 on the Sheikh Zayed Road in Safa, a few miles south of the city center where the club is located, suffers from dangerous traffic, so take a taxi or car. It's a forty-minute drive from the airport.

DUBAI COUNTRY CLUB

The Clubhouse

Food: A fine-dining restaurant serving continental food, plus a cafe serving breakfast and lunch and a number of bars.

Changing Rooms: Separate changing rooms for the golf course, plus additional ones for the pool and sports hall.

Ladies' Facilities: Try aerobics, aqua aerobics, and spinning classes for women, plus golf classes and tennis tournaments.

Pro Shop: Well stocked with all the top-brand golf clubs, such as Titleist, and shirts for men and women.

Background to the Course

Type: Desert.

Landscape: Sand for miles around. It's amazing to visit at sunrise or twilight for blood red or hazy purple views of the city skyline against the palms and pale sandy dunes.

Course Facts:

• Dubai Country Club has always been host to the Dubai's Men's Open, Dubai's oldest championship, dating to 1976.

• Other golf courses in Dubai need up to a million gallons of water a day to stay green, but this desert course only requires 10,000 gallons a week.

• Dubai Country Club is the region's oldest golf club, even though it only opened in 1971. It currently has more than 500 members.

• The club was named in *Golf World* as one of the world's unique golfing destinations.

Playing the Course

Playing off the tees, two lines of pegs denote the edges of the fairway. Land within those markers, and you can place your ball on your mat and play on as normal; land outside, and you have to play the ball as it lies, which is invariably off the sandy scrub ground. Once the green—or

rather, brown—is reached, you putt onto a mixture of sand and secondhand engine oil compressed with rollers. This surface holds a pitching ball surprisingly well; although the putt is quite slow, it will run true. After putting the golfer is expected to brush around the hole with brooms to smooth out footprints for the players behind. Players have to contend with numerous *dhubs*—burrows dug by desert lizards.

Score Card

Address: Dubai Country Club, P.O. Box 5104, Dubai, UAE

Phone: +971 4 3331155

Fax: +971 4 3331409

Web Site: www.dubaicountryclub.com

Courses and Lengths: Two courses: Al Awir, a par-71, 6,346-yard, eighteen-hole course, and the Creek Course, a par-32, 2,270-yard, nine-hole course.

Course Dress Code: Rubber but no metal spikes allowed. Shirt with collars and sleeves.
Tee Times: From 8:00 A.M. until twilight (about 7:00 P.M. in summer or 6:00 P.M. in winter) but tee times can be booked earlier if requested.
Handicap: No certificate required.
Green Fees: Nonmembers can only play at the invitation of a member and payment of a fee of about 91 AED (US$25). Groups of nonmembers can play Sunday to Wednesday from 8:00 to 10:00 A.M. by prior arrangement.
Packages: Three golf packages are available ranging between 100 AED (US$27) to 200 AED (US$54), all inclusive of food.
Other Costs: Buggies are 75 AED (US$20) for eighteen holes or 50 AED (US$14) for

nine holes. A bucket of balls is 10 AED (US$3.00), and club rental is 20 AED (US$5.50). No caddies allowed.
Facilities: A twenty-four-bay floodlit driving range, practice "brown" for putting, well-equipped pro shop, club repair center, and PGA pro tuition. Outside of golf, there's a sports hall offering badminton, squash, and a gym; one family and two sports-training pools; and outdoor tennis courts and football and rugby pitches.
Location: Ras al-Khor Road, Ras Al-Khor, just south of the Dubai Creek and a mile southwest of the city center. It's a fifteen-minute drive from the city center or thirty minutes from Dubai International Airport.

Ian's Opinion

Dubai Country Club is an ex-pat resort with great facilities and the best place to try out the craziest golf in the world. The experience of playing true desert golf is something every adventure golfer should try—although maybe only once. In desert golf the greens are known as "browns," and it's amazing to hit the ball off the Astroturf mats that you carry around with you. Desert golf is great fun, but be warned: Take some water with you, as it can get hotter than hell out there.

OTHER RECOMMENDED GOLF COURSES IN UNITED ARAB EMIRATES

1. ABU DHABI GOLF CLUB BY SHERATON, NATIONAL AND GARDEN COURSES

Address: P.O. Box 51234, Umm Al Nar, Abu Dhabi, UAE

Phone: +971 2 5588990

Web Site: www.adgolfsheraton.com

Only a fifteen-minute drive from Abu Dhabi International Airport, these two eighteen-hole, par-72 grass courses are beautifully maintained and prove a fine test for golfers of all standards. Superb for the summer, night golf is available on the back nine of the floodlit Garden Course. The customary UAE innovative design and luxurious clubhouse can only be described as magnificent. Many facilities are available, from swimming to floodlit tennis.

2. ABU DHABI AIRPORT GOLF CLUB

Address: Al Ghazal Golf Club, P.O. Box 4555, Abu Dhabi, UAE

Phone: +971 2 5758040

Only two minutes from Abu Dhabi International Airport, this eighteen-hole, par-71 sand course is said to be the best example of a desert course anywhere in the world. Wayward shots are played from the largest bunker in the world!

3. ABU DHABI GOLF AND EQUESTRIAN CLUB

Address: P.O. Box 33303, Abu Dhabi, UAE

Phone: +971 2 4459600

Web Site: www.adec-web.com

This club combines an immaculately presented nine-hole grass floodlit golf course with range and an international standard racecourse and show-jumping arena. It's moderately priced at $60 for eighteen holes (two times nine). With lots of water in play and a challenging par 5 in excess of 600 yards, this par-72 course is no pushover.

4. AL AIN GOLF CLUB

Address: P.O. Box 18945, Abu Dhabi, Al Ain, UAE

Phone: +971 3 7686808

The Hilton International, one of many top-class hotels in Al Ain near the eastern Oman border, has its own nine-hole, par-3 golf course. The short course would not test a professional, but for the average golfer, it certainly isn't easy, and it comes cheap—just a few dollars to play, even for nonhotel guests.

5. AL BADIA GOLF RESORT

Address: P.O. Box 49776, Al Rebat Street, Ras Al Khor, Deira, Dubai, UAE

Phone: +971 4 2855772

Web Site: www.albadiagolfresort.com

Opened in early 2005, the Al Badia features a brand new Robert Trent Jones II–designed par-72, eighteen-hole grass course along the banks of Dubai Creek. With water just about everywhere on this championship course in the heart of the acclaimed Dubai Festival City, this is already a mouthwatering prospect.

6. ARABIAN RANCHES GOLF CLUB

Address: P.O. Box 36700, 311 Emirates Road, Dubai, UAE

Phone: +971 4 8846777

Web Site: www.thedesertcourse.com

Arabian Ranches is a formidable eighteen-hole desert course almost 7,700 yards in length from the back tees and still only a par 72! Designed by Ian Baker Finch and Jack Nicklaus, this brand-new course has no water hazards—just lots and lots of sand. It's already been chosen to host a qualifying round in the UAE Golf Association (UGA) Order of Merit.

7. JEBEL ALI GOLF RESORT AND SPA

Address: P.O. Box 9255, Dubai, UAE

Phone: +971 4 8836000

Web Site: www.jebelali-international.com

The superb Jebel Ali Hotel is in a magnificent setting beside the Arabian Gulf. Among its many facilities, which include camel rides, you will find the grass championship standard nine-hole, par-36 Resort Course. For greater variety, and to encourage visitors to play eighteen holes, each hole has four tees. With a large central saltwater lake, which seems to come into play on most holes, this is a tough and interesting challenge.

8. THE MONTGOMERIE DUBAI

Address: P.O. Box 36700, Dubai, UAE

Phone: +971 4 3905600

Web Site: www.themontgomerie.com

Opened in 2002 and named after one of its designers, the eighteen-hole, par-72 Montgomerie is another essential visit while in Dubai. Built in a traditional Scottish links style, there are many memorable holes—not least the par-3, thirteenth, which is said to have the largest single green in the world. It's nine times larger than your average green; 200 yards long and approachable from a 360-degree teeing ground, which means the hole can be totally different every time you play it.

9. TOWER LINKS GOLF CLUB
Address: P.O. Box 30888, Ras Al Kaimah, UAE
Phone: +971 7 2279939
Web Site: www.towerlinks.com
Ras Al Kaimah is the most northerly and the least developed of the seven emirates. This is their very first golf club. Constructed in 2003–2004, Tower Links offers a 7,000-yard, eighteen-hole, par-72 championship course, a golf academy with the latest computerized swing analysis run by PGA pros, and a floodlit back nine holes and driving range.

GOLF COURSES FURTHER AFIELD

10. DOHA GOLF CLUB
Address: West Bay, P.O. Box 13530, Doha, Qatar
Phone: +974 4 832338
Web Site: www.dohagolfclub.com
Qatar is the next state west of UAE on the Arabian Gulf, and Doha Golf Club, around 80 miles northwest of UAE's western border, is *the* place to play golf here. Its two courses cater to all abilities: the 7,300-yard, eighteen-hole, par-72 Championship Course has been home to the Qatar Masters since 1998, and there's an easier, nine-hole floodlit Academy Course. The club features a magnificent clubhouse with full facilities and beautifully manicured courses.

11. RIFFA GOLF CLUB
Address: P.O. Box 39117, Kingdom of Bahrain
Phone: +973 1 7750777
Web Site: www.riffagolfclub.com
The Kingdom of Bahrain is a small island off the Arabian peninsula, about 150 miles northwest of the UAE's western border with Saudi Arabia. Only a short drive outside of its capital, Manama, Riffa Golf Club is the country's only eighteen-hole championship golf course and its only club where the back nine holes are floodlit, allowing play through midnight. Beautifully etched into the unforgiving desert, this delightful par-72 course, which has five lakes and more than seventy bunkers, is managed by Scotland's Gleneagles Hotel.

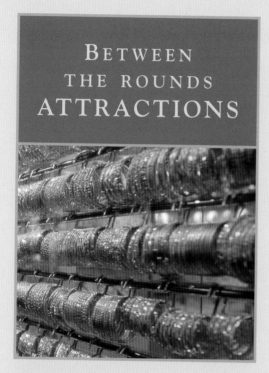

BETWEEN THE ROUNDS ATTRACTIONS

Architecture

Burj al Arab Hotel: Half boat sail, half rocket, there can be no doubt that the Burj al Arab Hotel is one of the most impressive symbols in hotel history and the iconic image of Dubai. It was built in 1999 by UK architect W. S. Atkins at the request of Dubai's rulers, who wanted to create a landmark for Dubai to rival the Eiffel Tower or the Sydney Opera House. Floating like a giant spaceship in the Arabian Gulf, it's a palace of technology entwined with luxury, making this one of the top places in the world to stay. The hotel is built offshore on an artificial island from the Jumeirah Beach Resort, 10 miles south of Dubai City. Burj al Arab is a record breaker: not only is it the only seven-star hotel in the world, but it's also the tallest, at more than 1,000 feet with the largest atrium (courtyard).

The hotel has 202 luxury suites containing from six to thirty rooms, which all come with their own butler, a 42-inch plasma screen, laptop computer, fax machine, and a Jacuzzi. The Burj al Arab literally drips with gold: There are 3,000 square feet of gold leaf on the pillars and fittings. It's a palace of glossy, golden, high-class kitsch that some may find tasteless, others heavenly. Decadence is apparent in every detail: the rooftop helipad, the 100-foot fire and water displays, a restaurant accessible by a three-minute submarine voyage, the hotel's own fleet of white Rolls

Royces, six world-class restaurants, and a pampering spa. You feel like a millionaire while you're there, but bankrupted when you check out.

Address: Burj al Arab Hotel, Jumeira Road (south end), Umm Suqeim, UAE
Phone: +971 4 3017777
Fax: +971 4 3017000
Web Site: www.burj-al-arab.com
Costs: The least expensive suite costs about 2,500 AED (US$700) a night, rising to 5,500 AED (US$1,500) for a two-bed suite, dining area, kitchen, and luxury toilet.

Bastakia Wind Towers: The Bastakia Quarter, on the waterfront east of the Dubai Souk, is distinguished by its cluster of traditional wind tower houses built at the turn of the twentieth century. They were the homes of wealthy Persian merchants who were attracted to Dubai by the city's laid-back trade tariffs. The wind towers, a form of nonmechanical air-conditioning, kept the houses cool in the burning heat of the summer by catching breezes and channeling them down into the room below (usually positioned above the living room or master bedroom), where the air temperature drops through a process of convection. The towers, which rise about 20 feet above the house, were built from *saruj*, a mix of red clay from Iran mixed with manure, and are decorated with coral rock, limestone, or plaster.

Shopping

Malls: With twenty-eight modern malls to choose from (and more on the way), Dubai is the ultimate city to shop till you drop. You'll find a lot of the retailers from back home, like Virgin Megastore, Hallmark, and IKEA, along with top-style names like DKNY, Cartier, and

Tiffany and Co. The boutique-style malls invariably offer a gift-wrapping service, and no mall is complete without its own prayer room. Typically malls are open from 10:00 A.M. to 10:00 P.M. Modern mall buildings often combine retail space, offices, luxury flats, and leisure activities, like a gym, arcade games, and cinema. Mall architecture ranges from impressively space age to downright tasteless. Of note is the Mercato Mall near Dubai Zoo with its Renaissance-style Mediterranean architecture, including Italian-style wall paintings, and the Wafi City Wall, which offers in-line skating, a 3-D motion cinema, a crystal maze, and copious shops amid its pyramid-shaped atrium and mock-Egyptian pillars. It's part Tutankhamen, part *The Mummy*. Remember that most outlets in malls operate on a fixed-rate, no-haggle basis.

Dubai Shopping Festival: Every year for a month, from mid-January to mid-February, the Dubai Shopping Festival heralds a celebration of nonstop shopping bargains and store giveaways that attract up to three million visitors. The festival is part of Dubai's bid to build on its trading heritage and become one of the world's greatest marketplaces, with retailers attending from more than thirty countries.

During the festival artists and entertainers come from all over the world to perform every day and night throughout the city. There are firework displays, laser and light shows, concerts, exhibitions, endless street entertainment, and some world-class sporting action. But of course the main attraction is the shopping. You can find fantastic deals on everything from haute couture and jewelry to home electronics and carpets. Dubai's desert roots are preserved at the Heritage Village, showcasing traditional arts and crafts. At the ever-popular Global Village, you can buy almost anything from around the world, and every night you have the chance to win not one but two Lexuses, worth $30,000 each, in the Lexus Mega Raffle. Although it costs about $60 to enter, if you don't win, you're entered into the grand draw at the end of the festival to win 1 million AED—about US$300,000.

The companies that sponsor the festival offer special discounts and deals that include flights, accommodation, meals, all transfers, and sightseeing at bargain rates. Airlines like Emirates offer discounted fares and an extra baggage allowance so you won't be taxed for your massive postfestival booty. Your credit card, however, may feel a little worse for wear.

Dubai Souks

The souks—traditional open-air markets—are one of Dubai's biggest attractions. It has a good selection of them, all alive with dazzling colors, intoxicating scents, and the hustle and bustle of hagglers and hawkers. Deira, the business and commercial quarter, is home to

frankincense, and dried fruit, imported from across the Middle East. Produce is sold straight out of large open sacks, and friendly shopkeepers are never too busy to introduce their wares to visitors.

Carpet Souk: The plentiful carpet and rug souk in Deira Tower Shopping Mall, al-Nasr Square, is one of the best places outside of Iran to buy Persian carpets. The quality is judged by the type of dyes used (natural being more desirable than synthetic), the number of knots per square inch, size, and the family name of the makers. Silk carpets are considered the most valuable, with carpets from Iran

the best souks, which are organized according to what they sell: gold, electronics, fish, spices, perfume, and carpets. The Deira Covered Souk sells Indian-style textiles, clothing, and henna. Most stalls are closed from midday to 5:00 P.M. Bargaining is the norm in all. Don't accept the first price, and be sure to shop around.

Gold Souk: A trip down to the famous Gold Souk shows why Dubai has earned itself a reputation as the City of Gold. The souk attracts buyers and browsers from around the world to its lattice archways, where the sheer scale and variety of gold on offer, at marked-down prices, is a truly dazzling display. Just about every conceivable kind of gold

jewelry is for sale, such as earrings, rings, necklaces, bracelets, and pendants. Designs can be traditional or modern, bold or conservative, chunky or delicate. To entice you further, many different shades of gold are also available. Craftsmen can alter the composition of alloys in the gold to create pink, white, yellow, or green hues in one piece. Prices vary depending on weight and whether the piece was made by machine or a craftsman.

Spice Souk: Adjacent to the Gold Souk, the Spice Souk (or Deira Old Souk) is saturated in a myriad of Arabic fragrances and seasonings. The narrow, dusty lanes are filled with aromas of cloves, cardamom, ginger, cinnamon,

commanding a higher price than those from Kashmir or Turkey. You can also find some lovely Turkish kilims and Turkoman, Kashmiri, and Afghan rugs. Whenever you buy a carpet or rug, you will be given a certificate of authentication guaranteed by the Dubai Chamber of Commerce and Industry, which ensures that your expensive carpet is actually worth its price. For a tourist buying a carpet in Dubai without getting ripped off takes great skill and patience. Do not feel embarrassed or obliged to buy just because the shop attendant has unrolled forty carpets for you.

Perfume Souk: Here you will find thousands of aromas, but if you can't find one you like, shopkeepers can conjure up a unique concoction to suit your tastes. Arabic perfumes or *attar* are very strong and spicy, unlike Western perfumes, which tend to be flowery and light. They are oil based, and they can leave a mark on your clothes. The perfume shops usually sell an enormous amount of incense, frankincense being the most common, which can be in the form of compressed powder, crystal, rock, or wood.

Mosques

Jumeirah Mosque: The Jumeirah Mosque is a stunning and much-photographed example of modern Islamic architecture. Located on Jumeira Road, it's built along medieval Fatimid lines and recognizable by its massive central dome flanked by two minarets. Mosques in Dubai are not open to non-Muslims, but it is possible to visit Jumeirah as part of a guided tour every Thursday morning with the Sheikh Mohammed Center for Cultural Understanding (Phone: +971 4 3536666, fax: +971 4 3536661). The best time to see its exterior is at sunset, when its stone gives off a golden glow, or at night when it is lit up.

Grand Mosque: The multidomed Grand Mosque, built in a variation of the Anatolian style, boasts Dubai's tallest minaret at 231 feet. Situated on Ali bin Abi Talib Street in Bur Dubai near the Ruler's Court, its vast space, with nine large domes and forty-five smaller ones, can house as many as 1,200 Muslim worshippers. Although the Mosque appears to be immaculately restored, it was only built in the 1990s as an exact replica of the Grand Mosque that stood on this site from 1900 to 1960. Its sand-colored walls and wooden shutters blend elegantly with its surroundings.

Outdoor Activities

Falconry: Falconry, or hawking, was once the traditional art of the Bedouin, who used peregrine and saker falcons to provide themselves with additional game like dove, sandgrouse, and the houbara bustard. Traditionally a wild falcon is caught and trained

in time for the migration of the houbara bustard, which is now a protected species. Capturing wild falcons is also illegal now, so often a combined saker and larger gyr falcon is taken from a controlled breeding program.

The rules of the sport are governed by strict federal laws, and now some falcons are returned into the wild at the end of each season. In the Arab Gulf it's now the sport of princes, sheikhs, and the elite. Birds, which are treated like pampered dogs, fetch more than $6,000 a piece.

Arabian trainers are considered to be the best falconers in the world, training a bird to hunt in as little as two weeks. The trainer builds up a relationship of trust with the bird, through practice, feeding, and sleep deprivation. The quarry must be killed according to Islamic law, so the falcon must learn to capture its prey live whereupon the throat can be slit. The falcon perches on a *wakir*, a highly decorative wooden pole. When not hunting its head is covered in a *burqa*, a leather hood. Falcons can be surprisingly strong. In 2003 a bird owned by Sheikh Mohammed downed a deer many

times its own weight and lifted it into the air. The Falcon Hospital (Phone: +971 3377576) in Dubai treats more than 12,000 damaged birds who have been hurt during hunting or conditions brought on by overpampering or lack of exercise.

In contrast to the traditional camel treks into the desert, the Emirates hunting elite and their falcons travel by four-wheel drive to hunt in the desert in massive groups. You can experience falconry, without the hunting at a desert safari organized for tourists. An Arabian barbecue accompanies an awesome sunset followed by belly dancing, smoking hubbly-bubbly pipes, and displays by the falcons.

Dune Bashing: Dune bashing, the white-water rafting of the desert, is an increasingly popular activity in Emirates. It's an excuse for the rich and elite to take their flashy four-wheel-drive machines into the desert for some serious fun on an exhilarating ride up and down sand dunes. The desert proliferates in all the Gulf states, so adventure sports related to sand are widely popular, and dune bashing is a great way to enjoy the beauty and peace of the desert in the comfort of an air-conditioned four-wheeler.

The Liwa Oasis in Abu Dhabi is a playground for dune bashing, but any decent sand dune will do. The ride is a real adrenaline trigger as the vehicle careers between the cuts

and curls of the sand dunes. The soft sands can make driving very tricky, and learning how to get unstuck in the treacherous sand is just as important as learning how to drive in the desert. Inexperienced drivers should book a trip with tour operators who specialize in dune bashing. Getting stuck is hard on your expensive vehicle and can leave you stranded in the sand for hours trying to rescue your car. Most drivers plan their route in advance and look for camel excretion or footprints, as these are sure signs of hard and compacted sand.

Dubai Creek by Dhow: Taking a boat down the Dubai Creek is the best way of seeing this great trading city. There are plenty of cruises, or you can take an abra to the Al-Makhtoum Bridge and back. Also make a visit to the dhow wharfage on the Deira side of the creek, where you can watch dhows unloading goods from countries around the world. If you're intrigued by these graceful boats, make a visit to the Dhow Building Yard, 1 mile south of Al-Garhoud Bridge in the Jaddaf District. Here they're made in the traditional way, working from the outside of the boat inward, by using simple hand tools. The only concession to modernity are the modern engines, now used instead of sails.

Further Afield

Hajar Mountains: The rugged Hajar Mountain Range stretches south from the Oman border with Emirates to Fujairah some 180 miles north near the coast. Along the route are gorges and water holes where, with a four-wheel-drive vehicle, you can try your hand at wadi bashing—off-roading on the dried-out riverbeds. Hatta, 70 miles from Dubai City near the Oman border, is a favorite spot for weekending ex-pats. Its main attraction is Heritage Village, a free-entry recreation of a traditional mountain village. From here you can access the magnificent rock pools over the border in a small canyon that fills with water all year round. It's just the place to share a cool dip with the toads or swim around the corridors of intricately carved rock and waterfalls.

Sharjah: Sharjah City is an easy 6 miles up the coast from Dubai City. The most important port on the Arabian side of the lower Gulf until it was eclipsed by Dubai, it now markets itself as the cultural capital of the Emirates. The city is an urban sprawl, but its center is worth visiting for its heritage area. There are several museums, art galleries, and the great Al-Arsah Souk, a charming market with traditional palm frond roof and carved doors, which is a good place to pick up Arabic and Bedouin gifts. Be sure to visit the Al-Hisn Fort; restored to its 1820 design, it houses photos, artifacts from the 1930s Al-Qasimi family, and a display of weapons, jewelry, and items used in the pearl trade.

Kalba Fishing Village: For immersion in a lifestyle that's long gone on most of the Gulf Coast, head to the traditional fishing village of Kalba in the Sharjah Emirate. Fishermen go about their daily business of pulling in their nets morning and evening, and *shasha* (canoe-like fishing boats made from palm frond) line the beach.

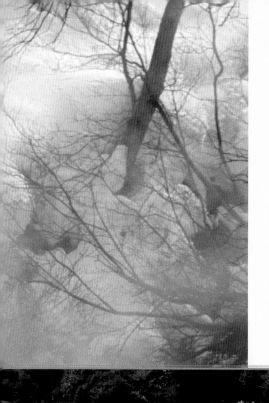

Golf in Japan is an untapped gold mine yet to be discovered by the West. The Japanese are well known for taking a good idea and creating the ultimate—and golf has proven no exception. Take the best golf course designers in the world—Jack Nicklaus, Robert Trent Jones Jr., Arnold Palmer, Gary Player—give them an unlimited budget, and tell them to design to their hearts' content. Then ask architects to create clubhouses with one goal: not to be outdone by anyone. This foolproof combination

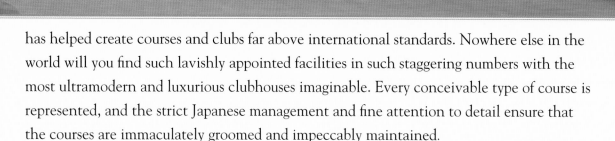

has helped create courses and clubs far above international standards. Nowhere else in the world will you find such lavishly appointed facilities in such staggering numbers with the most ultramodern and luxurious clubhouses imaginable. Every conceivable type of course is represented, and the strict Japanese management and fine attention to detail ensure that the courses are immaculately groomed and impeccably maintained.

For ninety years golf saw steady growth and was a safe and solid place for Japanese to invest their money. Investors happily injected the capital needed to gain the highly sought-after memberships they required to be effective in business. During the economic bubble years of the 1980s, backed by big banks, course design reached a peak of feverish construction. For golfers this means world-class courses galore and many to choose from. Playing a course per day, it would take six years to play all of Japan's courses. Since the bubble-bursting deflation of the 1990s, costs are down to a realistic level; coupled with public access to many formerly elite private courses, the future is bright for international golf.

Open-air bath at Zao Onsen Ski Resort (left)
Ishioka Golf Club (above)

Japanese golf is a slight twist from the old game: Experience electronic, remote control carts with global positioning systems (GPS), or airport-style escalators and conveyer belts that whiz you around the course. Just think like a samurai, clear your schedule for a full day (golfers break after nine holes for a long lunch, regardless of the time of day), substitute your scotch whiskey with sake, and you'll be ready for an unforgettable golfing experience.

About Japan

Japan is made up of more than 3,000 islands along the Pacific Ring of Fire. Here you can experience the natural extremes of typhoons, earthquakes, volcanic eruptions, and tsunamis within mesmerizing scenes of snowcaps, deep lakes, and lush greenery set among mostly uninhabitable mountains. Japan offers the most visually stunning and serene golf landscapes in the world.

Even beyond geography, Japan is a land of extremities, blending the old traditions with visions of the future, often side by side. The enigma of Japanese culture, traditions, and manners—often the polar opposite of Western behavior, can confuse the humble westerner and lead to many *Lost in Translation* moments. Blend with the crowds among the futuristic, efficient, and sanitized worlds of Tokyo and Osaka; scale the majestic heights of Mount Fuji; take in an ancient tea ceremony or Kabuki theater show; or just enjoy rural tranquillity. From ancient Shinto shrines to futuristic skyscrapers, from sumo wrestling to sushi, Japan will peel back your eyelids and astound you.

Festival float (above)

Senso-ji Buddhist temple (right)

Activities and Attractions

Castles and Palaces: Japan is bountiful with striking castles. Most are copies of original fifteenth-century mountain fort defenses, as many were destroyed in the nineteenth-century Meiji era and World War II. By the sixteenth century more sophisticated castles built on plains became administrative quarters. The black Matsumoto "Crow" Castle has a 400-year-old keep and exhibition of matchlocks and samurai armor. Himeji Castle is said to resemble a white heron in flight, with moats, turrets, and labyrinthian passageways. Be warned of enemy intruders by the creaking

floorboards of Nijo Castle. Seventeenth-century Matsue and Matsuyama are two of the few original, nonreconstructed castles with artifacts of the ruling Matsudaira clan. Sumptuous palaces and villas also offer stunning gardens, architecture, and history, such as fourteenth-century Kyoto Imperial Palace and the seventeenth-century Katsura Imperial Villa, built during an era when noble leisure pursuits included moon viewing.

Onsens: The Japanese capacity to bathe is matched by no other race on earth. Volcanic spring resorts (*onsens*) are a good way to unwind from the heat and hectic pace of Japan's wild cities. Some are heated by thermal waters, some are artificially heated and enhanced with therapeutic herbs, and others can be foul smelling and sulfurous. Purposes range from curing ailments to bathing amid the outdoors. There are many varieties to try: an outdoor stone bath by a river, thermal mud or sand baths, and even onsens inside cable cars. Try a natural onsen in the mountains to relax after hiking. Onsen hotels and even whole resorts develop around the baths, from isolated villages to entire complexes.

Pools are usually single sex, with mixed-sex bathing sometimes acceptable at night time. The centuries-old bathing customs are based on Shinto purification rituals. Wear a *yukata* (lightweight bathing kimono) to get to the pool, then shower thoroughly and remove all residue of soap before getting in. Bathing is almost always done naked. After a short soak, wash, shower, soap, and rinse again before reentering the bath. When you get out, do not rinse so that you absorb the full effect of the minerals.

Gardens: Landscaping has been an important art in Japan for centuries. The tradition originated from the Shinto love of nature and the Buddhist visions of paradise. There are three types of gardens: hill gardens with ponds, streams, and bridges to imitate natural scenery; dry gardens, using stones, sand, and moss to depict nature abstractly; and Zen meditation and tea gardens for the simplicity needed for a tea ceremony. The moatlike Hama Rikyu Garden, a feudal lord's retreat and duck-hunting ground, is considered the best oasis in Tokyo. The Sankei-en Garden in Yokohama with tea arbors, villas, and a pagoda is considered the nation's most picturesque. The Ryoanji Temple Zen Rock Garden in Kyoto, made from moss-covered boulders and raked pebbles, is a great place for meditation. Also in Kyoto at the Saihoji Moss Temple, are 100 varieties of moss that come into full color after a rain shower.

Skyscraper (above left), Lanterns (above)
Traditional rock garden pool (below)

Mountains and National Parks: Japan is one of the most geologically active places on earth. The combination of sixty active volcanoes, hot springs, lakes, and thousands of small mountains and hills make for fantastic outdoor and hiking experiences. The Japanese Alps in Central Honshu, site of the 1998 Winter Olympics, are full of resorts for Japan's favorite winter sport: skiing. Expect the best ski slopes to be very crowded. Japan is hiking heaven, with well-kempt trails and detailed signs. There are numerous national parks, the most visited being Fuji-Hakone-Izu, where ascending Mount

Mount Fuji

Fuji in its summer climbing season is a must. The seaside park of Ise-Shima is famed for its pearl diving. At Mount Fugen enjoy taking a high-altitude spring bath, walking through "the Hells" sulfur springs, or playing golf at one of Japan's oldest courses. Much of north and west Japan can only be hiked in summer and early autumn. For safety stick to the designated climbing season for each mountain.
Shrines and Temples: Buddhist temples contain a lecture hall, a decorative pagoda structure, an elegant gate, and sacred objects of worship like statues. Visit Tokyo's lively Sesonji Temple, with its fortune-telling and kitsch trinkets. Kamakura is the home of numerous Zen Buddhist temples, including the famous outdoor Great Buddha, but you'll find Japan's biggest Buddha in Todaiji Temple in Nara. The dominating and popular Kiyomizu Temple affords epic hillside views over Kyoto, but on a bright day, across the city, be dazzled by the Temple of the Golden Pavilion with its shining gold leaf and bronze phoenix.

Shrines are Shinto places of worship where the *kami*, Shinto gods, dwell. Pray here for good fortune, and celebrate festivals and special events. You'll notice a Torii entrance gate and the Komainu, a pair of guardian dogs, by each shrine's entrance. Some shrines have stages inside for displays of bugaku dances or No theater. You should clean your hands and mouth before entering the offering hall in accordance with Shinto purification rules. Inside pick Omikji fortune-telling paper slips, and write your wishes on Ema wooden plates. You'll find shrines to the gods of rice, war, scholars, the goddess of Mount Fuji, and other clans or local gods. Some of the best are the Toshogu Shrine in Nikko, made of millions of sheets of gold leaf in a forest of cedar trees; Tokyo's refuge of Meiji Jingu, surrounded by a dense forest in the heart of the city; the Shinto pilgrimage site of Ise Grand Shrines, whose inner shrine is reconstructed on a new site every twenty years according to Shinto rules; or the tranquil island of Miyahima, where the red Torii stands in the sea.

Motorized golf carts near Gotemba

History of Golf in Japan

The Japanese are crazy about golf, and it's no recent phenomenon. It has been played here for more than a century, and it's long been an intricate part of business culture. The first course in Japan was carved on a hilltop in Kobe city in 1901 by British businessmen and originally consisted of a mere four holes. These early ties to international business kept golf reserved for only the elite of Japanese society, a stigma that remains with the game today. The more money the affluent pumped into clubs and courses, the more interest it created in the game, thus starting the cycle that fed, nourished, and supported the industry throughout the twentieth century to become the mania we see today. Currently seventeen million of the fifty million golfers in the world raise clubs at more than 2,000 golf courses in Japan.

When to Go and What to Bring

Japanese summers and winters are long seasons, with a short spring and autumn between. The summers are so hot that they suck your energy and drain your body of essential fluids rapidly. Luckily drinks are available in the snack bars (or "tea huts") on the courses. If you don't mind the heat, this will greatly lengthen the golf season for you. The best time to visit is during the spring's cherry blossoming, advancing from Okinawa in the south in February to Hokkaido in the north in May. June and early July are fine temperature-wise, but the rainy season beckons, making playing conditions somewhat hit or miss. Layering of clothes is your best bet, and keep some rain gear tucked away in your bag. From late August into September Japan gets hit by a series of typhoons. This doesn't usually affect the hearty Japanese golfer, so don't let it bother you either. Just keep abreast of the local weather forecast when planning your excursion. In the autumn, October and November are usually mild, and the humidity levels drop, making it perfect for golf, but a Windbreaker is indispensable. In winter, inland courses will see snowfall, but you could try courses near the ocean or Kyushu's southern Kagoshima area, which has pleasant year-round conditions.

Costs

Japan's incredible course facilities, once enjoyed only by their financially elite membership, are now open to the public at vastly discounted prices. It's a far cry from the days when memberships soared above the $200,000 mark. Considering the caliber of courses for your golfing dollar, Japan is now priced in line with, or perhaps even below, international levels. Expect to pay 10,000 yen (US$93) for a weekday round at a top-notch facility. The same club on a weekend will run to nearly double the price—in some cases more. Drive a couple of hours from the cities, and you can almost half the prices. Club rental costs 3,000 yen (US$30) to 5,000 yen (US$49). Shoes are usually available, but don't expect to find anything larger than an American size 10. If you are lucky enough to get invited by a member to a private course, be warned: You will probably be paying close to $400 a round, but you might not see the bill, as it is customary for the person who invited you to pay. Outside of the major cities, stock up on plenty of cash in yen for golf courses as well as hotels.

Hotels

All travel and living in Japan is astronomically expensive, but this particularly applies to luxury hotels. Book in advance for popular destinations. There are many options, from a quickie short stay at a love hotel to indulge fantasies, to coffin-sized Capsule Hotels for city workers too drunk to make the last train. Western hotels are generally the safest bet; expect to pay from 10,000 yen (US$93) a night for a single, 12,000 yen (US$110) for a double, and about one-third more for the better-rated hotels (you'll find all the deluxe major American chains here). Some hotels give you the option of traditional tatami-mats or a less harsh Western mattress, and they mix and match Japanese and Western cuisine. Do try and stay at a traditional Ryokan inn during your visit. Often found in mountain hamlets, they offer a view into traditional Japan. Prices range from 4,000 yen (US$38) to about 25,000 yen (US$235), depending on luxury and location; full board with superb local cuisine is always included. Ryokan etiquette is highly complex and centered on detailed serving; be meek, observant, and always wait to be directed to avoid offense. On arrival leave your shoes at the door, and change into slippers. The maid will show you to your room, serve sweet tea, dress you in your *yukata*,

Girls in the trendy Harajuku fashion district, Tokyo (above)

Tokyo cityscape (below)

and show you to the communal bath. Later she will lay out the futon mattress on the tatami-mat where you will sleep.

Travel

Airports: Air travel into Japan is easy. There are many airports served by regular flights from around the world, making air a convenient way of navigating the country, as national carriers offer decent discounts for flights to different domestic destinations. The main gateway for international travelers is Narita Airport (NRT) near Tokyo and Kansai International (KIX) in Osaka.

Car Rental: Renting a car offers the greatest flexibility and is very safe, but private toll roads—costing between 100 (US$1.00) and 10,000 yen (US$93)—can make the experience expensive. You will need an international driver's license. Modern rental cars let you put in the map codes and direct you, which avoids the chaos of trying to read Japanese road signs. Driving and taxis are best avoided in gridlocked Tokyo, where it is said that if a thief steals your car in the morning, by the afternoon he will only have driven a block away.

Other Transport: The transport network is so well organized that people are used to schedules requiring split-second timing. In the rare event that trains are delayed in the phenomenally crowded morning rush hour, staff give out apology slips to workers to show their superiors! Rail travel is extremely fast, efficient, clean, safe, comfortable, and expensive. Services range from local lines to the famous super-fast *shinkansen* "bullet" trains, which travel up to 180 miles an hour and have signs and announcements in English. You can purchase an unlimited Japan Rail Pass, which lets you use any Japan Rail service for up to twenty-one days, but it can only be purchased outside of Japan. Major inner-city train routes often have display screens giving information in English, but this varies enormously between the major cities, with Kyoto faring better than Tokyo. In the big cities, undergrounds, monorails, trams, and buses give plenty of options to get around from 5:00 A.M. to midnight, with taxis taking you through the night, but realistically you'll need to understand Japanese for anything other than the color-coded undergrounds.

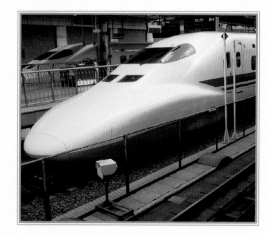

Bullet train

Regions and Golfing

Tokyo Area: On the face of it, Tokyo seems to conform to all its stereotypes: overwhelmingly big (55 miles wide by 15 miles long), frighteningly modern, constantly evolving, and frantically paced. Here consumption is king. Everything is a commodity, from clothing and gadgets to cultural pursuits and leisure activities. Visit the Imperial Palace, an oasis of calm in the city center; bid in the 5:00 A.M. tuna auction at Tsukiji, the world's biggest fish market; try fortune-telling at the Senso-ji Buddhist temple; indulge in the Japanese pastimes of drinking, karaoke, and pachinko in the Roppongi red light district; dine at one of the 100,000-plus restaurants; explore the *Blade Runner*–like modern architecture of Shinjuku; or play with technogadgets in futuristic Odaiba, where man-made beaches are stacked with Australian sand and you can test drive the latest Toyotas on a track. In short,

The suggested itinerary is for active days of about seventeen hours. If you prefer a more leisurely trip, pick and choose your favorite activities. You'll need to allow more time in Japan for your golfing trips. Travel is slow because traffic is heavy, and the regions surrounding Tokyo are mountainous and misty. It's often customary to break for lunch after nine holes. The game is slower, so allow extra time for a round.

Day 1: A.M. Fly into Narita airport (NRT) near Tokyo, preferably overnight. Spend the day exploring the world's craziest city. Be sure to visit the Imperial Palace and gardens and the Senso-ji Buddhist temple. Go shopping in futuristic Shibuya. There are no real golf opportunities in Tokyo—and it's a full day's travel just getting in and out of the city—but if you're itching to get started, head to the Chiba prefecture just east of Tokyo to play at Oak Hills, Abiding Club Golf Society, Ichihara Korakuen, or Academia Hills Country Club. **P.M.** If you like serious theater and can stay awake, take in a traditional Japanese performance at the Kabuki-za theater in Ginza. If five hours for a show is too long, just see one act from the gallery. For a novelty spend the night in a love hotel.

Day 2: A.M. Drive or take a train out to play the Jack Nicklaus–designed Ishioka Course on the Ibaraki prefecture 50 miles northeast of Tokyo. Allow more than two hours each way for travel.
P.M. If you have time, play nine holes at one of the many great courses in nearby Chiba. Then rest your weary laurels back in Tokyo's bustling metropolis after indulging in drinking, crazy clubbing, or pachinko gambling in Roppongi.

Day 3: A.M. Drive or take a one-hour journey by train to the Kanagawa prefecture. There are lots of golf courses to enjoy. We recommend Atsugi Kokusai Country Club, but it's impossible to get onto during weekends.

Akashi-Kaikyo Bridge, Tokyo

P.M. Visit Kamakura, a historic beach town with sixty-five amazing Buddhist temples and nineteen Shinto shrines, including the famous outdoor bronze Great Buddha. Spend the night in a traditional Ryokan inn in the hills.

Day 4: A.M. Drive to Gotemba in Kawana's neighboring prefecture Shiizuoka, 50 miles west, a two-hour journey. Play Gotemba Golf Course.
P.M. Enjoy a stunning view of Mount Fuji from the surrounding Fuji Five Lakes recreational area, with amusement parks, water sports, and waterfalls. Or play a second round at Belle View Nagao Golf Club, also in Gotemba. Drive 25 miles southeast to Hakone, a journey of ninety minutes.

Day 5: A.M. Enjoy hot springs, lakes, rock carvings, and nature trails in Hakone, the "valley of great boiling." Alternatively, head to Kago Saka Golf Club in Oyama cho, and play a round of golf on the slopes of Mount Fuji! **P.M.** Head 25 miles south to Ito city, a journey of ninety minutes. Play Kawana Golf Course. You'll need to stay the night in the opulent old English country estate Kawana Hotel in order to play Kawana.

Day 6: A.M. Head out early, and fly or take a bullet train 400 miles southwest to the island of Kyushu. Your final destination is the southeast city of Miyazaki.
P.M. If you make it before twilight, play one of the nine-hole courses at Phoenix Seagaia. Stay at the luxurious 500-foot-tall Sheraton Grande Hotel, with all rooms offering a spectacular view of the Pacific Ocean and surrounding pine forests.

Day 7: For a strange beach experience, enjoy an invigorating hot sand bath in Ibusuki near Kagoshima in the far south, 50 miles southwest. Otherwise, stay at the Phoenix. Take the family to Ocean Dome, the world's biggest indoor water park, or play the tropically challenging Tom Watson course and the other two nine holes at the Phoenix. Take a connecting flight home from Miyazaki.

FIVE-DAY EXECUTIVE STRESS BUSTER

Day 1: **P.M.** Fly into Narita airport (NRT) near Tokyo. Drive to Gotemba in Shiizuoka, 40 miles southwest of Tokyo, a two-hour trip.

Day 2: **A.M.** Play Gotemba Golf Course. **P.M.** Enjoy stunning view of Mount Fuji from the surrounding Fuji Five Lakes recreational area with amusement parks, water sports, and waterfalls, or play a second round nearby at Belle View Golf Club, also in Gotemba. Drive 25 miles southeast to Hakone, a journey of ninety minutes.

Day 3: **A.M.** Enjoy hot springs, lakes, rock carvings, and nature trails in Hakone, the "valley of great boiling." Alternatively, head to Kago Saka Golf Club in Oyama cho—and play a round of golf on the slopes of Mount Fuji! Head 25 miles south to Ito city by road, a journey of ninety minutes. **P.M.** Play Kawana Golf Course. Make like Joe DiMaggio and Marilyn Monroe on their honeymoon, and stay the night in the opulent old English country estate Kawana Hotel. You'll need to stay here in order to play Kawana.

Day 4: **A.M.** You'll love Kawana and will almost certainly want to stay in the luxury hotel and play another round. Otherwise, try one of the other superb courses in the Shizuoka prefecture–Belle View Nagao Golf Club or Mishima Country Club—all with great views of Mount Fuji.

P.M. Drive back 50 miles to Tokyo. If you make it back by evening, take in a traditional Japanese performance at the Kabuki-za theater in Ginza. If five hours for a show is too long, just see one act from the gallery. For a novelty spend the night in a love hotel.

Day 5: **A.M.** If sightseeing, be sure to visit the Imperial Palace and gardens and the Senso-ji Buddhist temple. Go shopping in futuristic Shibuya. If golfing, play one of the many great courses in nearby Chiba prefecture, like Oak Hills, Abiding Club Golf Society, Ichihara Korakuen, or Academia Hills Country Club. **P.M.** Fly home from Narita International Airport.

Phoenix Country Club Course

Tokyo at night (above)

Gotemba Golf Club (opposite)

Tokyo amazes. Just outside of the city, take day trips to the Toshugo Shrine in Nikko; the numerous shrines, temples, and Great Buddha of Kamakura; and Mount Fuji and the Hakone cultural and hiking park. The exuberant waterfront glitz of Yokohama is just thirty minutes away by train.

Tokyo and its surrounding prefectures enjoy the largest concentration of high-quality golf courses in Japan. Ibaraki, Saitama, and Chiba all have copious numbers of top-notch facilities. Their close proximity to the city equals high demand, and this is reflected in their sky-high green fees. It can also be harder to get a tee time at any price, as people plan their golf outings months in advance and there remain a lot of members-only clubs. All the courses in this area are world-class properties. They have large clubhouses that include spas with business and leisure facilities within a country club atmosphere. Most have back-massage chairs, foot-massage machines, and about every luxury imaginable. Some even offer a shoe-shining service so you can strut away in style. Even at exorbitant prices (US$250 to $400 per round), these clubs sell out on weekends, so expect to be forced to wait, sometimes nearly two hours, at the turn. This has long been accepted practice, and people usually use this time to do business, have lunch, and, for the most part, just get plain drunk! Less busy weekday rounds are the best bet at about half the price.

Honshu and Hokkaido: Honshu is mainland Japan, where the majority of people live and work. In Central Honshu go skiing in the Japanese Alps, buy wood crafts in traditional Takayama, explore castles in Matsumoto and Inyuama, or navigate the remote agricultural Shokawa Valley. Kansai and West Honshu are full of history and culture, such as in the imperial cities of Kyoto and Nara, crammed full of palaces, temples, and shrines. See great feudal castles in and around Kobe or Japan's most sacred Shinto shrine of Ise-jingu. For recent history visit the now-vibrant city of Hiroshima, scene of the world's first nuclear attack. More crazed Japanese culture and funky nightlife can be experienced in Osaka city. Northern Honshu, once known as "the end of the road," is little developed but entirely unspoiled. Think outdoor adventures, and think remote: Enjoy hikes on rocky coastlines and mountains full of warming hot springs, explore the tranquil island of Kinkasan, or take the pilgrimage hike to the three sacred Dewa Sanzan Mountains.

Hokkaido is the great north of Japan, rich with snowcapped mountains, wildlife, and the great outdoors. Discover the crystal clear lakes of Akan National Park, explore the pristine wilderness of Shiretoko-hanto, meet the indigenous Ainu tribe, ski or visit the February Snow Festival in Sapporo, or hike through volcanic remains in Toya-ko.

Golf in Japan started on Honshu, the "main island," which plays host to the majority of courses and tour events. Courses in this region are plentiful. If you are willing to travel a few hours away from any urban area, you can get some great deals that will leave you thirsty for more. Some courses in Hokkaido offer one price for all-you-can-play days; courses on Honshu are open twenty-four hours a day and offer night golf with stadium-like lighting.

Kyushu, Shikoku, and the Southwest Islands: The large southerly island of Kyushu was the point of entry for foreign traders and conquerors and the site of the earliest Japanese settlements. After passing through the cosmopolitan city Fukoka/Hakata, hike through the volcanic caldera of Aso-san, take a dip in Beppu, Japan's hot spring center, or have a hot sand bath in Ibusuki before enjoying the magnificent gardens and castles of nearby port city Kagoshima. Finally, sober up in Nagasaki and learn about the horrors of nuclear warfare.

Shikoku is mainly rural and off the typical tourist map, making it ideal for a peaceful and spiritual experience. Step onto the ancient pilgrimage trail of the eighty-eight Sacred Temples of Shikoku, take a hike up the sacred mountains of Tsuraugi-san and Ishizuchi-san, or climb the 800 granite steps to the shrine of Kopira-san in Kotohira. As a respite hike the deep gorges of the Iya Valley, or try sea kayaking the Inland Sea.

In the East China Sea, en route to Taiwan, lie the Southwest Islands, known collectively as Okinawa. Because of their warm climate, the islands are still favored as a vacation resort by the Japanese, proving great for diving, snorkeling, cycling, and sunbathing. Notorious for its tragic World War II naval battlefields and tunnels, it's also home to Iriomote-Jima, Japan's only tropical jungle.

Japan's southwest islands are a golfer's treat. The people and courses are friendlier here than in other parts of Japan; they see fewer foreigners and so will often treat you like a dignitary. Kyushu's lush green forests and vegetation sprout up from dark volcanic soil. The landscape lends itself well to the construction of golf courses, and there is plenty of coastline boasting a variety of seaside and ocean-view courses. The climate is mild in Fukuoka and semitropical near Kagoshima on the southern tip. Its warm weather has made it home to two major golf tournaments in November: Dunlop Phoenix in Miyazaki and Casio World Open in Kagoshima. Because of the area's volcanic nature, there are lots of natural hot springs, earth tremors, and earthquakes, so you may want to wait an extra few seconds before tapping in that ball hanging over the lip! Many clubhouses use the natural hot springs in their baths.

THE GOLF COURSES
ISHIOKA

The Clubhouse

Food: Serves a Japanese-style lunch menu, including curry rice and udon or soba noodles.

Changing Rooms: Impeccably clean and spacious with Japanese-style hot baths, towels, and toiletries.

Ladies' Facilities: Immaculate changing rooms and equal access.

Pro Shop: An impressive display of the latest designer golf wear by Nike, Boss, Ashworth, and Burberry.

Interior and Exterior: A small, modern clubhouse with elegant mahogany decor throughout.

Background to the Course

Architect: Jack Nicklaus built the course in 1994.

Type: Parkland.

Landscape: Play a relaxing game in breath-taking scenery with trees and lakes surrounding the fairway and greens. Serenity, however, can be disrupted by the nearby Self Defence Air Force base if they are on practice. Cut out of the Kogama Forest, the course lies almost flat, with only a 4-meter variation between its highest and lowest points.

Playing the Course

The 7,071-yard Ishioka is a beautiful new parkland course near Tokyo. It was voted best public golf course in Japan for 2002 and 2003

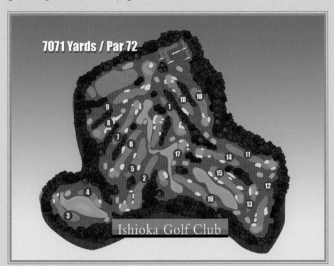

7071 Yards / Par 72

Ishioka Golf Club

by *Par Golf*, *Golf Digest*, and the Japan Golf Tour Organization (JGTO). Ishioka is dominated by tight fairways closed in by mature trees. Nicklaus added to the challenge by placing some heavy rough in key areas around the course. Areas of water on the course, as well as vast bunkers, add to the hazard count.

Score Card

Address: Ishioka Golf Club, 1050-1 Seraku, Ogawa-machi, Higashi-Ibaraki, Ibaraki 311-3401, Japan
Phone: +81 299 58 5111
Fax: +81 299 58 5119

E-mail: ishioka@accordiagolf.com
Course and Length: Eighteen holes, 7,071 yards, par 72.
Tee Times: 8:00 A.M. to 3:00 P.M.
Handicap: No certificate required.
Green Fees: Self-play weekday 10,800 yen (US$100), caddy service weekday 13,800 yen (US$125), weekend/national holiday with caddy 20,800 yen (US$190). Credit cards accepted. Buggies (golf carts) are free.
Facilities: A driving range, caddy service, buggies. Afterward relax in a Japanese onsen-style hot bath.
Location: Ishioka is 60 miles from Tokyo and 10 miles from the Ishioka Interchange on the Joban Expressway. By train it's fifty-two minutes on the JR Tokyu Super Hitachi from Tokyo Ueno Station to Ishioka Station, then a twenty-minute taxi ride to the course.

Ian's Opinion

This beautifully maintained and virtually flat course is as challenging as you'd expect from Nicklaus. Scattered en route are a few lovely teahouses, designed in the old style, which make great resting points for a refreshment break and to take in the experience. Meander over the pretty Japanese bridges crossing the streams. The sixteenth hole is one of the most scenic; play up a long fairway bordered by a lake, then pitch up to a green that sits above a creek. Like many courses in Japan, Ishioka had an amazing amount of investment before the financial bubble burst when it then became semiprivate. Today it remains as uncompromising and gorgeous to play as the sumptuous clubhouse is to dine in.

GOTEMBA

The Clubhouse

Food: Standard Japanese-style lunch menu including curry rice, udon or soba noodles, plus European favorites like pizza and pasta.

Changing Rooms: Impeccably clean with towels, toiletries, and a communal onsen bath.

Ladies' Facilities: Every Monday is ladies day, when they can enjoy any lunch on the menu for free. Ladies can play from the men's tees if they keep a reasonable flow of play.

Interior and Exterior: This ultramodern $40 million clubhouse built on the side of a hill offers panoramic views of the course and Mount Fuji. This could almost be the headquarters of a tyrannical James Bond archvillain—watch out for flying rockets during your round!

Background to the Course

Architect: Shiro Akaboshi, Japan's most revered golf course designer, built Gotemba in 1971.

Type: Traditional Japanese hillside course.

Landscape: Gotemba offers stunning views from the course itself, with contoured fairways surrounded by forests, bridges over ravines, and Japanese ponds. Its surroundings are even

more spectacular, with the snowcapped and enigmatic Mount Fuji looming in the distance.

Course Facts:

• Gotemba's club champion is in his sixties. Perhaps this is because Gotemba is a course that tests every facet of a golfer's game and requires many years of study to master. Businessmen bring their protégés here to test their mettle on this unforgiving course.

• If you can hack the cold and ice, January to April is a picturesque time to play here, when snow falls on Mount Fuji and you can benefit from reduced green fees.

Playing the Holes

Signature Hole: Gotemba's signature first hole (462 yards, par 5) starts you down the sloping valley toward the green in the distance. This par 5 will really test your course management and shot-making ability. The left side slopes

5887 Yards / Par 72

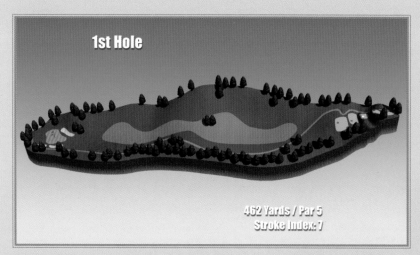

1st Hole

462 Yards / Par 5
Stroke Index: 7

away toward the out-of-bounds zone. Also factor in the downhill slope, and you are left with a few challenging shots to make the green in regulation. Watch out for the pine tree about 200 yards from the tee, sitting bang in the middle of the fairway. The smart player will lay up near the 150-yard mark, leaving him- or herself the most flat lie from which to execute the approach shot. Add to this the breathtaking views, and it can be tough to stay focused!

Best Golf Hole: The members' favorite hole, the sixteenth (150 yards, par 3), has out of bounds to the right. Any shots played short will not kick on, as there is a slight upward slope. The green, with its three tiers, is three times as deep as it is wide, so the right choice of club and strength of shot is key here.

Toughest Hole: With its stroke index of 2, the massively long eleventh (618 yards, par 5) is a monster of a hole that can destroy your round. Although the tee shot is downhill, the fairway is still very tight, with out of bounds

on the right. It is advisable to take a shorter club off the tee and then a longer one for the second shot where there is greater margin for error. The fairway dogleg lies to the right 150 yards from the green, so the third shot to the small green, surrounded by pine trees, is likely to be at least 180 yards long.

Playing the Course

Gotemba, clinging to a tree-covered mountain, is one of Japan's most spectacular mountain courses. It is so steep in places that you use escalators to climb up to the next tee. Buggies are readily available and essential if you want to cope with the course and avoid a coronary.

Score Card

Address: Gotemba Golf Club, 1924-2 Kouyama, Gotemba-shi, Shizuoka-ken 412-0033, Japan
Phone: +81 550 87 1555
Fax: +81 550 87 1915
(English-speaking golf pro Bennett Galloway: Phone: +81 990 9892 4319, e-mail: ben-galloway@gotemba-gc.co.jp)
Web Site: www.gotemba-gc.co.jp
Course and Lengths: Eighteen holes, 6,320 yards (back tee), 5,887 yards (regular tee) (par 72).
Dress Code: No jeans, T-shirts, or beach sandals. A no-tattoo policy, intended to keep out the Yakuza and crime organizations, is still written on a sign outside the clubhouse. Unlike many courses in the area, spiked golf shoes are allowed.
Tee Times: 7:00 to 10:30 A.M. and 2:00 to 3:00 P.M. for twilight half rounds, with some flexibility on times on the weekend. On weekends, a one-hour, forty-minute lunch break is compulsory. Weekdays and some weekends through play (no lunch break) and 1.5 rounds are possible.
Handicap: No certificate required.
Green Fees: Weekdays 9,800 yen (US$90),

weekends 18,600 yen (US$170), public holidays 17,600 yen (US$160). Prices are slightly reduced in the winter between January and April.

Packages: 8,500 yen (US$75) self-play on Tuesdays; 14,500 yen (US$130) hotel, breakfast, and golf package on weekdays; 19,500 yen (US$175) dinner, golf, and hot spring weekday package.

Other Costs: 2,310 yen (US$20) per person for caddy (based on group of four sharing), or 3,675 yen (US$33) per person (based on two sharing). You can rent shoes for 700 yen (US$6.00) and premium clubs for 3,500 yen (US$31).

Facilities: Caddies, lessons in English and Japanese, buggies, chalets, parking, restaurant, and Japanese onsen bath. Near the golf course enjoy a factory outlet shopping mall, Fuji speedway go-cart track, Gotemba microbrewery for Gotemba Kogen Beer, mountain biking, tennis, hiking, horse riding, fishing, and hiking up and skiing down Mount Fuji.

Location: Gotemba is 60 miles from Tokyo. By car take the Tomei Expressway to Gotemba Interchange; then it's a fifteen-minute drive. By train it takes one hour, forty minutes on the Odakyu Asagiri from Tokyo Shinjuku Station to Gotemba Station; then take a free shuttle bus to the course.

Ian's Opinion

This is probably the most stunning golf course I've ever played. It's a mountain course with many steep hills and gullies, so don't even contemplate walking the course—unless you're working out for a marathon or want to train for climbing a mountain (like the nearby Fuji). Gotemba is beautifully manicured (like all Japanese courses), and the views are spectacular: On a clear day you can see Mount Fuji in one direction and the Pacific Ocean in the other. This is the most serene and peaceful golfing experience you're ever likely to have. The highland midges here bite in the summer, so bring an insect repellent, and don't wear shorts. On some holes there are big fans on the green to keep them cool and protect them from the intense humidity. Gotemba is the best first hole you'll ever play; from the top of the course looking down on the par 5 in the distance, it's like staring into an amphitheater.

FUJI COURSE, KAWANA

Landscape: Breathtaking views of the Pacific Ocean from the cliff tops, sunken fairways and elevated greens surrounded by woods, and Mount Fuji in the background of this picture-postcard setting.

Pro Shop: Find great souvenirs from the historic hotel, such as Kawana-branded golfing equipment, balls, clothing, and markers. Best buys are a tea set of Mount Fuji for 8,600 yen (US$80) or a funky golf cap for 3,200 yen (US$30). Like everything at Kawana, nothing comes cheaply.

Course Facts:

• The hotel was built by Baron Okura of the Okura Hotel family in the 1930s. One of his employees built the golf course without his permission, but thankfully for golfers, the baron allowed it to stay.

The Hotel

Food: Kawana's main dining room serves French cuisine. There's also a grill serving Western-style food, a tempura restaurant, a tearoom, and a bar.

Rooms: Rooms are spacious. Twin, double, and triple rooms and suites are offered, as well as Japanese-style rooms. The hotel's art deco design is based on an old English country estate but with a hint of a Spanish influence. The interior and decor is an eerie and enchanting combo of *Twin Peaks* meets *The Shining*: fantastic old fireplaces, stuffed animals on the wall, and an old movie projection room.

Facilities: Three swimming pools, a billiards room, tennis courts, a mah jong room, and car parking.

Background to the Fuji Course

Architect: Charles Allison designed the course, known as the Pebble Beach of Japan, in 1932.

Type: Seaside.

• Old Hollywood fell in love with the old Kawana style. John Wayne stayed here, and it was the setting for Marilyn Monroe and Joe DiMaggio's honeymoon.
• It was used as a base by invading Australian troops during World War II.

6192 Yards / Par 72

Fuji Golf Course

• Kawana hosts the Fuji Sankei Classic golf tournament.

Playing the Holes (Fuji Course)

Signature Hole: The signature hole at Kawana is the beautiful fifteenth (415 yards, par 5). It runs along the edge of the cliffs and out toward a peninsula shared by the fifteenth green and sixteenth tee. From the back tees the drive has to travel over the bay, risking a 100-foot drop into the sea below. If a shot is played too safely, however, it can be gathered into the nest of bunkers down the right-hand side of the fairway. Approach shots into its wide but shallow green are threatened by tall pines clinging to the edge of the cliffs, making this one of the most spectacular holes it is possible to play.

Best Golf Hole: The members' favorite hole at Kawana is the massively long eleventh (619 yards, par 5), with a left-hand dogleg 300 yards from the green. The hole plays out to the end of the spit of land on which the course is set. Behind the raised green is the symbol of Kawana—a lighthouse in the shape of a tee peg. Although it can be benign in good weather, this hole is exposed to any winds blowing across Sagami Bay, which change the complexion of the whole course.

Playing the Fuji Course

The Fuji Course is usually in A-1 condition, painstakingly maintained from green conditions to general manicuring. There are no buggies allowed. As there are some quite dramatic changes in elevation, it can be fairly hard work to play, but do persevere and you won't be disappointed. Take an escalator ride to get to the higher holes—an ultramodern contrast to the old-fashioned hotel. Definitely hire one of the women caddies, mostly in their fifties, who are very knowledgeable.

Score Card

Address: Kawana Golf Resort, 1459 Kawana, Ito City, Shizuoka prefecture 414-0044, Japan
Phone: +81 557 45 1111
Fax: +81 557 45 3834

15th Hole

415 Yards / Par 5

Web Site: www.princehotels.co.jp/kawana
Courses and Lengths: Two eighteen-hole courses, the Fuji Course (6,192 yards, par 72) and Oshima Course (5,711 yards, par 72).
Tee Times: Dawn until dusk.
Handicap: No certificate required.
Green Fees: To play the Fuji Course, you have to stay at Kawana Hotel, which costs 50,000 yen (US$450) per night on weekdays and 57,350 yen (US$520) on weekends. The Oshima Course self-play costs 20,000 yen (US$180).
Packages: 66,000 yen (US$590) for one round at Fuji with a caddy, a night in the hotel, and one round self-play at Oshima.
Other Costs: There are no buggies, but caddies cost about 9,000 yen (US$80) per round.
Location: From Tokyo by car take the Tomei Expressway to Odawara/Atsugi interchange, then take the National Highway 135 for 50 miles (about one hour, forty minutes). By train take the Tokaido Shinkansen to Atami, then JR Ito Line to Ito Station; from there it's a fifteen-minute taxi ride to the course.

Ian's Opinion

The Fuji Course is one of the most beautiful coastal courses in the world, and it is superlative in every sense. Although it lacks Gotemba's mountain altitude, its beautiful coastal setting—with most of the holes offering spectacular vistas across the Pacific Ocean—rivals it for scenery. You can only play this course if you're staying at the $500 per night hotel, so understandably it's not too crowded. A round of golf is included in your room fee. Kawana is an undiscovered gem for the traveling golfer, if your wallet is deep enough. The signature fifteenth hole, par 5, running along the coast, is one of the most spectacular golf settings you'll find anywhere. Teeing off the first provides a spectacular vista of the ocean below.

PHOENIX SEAGAIA

The Sheraton Grande Hotel

Food: Variety is the spice of life at Phoenix Seagaia. Choose your cuisine from restaurants serving Italian, Chinese, sushi, and tempura and teppanyaki; a bakery; and several bars with music from jazz to karaoke and a sophisticated cocktail bar.

Rooms: Surrounded by black pine forests and overlooking the Pacific coast, the forty-five-story, 500-foot tall Sheraton Grande skyscraper complex has 744 spacious rooms, including all-modern-conveniences singles, twins, triples, and suites, five-star luxury set on 700 hectares (1,700 acres) of land. Its prism design magically offers all rooms a magnificent view of the Pacific Ocean and the Miyazaki Mountains. The exclusive Grande Floor and Luxury Grande Floor have been designed as a hotel within a hotel. For a slightly lesser price tag, stay in one of the 290 Western- or Japanese-style rooms of the Sheraton Phoenix Golf Resort itself.

Facilities: If you like your attractions big and cosmetic, there's much to do in Phoenix Seagaia. A fitness center includes a pool, gym, Jacuzzi, and the Banyan Tree Spa; shops sell golf equipment, clothes, and crafts; and a bowling alley, tennis club and Hitotsuba beach will keep you amused.

Activities

Ocean Dome: What could be more enthralling than a trip to the world's biggest indoor water

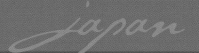

park? Listed for its enormity in *The Guinness Book of Records*, Ocean Dome measures 1,000 feet by 350 feet, with a tropically warming 86-degree Fahrenheit temperature year-round. On the pure white sand beach, enjoy an eternal summer in this indoor paradise, which could remind you of being trapped inside *The Truman Show*. Try surfing or body-boarding on the artificial waves with no fear of great whites or stinging jellyfish! There are many pools to choose from: the floating pool, a 100-degree Fahrenheit heated pool, a children's pool, or fast and thrilling steep-water flumes (Powerful Water Slider boasts speeds of up to 25 miles per hour, or plummet through mist and rain on Dragon Slider). Safety, fun, and comfort with beachwear, a 3-D motion theater, and local cuisine inside the center make this an ideal day to spend with the family. Bring flip-flops or sandals as outdoor shoes are not allowed on the beach area.

Spas and Baths: Located on the thirty-ninth floor of the Sheraton Grande is Japan's only Banyan Tree Spa, offering facials, body wraps, body scrubs, and a variety of massages. Banyan Tree Spas recreate a tropical garden spa, which incorporates oriental medicine to provide holistic, natural therapies that restore the harmony of body, mind, and soul. Treatments cost from 8,000 yen (US$70) to 29,000 yen (US$260).

For more ancient healing try the traditional Shosenkyu Onsen next to the Ocean Dome, with six private baths and two communal baths offering tranquillity and relaxation among the whispering pine trees. It is open from 6:00 A.M. until midnight daily, with priority given to guests at the Sheraton Grande. Make a reservation for a private bath.

Background to the Phoenix Country Club Course

Architect: Goukichi Ohashi; the course was constructed in 1971.

Type: Parkland course on the ocean.

Landscape: An evergreen course expertly blended into a 200-year-old black pine forest, where sounds of waves breaking on the nearby beach accompany your game.

Course Facts:

• Rated in the top one hundred courses in the world and within the top three in Japan.

• Phoenix Country Club has been host to the Dunlop Phoenix Tournament since 1974.

• It has the legacy of being the only course in Japan that Tiger Woods has played twice. See photos and signed caddie bags of visiting stars Woods and Sergio Garcia in the foyer of the elegant clubhouse, which is adorned with Miyazaki's famous Obi Japanese cedar.

Sumiyoshi · Takachiho · Nichinan

PHOENIX COUNTRY CLUB

3298 Yards / Par 36　　3422 Yards / Par 36　　3237 Yards / Par 36

Playing the Phoenix Country Club Course

The nine-hole Sumiyoshi played with either the Takachiho or the Nichinan course make up the eighteen holes of the championship course. Its location next to the turbulent sea, combined with strong coastal winds and thick, low pine forest cover, means judging the effect of the wind can be deceptive. Once you hit your ball above the level of the treetops, it is very difficult to control its distance or direction if the wind catches it. Buggies are not allowed on these courses, but it is flat and

not particularly strenuous to play (unless the temperatures soar, so avoid the heat of summer).

Score Card

Address: Phoenix Seagaia Resort, 3083 Hamayama, Oaza Shioji, Miyazaki-shi, Miyazaki 880-0122, Japan

Phone: +81 985 39 1301

Fax: +81 985 38 1188

Web Site: www.seagaia.co.jp

Courses and Lengths: Three nine-hole courses: Sumiyoshi (3,298 yards), Takachiho (3,422 yards), and Nichinan (3,237 yards). Also within the Phoenix resort is the tropically challenging Tom Watson course.

Dress Code: A smart jacket required in the clubhouse.

Tee Times: 8:00 A.M. until dusk.

Handicap: No certificate required.

Green Fees: Course visitors: weekday 31,465 yen (US$300), weekend 38,290 yen (US$370). Hotel guests: weekday 26,845 yen (US$260), weekend 33,145 yen (US$320).

Packages: ANA, JAL, JTB, KNT, and other travel agencies' vacation packages include golf and the hotel.

Other Costs: Caddy fee 3,700 yen (US$36). There are no buggies.

Facilities: A stylish and relaxing clubhouse and restaurant, pro shop, and David Duval's Academy, with coaching facilities and a driving range.

Location: A ninety-minute flight from Tokyo's domestic airport Haneda (HND), or a twenty-minute drive from local Miyazaki Airport (KHI).

Ian's Opinion

This is like playing in a giant Japanese garden. The course is embedded in a giant grove of what seem like massive bonsai trees—actually, black pine trees. The shape of the trees has been sculpted by the sea winds over the years, so they have fantastic rotund shapes. They were originally planted as camouflaging from Allied bombings in World War II. The woman caddies here are particularly industrious, with one lady caddy assigned to four male players. All about fifty years old, the ladies have been working on the course for the last thirty years since it opened. Many holes have fans to counteract the humidity, which can play havoc with the greens. Of the three courses, the Sumiyoshi and the Takachiho are the best. Even the superb Tom Watson–designed course nearby has now been designated a public course.

OTHER RECOMMENDED GOLF COURSES IN JAPAN

Players note: Watch out for the two-green configuration, which is unique to Japan. The yardage markers on either side of the course are accurate for the side's corresponding green. It's easy to forget, and hindsight won't help you when you are 10 yards short of the green!

Also, many golf course Web sites are in Japanese only. The Web site www.golf-in-japan.com is a fantastic resource, in English, and contains details of all of Japan's major courses, how to get there, prices, and online booking.

1. OAK HILLS COUNTRY CLUB
Address: 893 Karige, Kurimoto machi, Katori gun, Chiba prefecture 287-0014, Japan
Phone: +81 478 75 3131 (clubhouse)
Web Site: www.towa-golf.com
Built in 1981, this eighteen-hole, par-72 Robert Trent Jones Jr. course with lodge makes good use of bunker placement to really test your course management. It has a one-green design, and trees line most of the holes.

2. ABIDING CLUB GOLF SOCIETY
Address: 10 Takebayashi, Chonan machi, Chosei gun, Chiba prefecture 297-0155, Japan
Phone: +81 475 46 3300 (clubhouse)
Web Site: www.abiding.jp
Notes: Self-play available.
This eighteen-hole, par-72 course was one of the last courses to be designed by Desmond Muirhead in 1995. It is a well-balanced, tricky course with Scottish flair. It even has pot bunkers and a Tudor-style clubhouse to complete the effect and is accessible by a combination of train and golf course shuttle from Tokyo.

3. SUN MEMBERS COUNTRY CLUB
Address: Yamanashi prefecture, Kitasuzu-gun, Uenohara City, Inume 525, Japan
Phone: +81 554 66 2314 (clubhouse)
Web Site: www.sunmembers.co.jp
Notes: Self-play available.
This is a surprisingly flat eighteen-hole, par-72 mountain course accessible from Tokyo, featuring a two-green configuration. The greens are fast, and the fairways are like carpets on this very-well-groomed course. It's a fair course and quite wide open, so you can grip it and rip it on most holes.

4. RIVERSIDE PHOENIX GOLF CLUB
Address: 2606-1 Hirakata, Ageo shi, Saitama prefecture, Japan
Phone: +81 487 25 1441 (clubhouse)
Web Site: www.riverside-phoenix.co.jp
Notes: No caddies. Cash only.
This 1965-established eighteen-hole, par-72 course, located next to a slow-flowing river, is unusually wide and flat for Japan. It's maintained to a high standard, with power carts to make for a relaxing, worry-free round. Its close proximity to Tokyo makes it perfect for the busy executive.

5. KOCHI KUROSHIRO COUNTRY CLUB
Address: Kochi prefecture, Aki gun, 5207 Nishibunkou, Geisei mura 781-5703, Japan
Phone: +81 887 33 4333 (clubhouse)
Web Site: www.kochi-kuroshiro.com
Notes: Self-play available.
This semitropical par-72 course is home to the Japan Professional Golf Association Championship in May and the final stage of the Japan PGA qualifying school. A full thirty-six holes feature a one-bent green configuration and breathtaking views of the deep blue Pacific Ocean. World-class championship golf costs less than 8,600 yen (US$80) on a weekday and 20,000 yen (US$185) on a weekend, including a caddy.

6. ICHIHARA KORAKUEN GOLF AND SPORTS
Address: 603 Araoi, Ichihara shi, Chiba prefecture 290-0257, Japan
Phone: +81 436 37 8855 (clubhouse)
Web Site: www.ichihara.korakuengolf.co.jp
This eighteen-hole, par-72 millennium course challenges all levels of players and has an immaculate clubhouse. For a new course the greens are well seasoned, and it has the feel of a PGA championship course. It's a full 7,000 yards from the tips, so you may be tempted to hit a long iron to avoid trouble.

7. TOKUYAMA COUNTRY CLUB
Address: 1415 Nagaho Oji, Shunan shi, Yamaguchi prefecture 745-0125, Japan
Phone: +81 834 88 0500 (clubhouse)
Web Site: www.tokuyama.cc
Notes: Self-play acceptable.
This twenty-seven-hole, par-108 facility in southwest Honshu, carved on a hilly plateau an hour from Hiroshima, was designed by Peter Thompson in 1974. With lodging available and beautiful female Brazilian caddies, it couldn't get any better. Watch out for poisonous snakes on the course—although if you catch one, they make for a tasty barbeque!

8. APPI KOGEN
Address: Matsuo Mura, Iwate gun, Iwate prefecture 028-7393, Japan
Phone: +81 195 73 5311 (clubhouse)
Web Site: www.appi.co.jp
A thirty-six-hole, par-144 course surrounded by nature about forty minutes from Morioka city, adjacent to the superb Appi Ski Resort. The golf season sees an abundance of flowers, small streams, and ponds on this well-designed and well-laid-out course. It has been host to a Japan LPGA event. It offers a full-service hotel with a spa, horseback riding, and leisure sports.

9. NAKASU GOLF CLUB
Address: 798 Nakasu minami, Oji, Shunan shi, Yamaguchi prefecture 745-0512, Japan
Phone: +81 834 89 0011 (clubhouse)
Web Site: www.nakasu-golfclub.jp
This eighteen-hole, par-72 course has an Augusta-style feel with the stone bridge over the pond and the southern, laid-back atmosphere. It also has a great driving range and a picturesque waterfall. A one-minute walk from the clubhouse is the hotel, which features a natural hot spring and an outdoor pool. Rooms start at a modest 3,200 yen (US$30).

10. MISHIMA COUNTRY CLUB
Address: 1195 Tokuhara, Mishima shi, Shizuoka prefecture 411-0044, Japan
Phone: +81 559 88 0801 (clubhouse)
Web Site: www.accordiagolf.com
Notes: Self-play acceptable.
Situated on either side of a small valley with glimpses of Mount Fuji in the distance, this eighteen-hole, par-72 course makes good use of natural and man-made water hazards, and ninety bunkers keep things challenging. Enjoy the outdoor Japanese-style bath after your round.

11. ATSUGI KOKUSAI COUNTRY CLUB
Address: 1920 Shimo-ogino, Atsugi shi, Kanagawa prefecture 243-0203, Japan
Phone: +81 462 41 1311 (clubhouse)
Web Site: www.akkgolf.com
This meandering eighteen-hole, par-72 course features a two-green configuration and is the current site of the Daimler Chrysler Cup. After a round enjoy the immaculate baths with a view of the course and a steam room. Its proximity to Tokyo (30 miles from the Tokyo interchange) makes it pricey at about 3,200 yen (US$300) per round, and it's almost impossible to get on during weekends.

12. ICHINOMIYA COUNTRY CLUB
Address: 29-4303 Chiba prefecture, Choseigun, Ichinomiya machi, Torami 3166, Japan
Phone: +81 475 42 7200 (clubhouse)
Web Site: www.ichinomiya.co.jp
Notes: Self-play acceptable.
This thirty-six-hole, par-144 course is next to the ocean with cool breezes in the summer. It has a two-green configuration, with both a 6,556- and 6,640-yard par-72 course. Water hazards come into play on almost half the holes.

13. WINDSOR PARK
Address: 3473 Nakaimura, Ooazashioko, Nishi Ibaraki gun, Ibaraki prefecture 311-4401, Japan
Phone: +81 296 88 2221 (clubhouse)
Web Site: www.wpgcc.com
Notes: Self-play acceptable.
A luxurious country club that, as its name suggests, overflows with British country house–getaway charm. It's managed by CCA International, which owns nothing but first-class facilities. The eighteen-hole, par-72 forest-lined course, playing 7,007 yards from the tips, has swales and water hazards to challenge your intellect.

14. ACADEMIA HILLS COUNTRY CLUB
Address: 765-2 Onodia, Kimitsu city, Chiba prefecture 292-1151, Japan
Phone: +81 439 70 5111 (clubhouse)
Web Site: www.academiahills.com
Notes: Self-play acceptable.
The Isao Aoki–designed course makes good use of its surroundings to create a visually attractive eighteen-hole, par-72 course. The fairways are kept in immaculate shape and there is no shortage of challenging holes to test your savvy. You can usually play through, which allows time for an extra half round.

15. KASUMIGAURA COUNTRY CLUB
Address: 368 Shimohara, Tsukuba shi, Ibaraki prefecture 305-0063, Japan
Phone: +81 298 36 1155 (clubhouse)
Web Site: www.kasumigaura-kokusai-golf.co.jp
A well-established eighteen-hole, par-72 course playing 7,080 yards from the tips, with a strong member base. Be careful not to jump out of your shoes trying to fly your ball over the long fairways. Only forty-five minutes from Tokyo by car (traffic allowing), it's priced beyond the 3,200 yen (US$300) mark.

16. BRITISH GARDEN CLUB
Address: 1407 Asahibaba, Tsuru shi, Yamanashi prefecture 402-0014, Japan
Phone: +81 554 20 4211 (clubhouse)
Web Site: www.bgc.co.jp
Notes: Self-play acceptable.
One of the best-kempt courses you will find anywhere. The greens are fast, true, and hard. It's an eighteen-hole, par-72 mountain course that uses five elevators and countless conveyer belts to whisk you from green to tee, making the course hole by hole relatively flat, considering the terrain.

17. BELLE VIEW NAGAO GOLF CLUB
Address: 1918 Kouyama, Gotemba shi, Shizuoka prefecture 412-0033, Japan
Phone: +81 550 87 1112 (clubhouse)
Web Site: www.belleviewn-gc.co.jp
Notes: Self-play acceptable. For golf lessons in English, phone: +81 990 9892 4319, e-mail: ben-galloway@gotemba-gc.co.jp (English-speaking pro). This eighteen-hole course is fun to play. Not overly long—6,019 yards, par 71—but the hilly terrain makes it feel a little longer. With a chalet next to the clubhouse, friendly staff, and less than 10,000 yen (US$93) on weekdays, it makes an excellent golfing getaway for couples.

18. MISSION HILLS COUNTRY CLUB
Address: 686 Niyogedaira, Kunikami, Minato machi, Chichibu gun, Saitama prefecture 369-1622, Japan
Phone: +81 494 62 5511 (clubhouse)
This Pete Dye–designed eighteen-hole, par-72 course, completed in 1994, provides a good challenge for any golfer. Three-tiered greens, water-guarded greens, and greens with potato-chip undulations will test your putting stroke. A driving range, swimming pool, tennis courts, and lodgings are available.

19. KAGO SAKA GOLF CLUB
Address: 121 Subashiri, Oyama cho, Sunto gun, Shizuoka prefecture 410-1431, Japan
Phone: +81 550 75 4700 (clubhouse)
Web Site: http://fujiweb.co.jp/
This is as close to Mount Fuji as you can get—some of the holes are even on its upslope. Occasional outcroppings of volcanic rock can be seen on this relatively new eighteen-hole, par-72 course. Not a long course, but very well groomed, and the design works well with the natural landscape.

BETWEEN
THE ROUNDS
ATTRACTIONS

Kyushu and the Southwest Islands

Nagasaki Atomic Bomb Museum:
Nagasaki was the first city in Japan to establish links with the West in the sixteenth century, when visiting Portuguese traders and Christian missionaries influenced its culture. East/West relations took a tragic turn during World War II, when one of the greatest atrocities of the twentieth century occurred, prompting the end of the war.

On the morning of 9 August 1945, Bock's Car, an American SB-29 Air Force bomber, unloaded a four-and-a-half-ton atomic bomb on northern Nagasaki. Seventy-five thousand people were killed immediately—one-third of the city's population—and another third were severely injured. Many later died from painful and crippling diseases caused by radioactive poisoning. As the bomb exploded 1,500 feet in the air over the suburbs, the death toll was much lower than the Little Boy atomic attack on Hiroshima three days before. Although the city of Kokura was the intended target, the bomber's course was abandoned because of cloud cover, thus sealing the sad fate of Nagasaki. The Allies' attacks were in part revenge for Japan's bombing of the Pearl Harbor naval base, in part to force the Japanese to surrender to minimize the huge loss of lives on both sides that had already taken place in Okinawa.

A black stone monolith in the Hypocenter in Urakami marks the place of the explosion. Here you can see relics of the bomb blast, including a section of the wall of Urakami Cathedral, which was flattened in just three seconds after bearing the brunt of the bomb when it missed its target of the shipyard. The fireball created by the bomb, 1,000 degrees centigrade hotter than the surface of the sun, reduced the surrounding area to a barren ground of burnt rubble. Experts incorrectly thought Urakami would have no vegetation for nearly a century, but today the peaceful leafy suburb disguises the destruction of its recent history.

Since the war Nagasaki has been completely rebuilt, making it difficult to believe that these unthinkable atrocities occurred in this peaceful and innocent place. The city has become a focal center for peace campaigns; people from all over the world come to show solidarity with the people of Nagasaki and visit its museum. The exhibition includes live footage of the bomb blast and details of the loss of life and destruction of the city, together with reports on the current status of nuclear weapons worldwide. Objects on display include a clock stopped at exactly 11:02 A.M., the time of the bomb's blast; mangled spectacles and clothing; and photos of severely burnt victims. Videos of disfigured survivors are further testament to the horrors of nuclear warfare. A visit to the museum is a somber and sobering experience, but very worthwhile.

Other monuments to peace in Nagasaki include the Nagai Takashi Memorial Museum, a tribute to one man's work aiding bomb victims, and the Peace Park, with symbolic sculptures donated by nations around the world, including Nagasaki's sister town of St. Paul in Minnesota and the GDR (formerly East Germany).

Address: Nagasaki Atomic Bomb Museum, 7-8 Hirano-machi, Nagasaki 852-8117, Japan

Phone: + 81 958 44 1231
Hours: 8:30 A.M. to 5:30 P.M. daily
Admission: 200 yen (US$2.00) adults, 100 yen (US$1.00) children, audio guide 150 yen (US$1.40).

Ibusuki Beach: On the southernmost point of the Kyushu region, in the shadows of active volcano Mount Sakurajima, lies the balmy and chilled-out city of Kagoshima, known as "the Oriental Naples." Just south of the city lies the lush beach town of Ibusuki, famed for its hot, volcanic black sands. The hot sands, with temperatures that reach 195 degrees Fahrenheit, are supposed to purify your blood and refresh your soul, providing a great therapy for alleviating rheumatism, arthritis, and gastrointestinal problems. Many locals come to the beach every day to improve their health.

To enjoy this "sand therapy," head to Yunohama Beach and the Sana Mushi Onsen (natural sand bath). Here you will pay 1,000 yen (US$9.00) for the privilege of being

buried up to the neck in scorching, hot sands. Spending just the prerequisite fifteen minutes in the sand bath is a sheer effort of will, but

you will be hauled out feeling rejuvenated. And you can always opt for a swim in the nearby hot springs of Kawaijiri-onsen overlooking the black sand beaches.
Address: Ten minutes' walk from Ibusuki Station, heading right along the beach.
Phone: + 81 993 23 3900
Hours: 8:30 A.M. to noon and 1:00 to 9:00 P.M.
Admission: 900 yen (US$8.50) for a sand bath, 100 yen (US$1.00) for rental of a yukata robe.

Okinawa Naval Headquarters: Southwest of Kyushu in the East China Sea lies a string of small islands leading to Taiwan. Once a buffer zone between China and Japan, the Southwest Islands maintained a unique culture and have been ruled by Japan since the nineteenth century. The largest of these islands, Okinawa, was the scene for the last and bloodiest battle of World War II.

On Easter Sunday 1945, the invasion Operation Iceberg saw the assembling of the greatest naval armada in history, when a half million Allied troops and a fleet of 1,300 ships set out to capture the island. After eighty-two days of horrific battles with huge losses from both sides, estimated at 250,000 Japanese (half of whom were Okinawa citizens) and 12,000 American troops, the Allies captured Okinawa. It remained in American control until 1972, although, controversially, there are still 50,000 American troops stationed here.

The Japanese used stealth tactics and willpower to delay their inevitable capture. They fought bravely in the six-week battle, using kamikaze suicide bombers, flamethrowers,

grenades, and bayonets to weaken the immense Allied army. The Japanese navy built a secret underground headquarters, dug by hand with pick-axes to carve out more than a mile of tunnels. These tunnels became deadly graves and the site of one of the biggest mass suicides ever known. At the command of Vice Admiral Minoru Ota, commander of the Japanese Navy on Okinawa, 4,000 Japanese naval men took their own lives by either *seppuku*, a ritual disembowelment, or hand grenade. Suicide was considered an honorable end compared with capture or death at the hands of the Americans, whom their command had led them to believe were barbarians.

Today at the Imperial Navy Underground headquarters, south of Naha City, you can wander through 250 meters of tunnels and see the commander's final words on the wall next to holes and scars from suicide grenade blasts. The tunnels are open 8:30 A.M. to 5:00 P.M. daily; entrance costs 420 yen (US$4.00).

Other attractions relating to the battle include Shuri Castle, a small-scale equivalent to Beijing's Forbidden City, which was the headquarters of the Japanese High Command. It was largely destroyed in the battle, and its ceremonial entrance gate is now a popular photo spot for tourists. The ruins at Cape Kyan, popular today with hang gliders, were used as a suicide jump spot during the battle when Okinawan civilians realized they must surrender to the Allies. On the south coast is Konpaku-no-to, a memorial to 35,000 unidentified victims whose bodies lay on the beach for months after the end of the battle. The Cornerstone of Peace in Mabuni Hill has memorials from every prefecture in Japan and the names of some of the battle's victims, with Okinawan civilians and Allied troops listed alongside Japanese military. You can learn the whole gruesome story of the three-month so-called "typhoon of steel" and the Okinawan repression at the hands of both the occupying Americans and the Japanese military at the Peace Memorial Museum.

Climbing Mount Aso Volcano: In the center of Kyushu lies the giant Aso volcano, the world's largest caldera, formed from a series of explosions over a period of thirty million years. The huge crater has a circumference of 80 miles, encompassing within it towns, villages, and even train lines. Within the ring are rolling hills, meadows, bamboo groves, forests, hot springs, and Japan's most fertile farmlands. This beautiful but little-visited region is famed for its sake, which benefits from the combination of purest volcanic waters and fire.

The Five Mountains of Aso, ranging from 2,000 to 3,000 feet within the outer rim of the crater, make for great hikes. The easterly Naka-dake is a sulfurous and steaming active volcano, earning the Kumamoto prefecture its reputation as "the land of fire." It can be ascended by cable car, aside from periods of violent volcanic activity, when the Volcanic Museum in the principal town of Aso shows live footage from inside the active crater. The Rice Mound, a hill looking like an inverted rice bowl, and the Kusasenri Meadows make for interesting diversions from the mountains. Visit in March for the Aso-jinja Fire Festival with spectacular dances, when the farmer's fields are set ablaze to cut back brush.

Yamagata Prefecture

Skiing in Zao Onsen: January to March is
peak ski season at Zao Onsen in the Yamagata
prefecture, one of the oldest ski resorts in Japan.
Having been around since the 1920s, Zao
Onsen has had time to develop its traditions.
You can ride the tram to the top of the mountain
to see the famous "Juhyoo" trees. Affectionately
known as "snow monsters," the trees are
covered with layers of thick snow and ice, blown
by the Siberian winds coming over the Japan
Sea, and evolve into fantastical-looking shapes.
It feels like you're flying through an alien
landscape.

Zao Onsen is huge—a conglomerate of
formerly feuding lift operators—with forty-two
ski lifts and slopes for all abilities. But it's also
popular, so it's best to book your ski lift tickets
the night before you hit the slopes. For the
intrepid skier, there's "The Wall," a steep terrain
with a 30-degree slope, although the course
is only 1,000 feet long. There are also some
fantastic opportunities for off-piste anarchy
with free-riding and crazy jumping on the
snow-monsters runs.

If the icy terrains get to be too much, you
can relax in the many steaming hot springs
situated throughout the resort town. The town
still retains the feel of a traditional Japanese
mountain village, something you won't find at
other Japanese ski resorts.

Hiking Dewa Sanzan Sacred Peaks:
Sanzan is the Japanese name for the Dewa
region's three mountains that are sacred to
the Yamabushi, pious followers of the
Shugendo sect. During the pilgrimage season
you will see white-robed pilgrims climbing

trails or sitting under icy cold waterfalls, a practice known as *misogi*, as part of their high-endurance spiritual training. Ascend Hanguro-san (Mount Black Wing) up 2,446 stone steps, a popular pilgrimage trail. The teahouse at the second stage offers spectacular views of the Mogami River. At the summit see the Dewa Sanzan Shrine with its huge thatched roof housing the tomb of the imperial prince-turned-priest Hachiko. It's the setting for several festivals, including the Hassaku Matsuri fire rites at the end of August and rituals for New Year's Eve. Enjoy a pleasant two-hour hike up Gassan-san (Mount Moon), with its alpine flowers and summer skiing. The sacred hot-water spring of Yudono-san (Mount Bath) is where pilgrims bathe their feet. Mummified priests—a now-banned practice in which they self-mummified by slow starvation before being buried alive—can be seen in the temples of Dainichibo and Churen-ji nearby. Entry to the tombs costs 500 yen (US$5.00).

Near Tokyo:
Mount Fuji Region (Kanagawa, Yamanashi, and Shizuoka)

Climbing Mount Fuji: Mount Fuji is undoubtedly one of the world's most famous mountains, but it's not Fuji's modest 12,390-foot height that has elevated its stature. Its perfect conical shape, which seems to rise out of nowhere, has given it a religious symbolism for the Japanese as the gateway between heaven and earth, making Fuji a global icon for the beauty of nature. Fuji has been a dormant volcano since 1707; it first erupted about eight to ten thousand years ago. The summit is completely devoid of greenery or water, with only a loose volcanic ash covering.

Fuji has been refused World Heritage status because of the litter left behind by the thousands of tourists who make the pilgrimage here every summer. It's worth climbing, but you certainly won't be alone. At the top climbers can visit the Sengen shrine, twenty-four-hour noodle stalls, a post office, an office for souvenir stamps, and a weather station! Traditionally the Japanese climb the mountain to reach the summit in time for the early morning sunrise. This can be very elusive in summer when the skies are cloudy, adding to its mystique. You'll need a permit outside of the climbing season of July and August; a festival in nearby Fujiyoshida city marks the end of the season. The trails are divided into ten stages, and climbers usually start at the fifth stage. It's a hard climb, as the steep volcanic cinder moves about under foot. After the eighth stage, altitude sickness can kick in, so if you develop a bad headache or nausea, descend immediately. The summit is very cold compared with the base, so bring some warm clothes. A traditional proverb says "A wise man climbs Fuji once, but only a fool climbs it twice."

The surrounding Fuji Five Lakes is a pop-

ular recreational area of amusement parks, water sports, and waterfalls.

Historic Kamakura: Kamakura, a populous resort town and historical center, makes for a great day trip from nearby Tokyo. It has no fewer than sixty-five Buddhist temples and nineteen Shinto shrines set in a dramatic natural amphitheater among woods on three sides and the sea taking center stage. Entry to each temple or shrine typically costs between 200 yen (US$2.00) and 300 yen (US$3.00).

Kamakura was built in the twelfth and thirteenth centuries by warrior Yoritomo Minamoto. He chose this location because it was far from the imperial court in Kyoto and easy to defend. It's the home of the Go-zan, the five famous Zen temples of Kamakura, which were inspired by the five great Zen temples of China. Kamakura soon became the Japanese center of the newly imported religion of Zen Buddhism.

But the real treasures are the Shinto shrines nestled among connecting trails and lanes in the mountains. Tsurugaoka Hachimangu Shrine, to the god of war, is situated at the end of a cheery tree-lined lane that stretches back to the crowded Yigahama Beach. The Keniarai-Benten Shrine is dedicated to the goddess of the arts, one of the "seven lucky gods." If you go on the zodiac day of the snake and wash your coins in the nearby cave's spring water, it is believed that the money will double or triple in the future.

The giant 37-foot Great Buddha of Kotokuin Temple, a bronze cast from A.D. 1252, is Kamakura's most famous postcard image. Set serenely outdoors with the hills as a backdrop, it has survived numerous earthquakes, tsunamis, and typhoons over the centuries. It's hollow, so you can even step inside. The Hase Kannon Temple's statue of the goddess of the sea has an interesting legend: Two statues were made from a giant camphor tree, one kept in Hase, the other cast into the sea, ending up in a town where all who touched it incurred bad luck. When it eventually floated to Kamakura, it caused no trouble, a sign that the goddess was content in her new home.

Kita Kamura (north Kamura) houses three of Kamikura's five great Zen Buddhist temples, where you can enjoy delicious Zen vegetarian food amidst the tranquil wooded gullies. Tokei-ji Temple, the "divorce temple" may interest wandering wives: Under old Japanese law only men could apply for divorce, but if a woman spent three years in the temple, she could choose to divorce her husband.

You can't miss the thousand or so statues of Jizo, the guardian of children. They are donated by grieving parents and usually represent miscarried, stillborn, or aborted babies, but are burnt every year to make way for new offerings.

Most weekends you can request an English-speaking volunteer student guide to show you the sights. Just get to the Kamakura station around 10:00 A.M. to grab one.

Nature in Hakone: Situated on the Kanagawa prefecture, Hakone is a hot-spring town that has been a crowded resort for more than a millennium. Part of the larger Fuji-Hakone-Izu National Park, the town is very close to Tokyo and heaving with visitors. Hot springs, mountains, lakes, rock carvings, and—on a clear day—spectacular views of Mount Fuji make this a popular day trip encompassing many modes of transport: mountain tram, cable car, ropeway, and boat. The attractions are both cultural and natural, with several museums in the area dedicated to art, sculpture, and natural science. Take a ropeway path on the Owaku-dani nature trail, the "valley of great boiling." If you can stomach the eggy smell of the sulfurous steam vents, do as locals do and celebrate the trip with a boiled egg, which you can buy along the trail.

In Tokyo

Imperial Palace and East Garden: The fifteenth-century Edo Imperial Palace, overlooking Tokyo Bay in the center of the city, is the most expensive piece of real estate in the world. During the 1980s boom it was valued higher than the whole of the state of California. The palace is only open for two days a year, December 23 and January 2. It's always possible to wander around the grounds, though, and take in the sights, like the Edo-jo Castle, formerly the largest castle in the world but now a 1968 reconstruction. The Imperial Palace East Garden is a welcome retreat with its tea pavilion, Japanese garden, lawns, and excellent photographic views of the famous double-arched stone Nijubashi Bridge. Entry to the park is free. It is open 9:00 A.M. to 4:00 P.M., except Monday and Friday.

Kabuki-za Theater: During your visit to Japan, you must take in a traditional Kabuki theater show. Originating in the seventeenth-century Edo period, *kabuku odori* translates as avant-garde dance. Its traditions have changed little since its conception. Invented by a Shinto maiden and popularized by prostitute-actresses, the genre was soon cleaned up with all parts played by men. Older men in drag play female characters, but unlike pantomime, the style is profound and serious. Using exaggerated gestures, elaborate costumes, and fanciful sets, the style is rich with symbolism and meaning—even the color of the actor's kimono lining is significant. It is a theater of spectacle, with the principle star being the actor, accompanied by a noisy percussive orchestra. Actors undergo many years of training to perfect this highly refined art. Kabuki's rituals, spirituality, and faces painted in fixed expression went on to influence late-nineteenth-century expressionist Western dramatists such as W. B. Yeats. Its repertoire of 350 plays take the form of historical opera derived from puppet theater, and feudal daily life, with a focus on the conflict between social obligations and personal emotions. The best place to see a show is the Kabuki-za theater in Ginza. Be warned: Performances can last up to five hours, but if you only want a taster, get a cheaper gallery ticket to watch one act. Watch for the *hanamichi*, an elevated pathway into the audience with a trapdoor through which supernatural characters appear.

Address: Kabuki-za Theater, Harumi-dori Avenue, Ginza, Tokyo, Japan

Phone: +81 355 65 6000

Web Site: www.kabuki-za.co.jp

Hours: Performances twice daily. Open 11:00 A.M. to 4:00 P.M. and 4.30 to 9:00 P.M. Closed last week of every month.

Admission: Varies from 2,500 yen (US$23) to 17,000 (US$160), and an extra 600 yen (US$6.00) for an earpiece with English translation (not available for gallery tickets).

Ueno-koen Park and Museums:

Ueno-koen is Tokyo's most popular setting for viewing the cherry blossom, usually in April. Within the park are several interesting shrines, pagodas, statues, and temples (Kiyumizu Kannon-do Temple is where women

who want to conceive leave a doll; they are burnt ceremonially every year on September 25). Tokyo's main museums are within the park: The Tokyo Metropolitan Museum has Japanese art in both traditional and Western techniques; the National Museum houses a huge art collection, a gallery of Eastern antiquities, and masks and scrolls from the Horyu-ji treasures; and Shitamachi History Museum is a celebration of downtown old Tokyo. Children will enjoy the park's small Ueno Zoo with its pandas. All attractions in the park are open Tuesday through Sunday, from either 9:00 or 9:30 A.M. until 4:30 or 5:00 P.M. Bag a bargain below Ginza prices at the lively Ameyoko-cho arcade, where loud

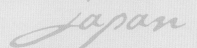

japan

145

River in A.D. 628 by two fishermen brothers. A seventeenth-century shrine to these men, the Asakusa-jinja, is located next door to Senso-ji and is the site of the annual Sanja Festival every May. Before the temple is a giant incense cauldron, the smoke of which is supposed to cure ailments by wafting the defective body part into the smoke. The spirituality of the postwar reconstruction temple draws visitors looking for more than a view of its architecture. Particularly popular at New Year's, try fortune-telling by lots: Deposit 100 yen (US$1.00) in a slot, and shake out a bamboo stick with a number, which corresponds to a drawer with a paper detailing your fortune, or misfortune, often in hysterically incomprehensible English translations. If the fortune is bad, disaster can be averted by tying the paper to a nearby post.

shopkeepers hawk their goods. For more serene hawking visit the Shinobazu Pond, with its many migrating birds.

Shopping in Ginza: Consumerist and futuristic Ginza was the first quarter to modernize after Japan opened its doors to the West in the second half of the nineteenth century. Brick buildings were erected, and other novel inventions, such as sidewalks and street lamps, were introduced. Nowadays the streets are lined with another elegant addition: the Ginza girls. These are ladies both young and old who wouldn't dream of leaving home without their Chanel suit and Louis

Vuitton handbag. Make sure you check out Mitsukoshi, one of Ginza's biggest department stores, where you'll find all the latest designer gear, as well as the Sony building, which showcases the company's latest models of cameras, PlayStations, and other gadgetry. Ginza is a test bed for Japanese corporations' latest technology, a place where you can test out and buy tomorrow's world today.

Senso-ji Temple: Tokyo's oldest temple has an impressive shrine to the Buddhist Kannon, goddess of mercy, where Kabuki actors and Sumo wrestlers regularly pray. Legend holds the statue was fished out of the Sumida-gawa

southern california

When Southern California meets golf you will find possibly the most perfect combination of terrain, weather, and sport in the world. There are more than 400 golf courses on the co-called "Golf Coast" of America—the land stretching from Los Angeles to San Diego in the south. Average year-round temperatures of 80 degrees Fahrenheit, long sunny days, breathtaking scenery, and numerous top-quality

championship standard courses make Southern California a must for anyone who loves the game of golf.

This region boasts an enormous diversity of natural landscape, from sweltering desert and snowcapped mountains to beautiful beaches and rolling parkland. Taking advantage of these natural features, developers spend millions upon millions of dollars here every year on building new courses based on classic designs from around the world. Links, desert, mountain, parklands—you will find them all. The quality and sheer opulence of the country club–style facilities that go with many of these new courses really has to be seen to be believed, but as more and more of them are private, or part of gated communities, you may not have that opportunity. For the traveling adventure golfer, however, there are more than enough magnificent public and semipublic courses that will welcome you so you may experience the delights of this iconic golfing region.

Big Sur coastline (left)
PGA West Stadium Course,
seventeenth hole (above)

About Southern California

In the south, it's easy to see how California got its nickname, the "Golden State." It has a potent mix of glitzy glamour, urbanity, and wilderness nature. Millions of Americans and international visitors flock here every year to shop till they drop in Los Angeles, flaunt it on stunning beaches, tuck into unique fusion foods, and get back to nature in this perfect vacation playground.

Activities and Attractions

Beaches and Offshore Islands: Beach life is synonymous with Southern California, and it's not hard to see why. The famous beaches of Los Angeles (Long Beach, Malibu, Santa Monica) and San Diego (Imperial Beach), plus the many beach cities in between, are the lifeblood of sun lovers everywhere. Stretching north from LA, the beaches become cooler and more urbane; the attractions broaden to include historic towns such as Santa Barbara and California's famed fusion food. Out to sea you'll find the favored ecotourism destination of the Channel Islands National Park.

National Parks: More and more of Southern California's varied environments are being put under the jurisdiction of the National Park Service to protect them. Choose from the marine reserves like the Channel Islands, where you can dive and snorkel, to seaside reserves like Torrey Pines outside San Diego, with its dramatic red-hued cliffs and spring wildflowers. Farther inland the terrain becomes desert, where you can experience the clear light and stark beauty of places like Joshua Tree and Anza Borrego.

Missions: In order to cement their empire in the eighteenth century, the Spanish decided to establish permanent settlements along the Californian coast with Catholic missions: a church and residences surrounded by vineyards, fields, and ranches. Twenty-one missions were constructed, ten in southern California. Nowadays the missions are a mixed bag, and some are more worthwhile to visit than others. Perhaps the most picturesque is San Juan Capistrano, its Moorish architecture lending it a romantic feel, whereas Mission La Purisima Concepción really gives a sense of nineteenth-century mission life.

History of Golf in Southern California

Golf was introduced into Southern California in the early 1890s when the West Coast was a popular destination for settlers traveling from the East to seek their fortunes. At that time some of the well-known and highly respected courses of today, like the Victoria Club at Riverside and Redlands, were constructed. Golf became the fastest-growing leisure activity. Since then, with the notable exception of the Great Depression and the two World Wars, the sport has flourished. California now has twelve of the top one hundred rated courses in the world and many of the world's top golfers living within its boundaries.

Pacific coast

When to Go and What to Bring

The best time to go depends on which region you're visiting. The inland desert region, out and beyond Ridgecrest, Palm Springs, and east toward Nevada, is very hot between March and October, with temperatures in the summer months rising to 130 degrees and above. This, however, is the best time to go to the coastal resorts, when the rainfall is much lower, and wall-to-wall sunshine—with very acceptable playing temperatures of about 85 degrees—is almost guaranteed. Sunblock, sunglasses, shorts, and a hat are all you need to pack. Remember, these are top-quality golf courses that expect the usual standards of dress.

Santa Ynez Valley

Costs

Green fees vary from $20 to $300, depending on the quality of the course and the day of the week you want to play. Clubs and golf carts are available for rent at reasonable prices at all courses, with a range of different quality and price options.

Hotels

The high season for the south falls in the winter months, when a quality hotel will cost upward of $120; don't expect anything top-notch for less than $250, and in places like LA, this will be double. Midseason falls in the shoulder periods between winter and summer and can mean reductions of up to 50 percent depending on the establishment.

Travel

Airports: The main southern Californian airport is Los Angeles International Airport (LAX), a hub for air travel from the Pacific Rim, the rest of America, and Europe (usually via a connecting flight). The John Wayne Orange County Airport (SNA) in Santa Ana is a viable alternative for the south, and Palm Springs (PSP) also has a domestic airport.

Car Rental: California is a pretty difficult state to get around without a car, so renting a vehicle is a must. The state has a wide array of rental agencies offering all types of cars, from budget to luxury. The cost of gas has fluctuated dramatically in recent years, but it costs considerably more here than in other states. When driving through the desert, make sure your car is in good order and that you have spare gas, oil, and coolant.

Regions and Golfing

Any discerning golfer visiting Southern California will soon realize that there are really only two kinds of golf course in this part of the state: superb and outstanding. Billions of dollars have been spent on importing and maintaining Scottish links and other overseas-style courses in the last twenty years, but for most clubs the regional differences still reflect the natural terrain and climate of each area.

Santa Barbara, San Luis Obispo, and Kern: The town of Santa Barbara is often called the Californian Riviera because of its wealthy population, Mediterranean architecture, and seaside location. Stay for a couple of days, as its downtown architecture, especially its mission and courthouse, warrants extensive exploring. Its pretty beaches and restaurants are top-notch. Farther north you'll

Santa Barbara cinema

The suggested itinerary is for active days of about sixteen hours. If you prefer a more leisurely trip, pick and choose your favorite activities.

Day 1: Fly into Los Angeles. Rent a car for the week, and head to the Palos Verdes peninsula near the Los Angeles harbor to play a round at Ocean Trails Golf Club. Spend the remains of the day shopping or sightseeing in Los Angeles. Check out the magnificent Frank Gehry–designed Disney Concert Hall and the buzzing atmosphere of Chinatown and Little Tokyo. Stay in the chic and showbiz Standard Hotel.

Day 2: A.M. Near Fox Studios, in the heart of the city, play Rancho San Marco ($22), the busiest course in the world. Arrive close to dawn because you can wait up to five hours for a round!
P.M. Go star spotting in Hollywood at the Walk of Fame, the Chinese Theatre, and the Hollywood Forever Cemetery. Drive two hours south on U.S. Highway 101 toward the resort town of Big Bear Lake. If you want to play more golf, stop in Beaumont for a round at Oak Valley Golf Club by the San Gorgornio and San Jacinto Mountains.

Day 3: A.M. Enjoy a few hours skiing in winter or hiking in summer in the San Bernardino Mountains or head to Palm Springs to play one of the five courses at La Quinta in the morning. It's a ninety-minute drive south to Palm Springs.
P.M. Play La Quinta PGA Stadium Course in Palm Springs. If you can afford $6,572 dollars

for three nights, stay in the height of legendary Hollywood luxury at Frank Sinatra's Twin Palms Estate. Otherwise, relax in the smart resort of La Quinta.

La Quinta

Day 4: A.M. Either play one of the other four courses at La Quinta, or just outside of Palm Springs, play Westin Mission Hills, Black Gold, Indian Palms, or the Desert Falls Country Club.
P.M. Take a desert tour of Joshua Tree National Park, but if your visit is in midsummer, when temperatures are deadly, take an aerial tramway tour up the San Jacinto Mountains for great views and hiking.

Head northwest to Santa Barbara on the west coast north of LA, a total three-and-a-half-hour journey of 200 miles. Take I–10 west, then merge onto the US 101 north. You may want to stop near LA for the night and continue the journey early morning.

Day 5: A.M. Play Sandpiper Course.
P.M. Go gliding in Santa Ynez Valley, wine tasting in the nearby vineyards, or golfing at LaPurisima, a great-value public course an hour's drive north of Santa Barbara. Head to the historic town of Solvang.

Day 6: A.M. Play Alisal Ranch golf course.
P.M. Explore historic Solvang and the Mission of Santa Ines. If you can find a member to take you, play the Nicklaus-designed Sherwood Country Club, between Santa Barbara and LA. Spend another night in Solvang. Or take a detour 50 miles north to play a round and spend the night at Ojai Valley Inn and Spa.

Day 7: A.M. Head back toward LA along US 101 south. It's just an hour's drive to the Lost Canyons course, 30 miles northwest of LA, to play one of their two championship links-style courses designed by Pete Dye and Fred Couples. If you want a second round, stay here as the golf's great—and it's conveniently located near the airport.
P.M. Take CA 118 east. Merge onto I–405 south, then I–10 west toward Santa Monica, a thirty-minute, 30-mile drive south. See and be seen on the style-conscious Santa Monica Beach, just north of LA. Drive back to Los Angeles International Airport (LAX) to head for home.

Day 1: P.M. Fly to LA. Rent a car and drive straight to Santa Barbara on US 101 north, a one-hour, 75-mile journey along the West Coast.

Day 2: A.M. Play Sandpiper Course. **P.M.** Go wine tasting in the nearby vineyards, or play La Purisima, a great-value public course an hour's drive north of Santa Barbara. Drive to the nearby pretty historic town of Solvang.

Day 3: A.M. Play Alisal's Ranch Course. **P.M.** Explore historic Solvang and the mission of Santa Ines. Alternatively, it's just an hour's drive from Solvang to the Lost Canyons course, 30 miles northwest of LA. Play one of their two championship links-style courses designed by Pete Dye and Fred Couples. Head back to LA along US 101 south.

Day 4: A.M. Near Fox Studios, in the heart of the city, play Rancho San Marco ($22), the busiest course in the world. Arrive close to dawn because you can wait up to five hours for a round!
P.M. If you've still got energy and time, go star spotting in Hollywood at the Walk of Fame, the Chinese Theatre, and the Hollywood Forever Cemetery. Otherwise, drive straight out to Palm Springs, a two-hour drive east on US 101 and check into La Quinta. You may have time for nine holes at one of the five resort courses.

Day 5: A.M. Play La Quinta PGA Stadium Course in Palm Springs.
P.M. Either play one of the other four courses at La Quinta, or just outside of Palm Springs, play Westin Mission Hills, Black Gold, Indian Palms, or the Desert Falls Country Club. Drive two hours back to LA to catch your night flight home—or fly directly from Palm Springs Airport (PSP).

Ranch Course

find San Luis Obispo, a quiet coastal town that makes a pleasant base for central California's biggest attraction, Hearst Castle, the over-the-top palace of publishing magnate William Randolph Hearst. For a real slice of the outdoors, head out to sea to the Channel Islands National Park, a chain of desert islands running north from Santa Catalina outside LA. Not only will you find excellent hiking trails but opportunities for fishing and scuba and skin diving through caves and shipwrecks. Between February and April you can whale watch.

Although this region is more than one-third of the coastline, it has far fewer golf courses than its neighbors, mainly because it has more mountains, 50 percent more rainfall, and a tiny population by comparison. There are many beautiful public courses to play, like La Purisima in Santa Barbara and Cypress Ridge in San Luis Obispo. There are also public courses in Kern, which is dominated by the southern end of the Sierra Nevada Mountains and the Mojave Desert.

Los Angeles and Ventura: Just farther to the south on the coast, Los Angeles and Ventura counties have between them a population of approximately eleven million people (30 percent of the whole state) in a relatively tiny area. With its sprawling, car-oriented culture and fake movie glamour, you'll either love LA or hate it, but there's more here than just Hollywood and *Baywatch* beaches.

Universal Studios

In downtown LA you'll find the magnificent Frank Gehry–designed Disney Concert Hall and the buzzing atmosphere of Chinatown and Little Tokyo. From the harbor take the ferry to Santa Catalina Island, one of the largest of the Channel Islands, for a guided tour of its unique ecosystem.

With the increasing popularity of golf in the last two decades, it is no surprise that so many new courses are being built in California each year, many of them in this small region. The conditions for golf are almost perfect, so there are dozens of top-class courses to choose from. With the attractions of Los Angeles city within comfortable driving distance, it would be a crime to miss this area.

San Diego and Orange: Farther south San Diego County comprises a great variety of landscapes across its 4,200 square miles, from the coastal mountains to the deserts of Anza Borrego. Highlights of laid-back San Diego city include Balboa Park with its zoo (housing more than 3,000 animals in beautiful enclosures); museums showcasing science, art, and history; and Mission Beach, *the* place to be seen and a great place for in-line skating, surfing, and strolling. Outside the city, North County has its fair share of attractive coastal communities, like Del Mar and Julian, and the Cuyamaca Rancho State Park is a wilderness area crisscrossed with attractive hiking trails. Torrey Pines is a seaside reserve with stunning cliff views and world-class golf. The Mexican border town of Tijuana is a day trip from downtown San Diego, although it hardly gives an authentic taste of Mexico.

Orange County is synonymous with the archkitsch of Disneyland, but there are other attractions. Laguna Beach, one of Southern California's favorite beach destinations, has secluded beaches, waterfront parks, and a lively arts community. The charming chapel and tranquil gardens of nearby Mission San Juan Capistrano, one of California's most beautiful, is a quiet oasis in this busy region.

The terrain, area, and climate in Orange and San Diego counties are similar to Los Angeles and Ventura, but with only half the number of people. Appropriately, Orange's coastline has been called the "Golf Coast" of California, with many of the courses sandwiched between a seemingly never-ending backdrop of mountains on one side and long sandy beaches and sparkling blue ocean on the other. Quality golf courses are so thick on the ground, the only problem is deciding where to go.

Imperial, Riverside, and San Bernardino: The lush coastal areas of the south are not all that's worth visiting. A couple of hours' drive east will reveal a stark landscape you will soon find beautiful. The Coachella Valley is home to the affluent resort cities, like Palm Springs, where golfing, swimming, and eating are the primary attractions. You can also take the aerial tramway up into the mountains or explore the Native American history of Indian Canyons. Joshua Tree National Park is a transition zone between high and low deserts and is famous for its distinctive Joshua trees and interesting rock outcrops. The Anza Borrego Desert has 10,000 years of human history and some of the most spectacular desert anywhere in California.

Sandpiper

Imperial and San Bernardino counties are almost entirely consumed by the Colorado Desert with fairly restricted golfing facilities and oppressive summer temperatures often rising to more than 130 degrees. In contrast half of Riverside County is in the desert, but the other half, including the golf mecca of Palm Springs, is very fertile. This is undoubtedly a playground for the rich and famous, and the standard of the golf courses that bring together the best of inland and desert designs reflect this everywhere you go. If you need to ask how much, don't even consider it.

RANCHO PARK

The Clubhouse

Food: The superbly retro, original 1950s diner (often used as a set for Hollywood films) serves up anything the hungry golfer demands, from granola and fruit breakfast plates to burgers, curries, omelets, and pancakes—all at reasonable prices.

Changing Rooms: Basic (think municipal swimming pool changing rooms) but clean. The complimentary golf magazines are a nice touch.

Ladies' Facilities: As a public course, Rancho Park doesn't restrict the movements of women; they have to queue up for tee times the same as men.

Interior and Exterior: A squat 1930s structure with a plain interior.

Background to the Course

Architect: William Johnson, manager of LA City Golf Courses, was responsible for the construction and development of the course, which opened in 1946. He was advised by the golf architect William Bell, whose courses include the Bel-Air, Riviera, and Los Angeles Country Clubs.

Type: Parkland.

Landscape: The course is far wider than you'd expect. This resolutely urban course has definite undulations, but the many tall trees don't obscure the towering Century City buildings next door or the surrounding million-dollar-plus houses.

Course Facts:

• The teenage Jack Nicklaus played here during his early career, finishing his game twenty-one shots shy of the winner.

• The course has experienced its fair share of disasters in its history, with an oil spill and a plane crash.

• It's the only American course to have hosted all three major tournaments.

• During his election campaign in 2000, former president Bill Clinton dropped in for a quick round. He's the only person to have been afforded special treatment and not made to wait his turn. There's a plaque commemorating the event outside the clubhouse.

• O. J. Simpson was famously booed off this course while he was on trial for murder.

• The annual Police Celebrity Golf Tournament is held here every May, when Hollywood stars and the Los Angeles Police Department join forces to raise money for charity. Past participants include Joe Pesci, Jack Nicholson, Martin Sheen, Jackie Chan, and Dennis Hopper.

• The killer hole is the eighteenth. When the LA Open was held here, the legendary Arnold Palmer made 12; he hit two balls into the driving range on the right and two into the street on the left trying to reach the green in two. There's even a plaque commemorating it!

Playing the Course

Rancho Park is an absolute phenomenon, facilitating up to 140,000 rounds a year. With so much traffic this course is in surprisingly good condition. On certain holes there are alternative greens to give the grass some respite, but generally the course copes remarkably well. Given its location, right in the middle of Los Angeles, it is very attractive, with generous well-tended fairways and undulating but true running greens.

Score Card

Address: Rancho Park, 10460 West Pico Boulevard, Los Angeles, CA 90064-2342, USA
Phone: +1 (310) 838–7373
Course and Length: Eighteen holes, par 71, 6,300 yards.
Dress Code: Usual golf apparel.
Tee Times: Course opens one hour before sunrise, with tee times at sunrise, and closes at sunset. A reduced "twilight" rate applies approximately three-and-a-half hours before sunset. It is reduced again at "super twilight," two hours before sunset. Tee times are set at six-minute intervals for foursomes only. Golfers are allowed to tee off on the back nine during the first hour each day. Holders of an LA city golf card are allowed to call seven days in advance to make reservations.
Handicap: No certificate required.
Green Fees: $22 on weekdays.
Other Costs: Electric golf carts are $24.00, club rentals $20.00, and Callaway Clubs $40.00 with driving range balls $5.00.
Facilities: Putting green, driving range, and clubhouse with restaurant with original 1950s fittings.
Location: Sandwiched in between two of Los Angeles's most exclusive golf clubs, the Riviera and the Hillcrest Club, in the heart of Hollywood.

Ian's Opinion

Rancho is a public course that claims to be the busiest in the world, with tee times happening every six minutes. This course is open 365 days a year from sunup to sundown. There is no tee time booking available for visitors, so people (including film stars from the Fox Studios across the road) start queuing up here at 6:00 A.M. The major downside is that it's not uncommon to have to wait up to four hours for a round during peak periods. Despite its overcrowding Rancho offers extremely high standards of golfing within well-maintained grounds. The golf is of a similar standard to the nearby Hillcrest Country Club, which is, like many in Los Angeles, a private course where membership costs $100,000 a year. Playing Rancho will set you back a mere $22. What a bargain!

SANDPIPER

The Clubhouse

Food: The snack bar serves up typical golfers' fare, ranging from burgers and fries to bags of potato chips. The outdoor seating on the veranda affords fabulous views of the coast.

Changing Rooms: Standard amenities with lockers and towels.

Ladies' Facilities: Women are welcomed at Sandpiper, and their facilities are equal to men's.

Interior and Exterior: The clubhouse is a small modern building with a clean but plain interior and a small pro shop.

Background to the Course

Architect: William Bell (in 1972), who also designed Torrey Pines and the Bermuda Dunes Country Club.

Type: Seaside.

Landscape: This course feels like a mixture of several varieties rolled into one. The first few holes are pretty flat and wooded, but by the back nine the course has started to alter drastically in elevation, with more water hazards and stunning ocean views. You're playing among palm trees with almost half a mile of ocean frontage. Five of the fairways are only a stone's throw from the lovely beach.

Course Facts:

• Sandpiper hosts several professional tournaments, such as the PGA Tour Tournament Players Series, the LPGA Tour Santa Barbara Women's Open, and the prestigious final stage of the PGA Tour Qualifying.

• It's rated by *Golf Digest* as one of the top twenty-five public golf courses in America.

Playing the Holes

Signature Hole: The tee of Sandpiper's signature hole, the eleventh (174 yard, par 3), is some 100 feet higher than the green. Only a line of palm trees protects the naked green

11th Hole   174 Yards / Par 3
Stroke Index: 12

from a stunning beach. With bunkers left and right of the green, the tee shot has to be pinpoint accurate, which is not easy given its distractions: wind blowing from the sea and the constant din from the oil-pumping station situated only yards from the tee.

Best Golf Hole: Sandpiper's tenth (354 yards, par 4) follows a natural ridge away from the clubhouse and out toward the beach. The opening shot is tricky as the fairway has a sharp left-hand dogleg halfway down its length. A drive hit too far will run out of fairway on the right, plus the ground contours away sharply on both sides of the fairway on the approach to the green. If the green, which sits out on its own spit of land, is missed, the golfer can be left with a wedge shot of some 50-feet elevation to get back on.

Toughest Hole: The long thirteenth (532 yards, par 5) is a real test of accuracy and length for any player. The hole runs directly alongside the cliff tops, with spectacular views across the Pacific. The drive and second shot have to be long and accurate, but it is the third,

over an 80-foot-deep ravine to a small green perched precariously on the cliff's edge, which is the real test of nerves. Left of the main green is an alternative green that is used during maintenance or bad weather. If it's in play, an easier game is to aim your shot here to avoid playing over the deeper part of the ravine.

Playing the Course

Sandpiper really is one of the best public courses in California. Dramatic changes in elevation and the approaches to the spectacularly located greens make for a special game. If the wind is blowing, this course can extend from a test of accuracy to a full-blown endurance test. Golf carts are used, which most golfers will be thankful for around the tenth to fourteenth holes, where it seems to be all up hill and down dale. The greens are

good for a public course and in the summer can be quite fast.

Score Card

Address: Sandpiper, 7925 Hollister Avenue, Santa Barbara, CA 93117, USA
Phone: +1 (805) 968–1541
Web Site: www.sandpipergolf.com
Course and Lengths: Eighteen holes, 7,068 yards (black), 6,597 yards (silver), 5,701 yards (copper).

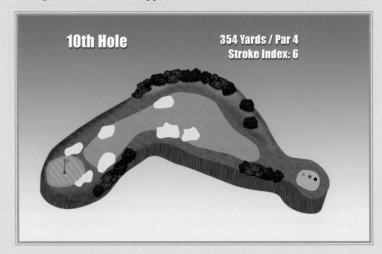

6597 Yards / Par 72

Sandpiper

Tee Times: From sunrise until the light gives out.

Handicap: No certificate required.

Green Fees: $55 to $130, depending on season, day, and time.

Other Costs: Golf cart rental is $15 a round, Titleist club rental is $50 per set.

Facilities: A clubhouse with restaurant and outdoor patio affords fabulous views of the course and coast. Small pro shop.

Location: Situated at the north end of Santa Barbara, easily reached via Highway 101 via the Winchester Canyon exit.

Dress Code: Soft spikes required, and no denim allowed. Men need collared shirt with sleeves, midthigh-length shorts. Ladies need a collared shirt with or without sleeves, as long as shoulders are covered, and shorts and skirts must be midthigh in length.

Ian's Opinion

Sandpiper is often regarded as the "poor man's Pebble Beach," an unjust reputation for this superbly situated seaside course set on a beautiful stretch of the central Californian coast just north of Santa Barbara. The opening nine holes aren't particularly spectacular, but the scenic tenth, eleventh, twelfth, and thirteenth run out alongside stunning beaches and craggy cliffs bordering the Pacific Ocean. This beautiful course is best played in the late afternoon, when you can witness the intense sun gradually setting over the ocean horizon.

THE GOLF RESORTS
PGA WEST, LA QUINTA

The Hotel

Food: There are three restaurants. Azur offers French cuisine with a modern twist, and the Adobe Grill serves up Mexican cuisine in the open air. Avoid Morgans—it's overpriced and lacks imagination.

Rooms: The original twenty casitas of the Hollywood Golden Age have now become 800 luxury rooms, suites, and villas. Many of them have their own private patios, and most of the rooms (which average 500 square feet) have king-size beds, working fireplaces, and large bathrooms with separate bath and shower.

Interior and Exterior: The hotel and its accommodations are Spanish hacienda in style, surrounded by genuinely beautiful grounds and a beautiful array of flowers, including delicately fragranced orange blossom. The lobby is elegantly styled with a display of photographs charting the rise of La Quinta as Palm Springs's preeminent resort.

Facilities: The hacienda-style spa is a substantial part of the resort. Golf and spa packages are offered. Specialities include the Just for Guys Facial, the Sports Pack Body Wrap (where warm mud is wrapped all over the upper body), the Golf Massage, and the Open-Air Celestial Shower. It has forty-one pools and fifty-three whirlpool spas dotted across the resort, and its twenty-three tennis courts have won accolades from *Tennis Magazine*.

Background to the PGA West Stadium Course

Architect: Pete Dye (1980), whose other courses include Tournament Players Club at Sawgrass, Florida, and the Punta Cana Golf Club in the Dominican Republic.

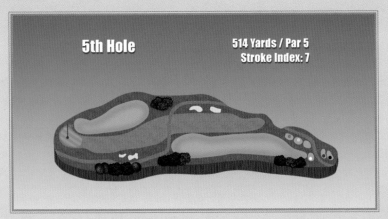

5th Hole

514 Yards / Par 5
Stroke Index: 7

Type: Parkland.
Landscape: The course is surrounded on two sides by the forbidding and rugged Santa Rosa Mountains. As with all the courses in Palm Springs, the greens *are* green (despite the heat), and the course is dotted with palm trees. Watch out for the fish in the water hazard at the seventeenth hole—if your ball goes in there, you'll never get it back!
Course Facts:
• Major tours played here include the Bob Hope Chrysler Classic, the Skins Game, and the PGA Tour Final Qualifying School.

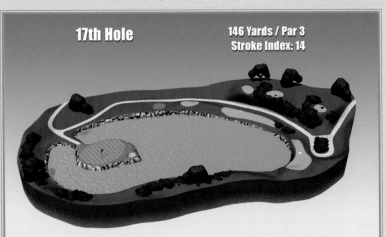

17th Hole

146 Yards / Par 3
Stroke Index: 14

• There are deep bunkers surrounding many of the greens that you need steps to get down. The bunker guarding the left of the sixteenth is the biggest at 18 feet. A former speaker of the House, Thomas P. "Tip" O'Neal, once took ten shots to get out of it.

• Alcatraz, the signature hole, built on an island green on top of rock, is very reminiscent of its namesake. Lee Trevino made Skins Game history here in 1987 with an ace. He hit a 6-iron 166 yards, turned, and hugged his caddy. A plaque beside the tee box commemorates his achievement.

Playing the Holes (PGA West Stadium Course)
Signature Hole: The seventeenth (146 yards, par 3) at the Stadium Course is known as one of the toughest holes in world golf. Called Alcatraz, the daunting green is built on a rocky island in the middle of a large lake. Designed by Pete Dye, it is short from tee to green but still manages to intimidate anyone who makes the climb up to the raised tee. The greens here are generally fast and quite firm to pitch onto, so hitting

and holding onto such a small target area is very difficult. The drop zone to the right-hand side of the lake still leaves a very tricky little chip for anyone unlucky enough to hit their tee shot into the lake.
Best Golf Hole: The long fifth (514 yards, par 5) has a drive across water, followed by a second shot that has to be threaded down the narrow fairway between two lakes with little margin for error. To hit the green in regulation will usually involve another shot over water onto a small, sloping putting area.
Toughest Hole: Voted by the PGA in 1986 to be among the eighteen toughest holes in America, the sixth (240 yards, par 3) certainly is a true test of club selection and shot accuracy. The small green is bordered by water at the front, left, and right, with a series of large mounds at the back of the green. The tee shot has a 230-yard carry over water. Any shot too long will require a chip onto a green that slopes away and back toward the lake.

Playing the PGA West Stadium Course
In the middle of summer the merciless heat can soar to temperatures of 120 degrees Fahrenheit, and golfers will need to cover up. All the golf carts are equipped with an ice-water container, which is fortunate, as there is not a lot of shade in the desert. The course was designed by Pete Dye to be one of the toughest tests in all golf, and it certainly succeeds. The first four holes are tight but not too threatening, and as you walk onto the fifth tee, you feel a premonition of things to come: large lakes and vast bunkers filled with fine sand punish

6739 Yards / Par 72

PGA WEST.
TPC STADIUM COURSE

any wayward shots. A round played to anywhere near your handicap really is a moral victory.

Score Card

Address: La Quinta Resort, 49-499 Eisenhower Drive, La Quinta, CA 92253, USA; PGA West TPC Stadium Course, 56-150 PGA Boulevard, La Quinta, CA 92253, USA

Phone: La Quinta Resort and Club: +1 (760) 564–4111; PGA West: +1 (760) 564–5729

Web Site: www.laquintaresort.com

Course Lengths: Five eighteen-hole, par-72 courses: La Quinta Resort Mountain Course (5,405 yards), La Quinta Resort Dunes (5,748 yards), PGA West Stadium (6,739 yards), PGA West Greg Norman (5,748 yards), and PGA West Jack Nicklaus Tournament Course (6,037 yards).

Dress Code: Appropriate golf attire, with no denim or metal-spiked shoes.

Tee Times: Start around half an hour after sunrise and end two hours before sunset, with seven tee times per hour on eight- to nine-minute intervals.

Handicap: No certificate required on any of the courses, but the starter will inquire as to the player's skill level and suggest the proper set of tees from which to play.

Green Fees: Rates range from $75 to $235, depending on the season. Resort guests receive substantial discounts as well as advanced booking privileges. Tee times are accepted three days before play. With an additional prebook fee, outside players may book up to thirty days in advance.

Packages: The most popular package is Best of the West, which includes breakfast and unlimited golf for one or two players on any of the five courses at La Quinta or PGA West. Packages change regularly.

Other Costs: The a la carte green fees and packages include shared cart and unlimited use of the practice facilities on day of play. A player can hit balls for three hours before play and another three hours afterward at no additional charge. Rental club choices are Callaway Hawkeye VFT or Callaway X-14 at $65 per set, including a sleeve of Callaway golf balls.

Facilities: The large clubhouse serves meals and drinks from 6:00 A.M. A world-class pro shop, with many items featuring the PGA West logo, will ship purchases to your address for a fee.

Location: La Quinta is 19 miles southeast of Palm Springs and 120 miles east of Los Angeles. Palm Springs Regional Airport is a thirty-minute drive and Ontario Airport a ninety-minute drive along Interstate 10.

Ian's Opinion

This tough nut is a qualifying course for American professionals on the PGA tour. If, like me, you're a medium- to high-handicap golfer, you will undoubtedly have difficulty getting onto the green of Alcatraz. Like many modern courses, particularly the one hundred-plus located in the Palm Springs area, the Stadium Course can be overly difficult to the novice, making for a frustrating golf experience. The sister courses designed by Jack Nicklaus and Greg Norman are equally challenging. Whatever your ability, the PGA's setting within the surrounding Santa Rosa Mountains is captivating.

RANCH COURSE, ALISAL

The Hotel

Food: The Alisal serves up what can only be described as hearty American fare with the accent on large steaks and fresh produce. The terrace at the restaurant overlooks the eighteenth green. Its breakfast diner is a popular eating spot for rich Solvang residents. For brunch try their mouthwatering hamburgers.

Rooms: The seventy-three guest rooms are fitted to reflect the ranch lifestyle with cozy furnishings and wood-burning fireplaces.

Interior and Exterior: The hotel buildings gel pleasantly with their surroundings. They're all wooden-fronted, gabled exteriors that perfectly conjure visions of the wild West. Inside it's inviting, with open timber roofs, stone-clad walls, and comfy, tasteful furnishings.

Facilities: A swimming pool, seven tennis courts, the Ranch Room, and a 175-seat main

dining room serving full-American breakfast and dinner daily. The Oak Room, an eighty-seat lounge and twelve-seat bar, serves nightly cocktails with live entertainment.

Activities

The Alisal dude ranch is a 10,000-acre working cattle ranch that's been in operation since 1843. It's been open as a retreat since 1946 for guests seeking outdoor pursuits like horseback riding, backpacking, fly fishing, and golfing at two championship golf courses—all with five-star hospitality and service. Since the Ranch is geared toward families, none of the activities require prior experience.

Horse Packing: The Alisal owns one hundred quarter horses, and there are 50 miles of trails to choose from through oak and sycamore trees along scenic canyons and verdant valleys.

Whatever your skill level or interest, you'll find something to suit you. One of the most popular activities is the morning trail ride out to the historic part of the ranch. At the Adobe Camp riders are treated to an outdoor pancake breakfast while being serenaded by a singing cowboy on guitar and a cowboy poet.

Cowboy Fun: The Alisal puts on lots of ranch-related activities and events. Rodeos are a popular tradition in which guests can take part in team penning, team sorting, pole bending, and steer branding. The wranglers will also put on quick-draw demonstrations and show off their rope skills. After all that activity you'll be treated to a hearty Western steak barbecue—and more country music than is good for anyone!

Other Activities: The Alisal has a private 100-acre lake in the foothills, which offers a

tranquil setting for guests to go fishing, boating, and kayaking. Other activities include tennis, bike riding, hiking, nature walks, and volleyball. The petting zoo is a family favorite. Guests can help look after ponies and bottle-feed goats, calves, sheep, and exotic miniature horses, as well as participate in egg gathering, grooming, and exercising the animals in the livestock enclosure.

Indoor Western evenings are another Alisal favorite. Guests are treated to an oak-barbecued dinner accompanied by country music and line dancing with instructors. Winemaker dinners are hosted by the Alisal's own vintners or some of the region's most eminent wineries, who serve their best reserves. You can also take organized tours of nearby wineries.

Solvang, a quaint Danish town, and the Santa Ynez Valley, famous for its winemaking.

Playing the Ranch Course

The Alisal Dude Ranch has two courses, the River and the Ranch. The latter is recommended if you only have time to play one. The Ranch Course has surprises in store. Following the line of the floor of a beautiful valley, it is home to hundreds of mature trees that form the major hazards on the course, along with *barrancas* (dried-out river beds), where you'll need to watch out for rattlesnakes if you lose your ball.

The Ranch is away from the coast and gives the impression of being shadier and cooler than many other courses in the area. Maybe it's because of all the trees, which force the golfer into exercising a certain amount of course management. This is neither a hilly course to play nor, with the ready availability of golf carts, strenuous—unless you find yourself fleeing from one of those pesky rattlesnakes.

THE ALISAL
Guest Ranch and Resort

6122 Yards / Par 72

Background to the Ranch Course

Architect: William Bell (in 1955), who also designed Torrey Pines and Sandpiper in California.
Type: Parkland.
Landscape: Although the heavily wooded course is hard to play, it's secluded and picturesque to walk. The sixth hole has good views of

Ian's Opinion

Although there's little water on the course, the main hazards are the beautiful oak trees, which are common throughout the valley and have matured in the five decades since the course was built. The back nine holes, particular the fourteenth through the eighteenth, are set in a spectacular and serene landscape. A peaceful round can be enjoyed here, but don't get too frustrated when the tight course punishes your wayward shots.

Score Card

Address: The Alisal Guest Ranch and Resort, 1054 Alisal Road, Solvang, CA 93463, USA

Phone: +1 (805) 688–6411

Web Site: www.alisal.com

Courses and Lengths: Two eighteen-hole, par-72 courses: Alisal Ranch, 6,551 yards (blue), 6,122 yards (white), and 5,752 yards (red); and River Course, 6,099 yards (white) and 5,710 yards (red).

Dress Code: Collared shirts, no blue jeans, and soft spikes only.

Tee Times: Tee times start as early as requested, generally 7:30 A.M., and can be scheduled as close as four minutes apart.

Handicap: No certificate required, but you have to be a ranch guest or a club member to play the Ranch Course. The River Course is open to the public.

Green Fees: $100 per round.

Packages: Golf Classic, Golf Getaway, Women's Golf Adventure, as well as packages geared toward ranch life, including Cowgirl and Mother-Daughter Cowgirl Boot camp.

Other Costs: Golf carts are $16 per rider.

Facilities: A driving range, putting green, practice bunker, clubhouse with restaurant and lounge, locker rooms with shower facilities, and a small but friendly pro shop.

Location: Thirty-five miles northwest of Santa Barbara just outside Solvang. It's halfway between San Francisco and San Diego and approximately a three-hour drive from Los Angeles along Highway 101.

OTHER RECOMMENDED GOLF COURSES IN SOUTHERN CALIFORNIA

1. Lost Canyons

Address: 3301 Lost Canyons Drive, Simi Valley, CA 93063, USA
Phone: +1 (805) 522–4653
Web Site: www.lostcanyons.com
Less than an hour from Los Angeles International Airport, Lost Canyons has two eighteen-hole, par-72 championship standard courses, Sky and Shadow, which are both open to the public and relativity cheap to play. Designed by Pete Dye and Fred Couples, the Scottish links-style courses, are both a great test of golf and a must to visit if you are in LA.

2. Westin Mission Hills Resort

Address: 71501 Dinah Shore Drive, Rancho Mirage, CA 92270, USA
Phone: +1 (760) 328–5955
Web Site: www.westin.com
Built into the desert on the outskirts of Palm Springs, Mission Hills has two magnificent eighteen-hole, par-70 championship courses. Between them they provide the total golf experience, contrasting peace and wildlife with mountains, waterfalls, and rock formations. This is the place to rub shoulders with the seriously rich. Cruise down Bob Hope Drive or Frank Sinatra Boulevard, then buy the logo golf shirt to wear when you get home.

3. Ocean Trails Golf Club

Address: 1 Ocean Trails Drive, Rancho Palos Verdes, CA 90275, USA
Phone: +1 (310) 265–5525
Web Site: www.oceantrails.com
Eighteen-hole Ocean Trails is built on some of the most desirable real estate in Southern California, the Palos Verdes peninsular by LA Harbor. In 1999, just before the par-71 course was about to open, a landslide took the eighteenth fairway into the ocean. The cost of putting it back in place was reportedly more than $20 million.

4. Oak Valley Golf Club

Address: 1888 Golf Club Drive, Beaumont, CA 92223, USA
Phone: +1 (951) 769–7200
Web Site: www.oakvalleygolf.com
Halfway between Los Angeles and the desert courses of Palm Springs, Oak Valley is not to be missed. Fewer than fifteen years old, the eighteen-hole, par-72 course is not expensive, the greens are faster than most desert courses, and the breathtaking backdrop of the San Gorgonio and San Jacinto Mountains comes highly recommended.

5. Black Gold Golf Club

Address: 17681 Lakeview Avenue, Yorba Linda, CA 92886, USA
Phone: +1 (714) 961–0060
Web Site: www.blackgoldgolf.com
Although the appropriately named Black Gold Golf Club is built on top of an oil field, it is actually very desirable. On the side of a hill overlooking Orange County and coastline, the par-72 course has eighteen very individual holes—a great test of golf with top-class facilities.

6. Pelican Hill Golf Club

Address: 22651 Pelican Hill Road South, Newport Coast, CA 92657, USA
Phone: +1 (949) 760–0707
Web Site: www.pelicanhill.com
Both eighteen-hole courses (par-71 Ocean North and par-70 Ocean South) at Pelican Hill consistently, and justifiably, get rave reviews from the golfing press, who consider them to be the best public golf facilities in Southern California. It isn't cheap, but worth every cent.

7. Reidy Creek Golf Course

Address: 2300 North Broadway, Escondido, CA 92026, USA
Phone: +1 (760) 740–2450
Web Site: www.jcgolf.com
Situated 20 miles from the ocean in northern San Diego County, par-54 Reidy Creek is a fun course to play. Its unusual feature is the eighteen equally challenging par-3 holes, which keep the feel of a championship course despite the omission of par 4s and 5s. Play here if you are still seeking your first hole-in-one—they had six in the first week it opened!

8. Landmark Golf Club

Address: 84000 Landmark Parkway, Indio, CA 92203, USA
Phone: +1 (760) 775–2000
Web Site: www.landmarkgc.com
At Landmark you will find two eighteen-hole, par-72 classic public courses that regularly host the best golfers in the world one day, then regular golfers the next. With holes called Jaws, Postage Stamp, and Brutal, no further description can do it justice. Green fees are priced less than $100 most of the time, and the online system for booking and payment of tee times couldn't be simpler.

9. Empire Lakes Golf Course

Address: 11015 Sixth Street, Rancho Cucamonga, CA 91730, USA
Phone: +1 (909) 481–6663
Web Site: www.empirelakes.com
Arnold Palmer's award-winning Empire Lakes is an eighteen-hole, par-72 championship course of stunning beauty. As you may expect, there is quite a lot of water and huge bunkers. A particularly pleasing feature is that it's relatively flat in contrast to the awesome 3-D backdrop of the San Gabriel Mountains.

10. LA COSTA RESORT AND SPA
Address: Costa del Mar Road, Carlsbad, CA 92009, USA
Phone: +1 (760) 438–9111
Web Site: www.lacosta.com
La Costa Resort, which describes itself as "the ultimate in rest and relaxation," offers far more than just a round of golf. The two fabulous PGA Championship courses are, like so many in this part of the world, terrific, but they are just part of a luxurious playground for the seriously rich. The eighteen-hole, par-72 Tournament Course uses the best holes from both the north and south courses.

11. TORREY PINES
Address: 11480 Torrey Pines Road, San Diego, CA 92037, USA
Phone: +1 (858) 552–1784
Web Site: www.torreypinesgolfcourse.com
No golf tour of Southern California would be complete without playing Torrey Pines. Both eighteen-hole, par-72 seaside courses are among the premier public golf facilities in the country and really worth the trip if you are not on a tight budget. Tiger Woods won the Optimist Junior World Tournament here when he was fifteen.

12. LA PURISIMA
Address: 3455 State Highway 246, Lompoc, CA 93436, USA
Phone: +1 (805) 735–8395
Web Site: www.lapurisimagolf.com
Although less fashionable, eighteen-hole La Purisima is one of California's top-ten championship public courses with all the style, quality, and beauty of its expensive neighbors. The par-72 course offers good value: Package deals include bed, breakfast, a round of golf, cart, and practice balls for less than $90 a head.

13. INDIAN PALMS COUNTRY CLUB
Address: 48-630 Monroe Street, Indio, CA 92201, USA
Phone: +1 (760) 347–2326
Web Site: www.indianpalms.com
Only half an hour's drive from Palm Springs International Airport, Indian Palms Country Club has three individual nine-hole, par-36 courses that are, for the average golfer, more forgiving than some of its more famous neighbors. The island

green on a short par 4 makes for a very challenging long-iron approach shot for the long handicapper.

14. SHERWOOD COUNTRY CLUB
Address: 320 West Stafford Road, Thousand Oaks, CA 91361, USA
Phone: +1 (805) 496–3036
Web Site: www.sherwoodcc.com
In comparison to its neighboring counties, Ventura seems to keep quiet about its great courses. The Jack Nicklaus–designed Sherwood Country Club is a very private members club with stunning views and many shots over waterfalls—the number depending on ability. Built in 1989, the eighteen-hole, par-72 course has received countless accolades from the golfing press. Worth a visit if you can find a member to take you.

15. DESERT FALLS COUNTRY CLUB
Address: 1111 Desert Falls Parkway, Palm Desert, CA 92211, USA
Phone: +1 (760) 340–4653
Web Site: www.desert-falls.com
A semiprivate eighteen-hole, par-72 course on the outskirts of Palm Springs, Desert Falls combines the deep bunkers of the traditional Scottish links course with the natural desert terrain and some very, very slick greens—one of which measures almost half an acre! Another unsung gem among many in this area.

16. OJAI VALLEY INN AND SPA
Address: 905 Country Club Road, Ojai, CA 93023, USA
Phone: +1 (805) 646–5511
Web Site: www.golfojai.com
A 1920s-built, eighteen-hole, par-70 resort course, Ojai Valley Inn and Spa has played host to numerous senior PGA Tour events. Expect beautiful views across the Ojai Valley, fast greens, and all the challenges of a mature course. Green fees are not cheap, but packages are offered out of season.

17. THE LINKS AT RIVERLAKES RANCH
Address: 5201 Riverlakes Drive, Bakersfield, CA 93312, USA
Phone: +1 (661) 587–5465
Web Site: www.riverlakesranchgolf.com
One of the few courses in Kern County, the eighteen-hole, par-72 links is set in fertile land at

the southern end of the San Joaquin Valley. Although close to the desert, there is a surprising amount of water. The man-made Friant-Kern canal is a constant companion, and there are a dozen or so lakes on the course. Unusual features include the cooling air misters around the clubhouse—a welcome respite in summer months.

18. CYPRESS RIDGE GOLF COURSE
Address: 780 Cypress Ridge Parkway, Arroyo Grande, CA 93420, USA
Phone: +1 (805) 474–7979
Web Site: www.cypressridge.com
Cypress Ridge is one of the new courses that have sprung up along the central Californian coastline. The eighteen-hole, par-72 course was designed to integrate existing wildlife and tree management and still make the course challenging. The result is an ecological success and some very interesting holes with great ocean views, but it would be better without the reality check of the ever-present real estate nearby.

19. DEL RIO COUNTRY CLUB
Address: 102 East Del Rio Road, Brawley, CA 92227, USA
Phone: +1 (619) 344–0085
Not to be confused with the Del Rio Golf and Country Club farther north in California, the eighteen-hole, par-70 Del Rio Country Club is a 1920s-designed, semiprivate course that was re-designed in 1978 by Robert Muir Graves. Most of Imperial County is desert and very, very hot in the summer, so Del Rio with its water hazards is a welcome oasis.

20. MONARCH BEACH GOLF LINKS
Address: 22 Monarch Beach Resort Drive North, Dana Point, CA 92629, USA
Phone: +1 (949) 240–8247
Web Site: www.monarchbeachgolf.com
Monarch Beach is a spectacular coastal course just south of LA. Revamped in recent years, this eighteen-hole, par-70 course is yet another Scottish-style links course that has traditionally hosted the Hyundai Team Challenge. This beautiful resort course is open to the public at all times (tournaments permitting), allowing players to follow in the footsteps of their golfing heroes.

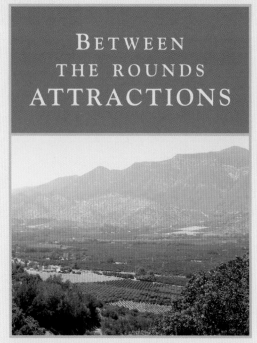

Near Santa Barbara

Gliding in the Santa Ynez Valley: Over the steep San Marco Pass from Santa Barbara is Santa Ynez Valley, a prime grape-growing area that makes for a good scenic drive. But even better, view it from the skies. For more than fifty years, gliding enthusiasts have been thrilled by the valley's favorable air currents and breathtaking views.

There are plenty of hang gliding and paragliding options. The best outfitter in the area is Windhaven Gliders, at the Santa Ynez Airport, where the expectation, like the dust, weighs heavily. Unless you have a gliding license, you will be paired with an instructor who will fly with you. You're towed by a sailplane for ten minutes and then released at the altitude you've chosen, which ranges from 2,500 to 5,820 feet—more than a mile high. The views are stunning, especially as you get above the Coastal Mountain Range and the silver surf of the ocean comes into view.

Address: Windhaven Glider Rides and Instruction, P.O. Box 625, Santa Ynez, CA 93460, USA

Phone: +1 (805) 688–2517

Hours: Wednesday through Sunday, 10:00 A.M. to 5:00 P.M.

Wine Tasting at the Rideau Vineyard: Grape growing and winemaking were first introduced to Santa Barbara County in the mission era. After a period of decline, the last three decades have seen a renaissance in the industry. There are now almost one hundred wineries in the county, primarily situated in the Santa Ynez and Santa Maria Valleys, operating a business worth $36 million annually.

Rideau Valley is home to the Historic El Alamo Pintado Adobe, which dates back to 1769 when it was on the famous stagecoach route that ran from Santa Ynez to Santa Barbara. It was then owned by the king of Spain and supervised by the Mission Santa Barbara. After changing hands over the centuries, it fell into disuse in the early twentieth century until it was rescued by Iris Rideau in 1998, who has made it into a stunning vineyard and wine-tasting venue.

Its most famous wines are Viognier and Tempranillo, as well as its award-winning Chateauneuf Cuvée, but you should come here as much for the atmosphere as the wines. The house has been exquisitely decorated with Edwardian furnishings, and the large wood-paneled kitchen turns out mouthwatering delicacies to sample with the wines. If you're lucky, you'll arrive on a day when the fabulously charming Iris is present.

Address: Rideau Vineyard, 1562 Alamo Pintado Road, Solvang, CA 93463, USA
Phone: +1 (805) 688–0717
Web Site: www.rideauvineyard.com
Hours: Vary; call for details.

Explore Historic Solvang: Solvang (meaning "sunny field") is a strangely Disneyesque town founded in 1911 by three Danish settlers who wanted to preserve their traditions for future generations by building a school to impart the basics of Danish culture. Although the Atterdag College has long gone, its spirit influenced the construction of the town. Today Solvang has a kitsch image with its windmills and wooded fronts, but its genuine appeal is its food. Try the Danish classic *rundstykker*, a savory hard roll often served with cheese and cold cuts of meat. The town is full of bakeries offering a range of authentic Danish pastries; seek out Solvang Bakery, renowned as the best in town. To learn about the history of Solvang and its early settlers, visit the Elverhoy Museum of History and Art. One weekend in mid-September Solvang celebrates Danish Days, with Danish folk dancing, music, parades, and food.

Explore Historic Mission Santa Ines: While in Santa Barbara County you must visit a mission. Solvang's Mission Santa Ines was established in 1804 at the height of missionary prosperity, number nineteen of California's twenty-one missions established by Franciscan priests from 1769 to 1823. The building has gone through several renovations over the years, but the trompe l'oeil green-marble trim

on the interior of the church walls is one of the best-preserved examples of missionary art. The museum houses many artifacts of the mission's past, including the largest and most valuable vestments from the fifteenth century to 1718; the emerald-green cope made from materials used at the court of France's Louis XIV is particularly beautiful. Relax in the courtyard, an oasis of tranquillity.

Address: Mission Santa Ines, 1706 Mission Street, Solvang, CA 93463, USA
Phone: +1 (805) 688–4815
Web Site: www.missionsantaines.org
Hours: Daily except Sunday, 10:00 A.M. to 5:00 P.M.

Near Los Angeles

The Standard Hotel: If you want to be at the center of the glitz and glamour of Sunset Boulevard, there's only one place to stay, and that's the Standard Hollywood Hotel. Owned by André Balaz, proprietor of the legendary Chateau Marmont (200 yards along the strip) and the stylish Mercer Hotel in New York, the Standard was conceived as an inexpensive yet innovative hotel for the sophisticated traveler. Its many quirky features have propelled it since its opening in 1999 to become one of the top places to stay in LA, as well as its coolest nightspot. These include the real-life model in a box behind the reception, blue Astroturf around the pool mowed by a performance artist gardener, a tattoo parlor in the barber's shop, and a twenty-four-hour restaurant. The rooms are minimal in a big-kid sort of way, so you'll find blow up sofas, beanbag chairs, CD players and a minibar stocked with must-have items like Oreos and Vaseline! If you just want to soak up the vibe, then make sure you rock up on a Wednesday, the day of the week when, according to local rituals, all the celebs turn up to party.

Address: The Standard Hotel, 8300 Sunset Boulevard, Hollywood, CA 90069, USA
Phone: +1 (323) 650–9090
Fax: +1 (323) 650–2820
Web Site: www.standardhotel.com

Star Spotting in Hollywood: There's no getting away from Hollywood in LA, so it comes as no surprise that the city's brimming with cheesy tourist attractions associated with it. You can't visit the Hollywood sign, but the best place to view it is to head up Beechwood Drive. A potent symbol of stardom, it's surprisingly been the jumping-off point for only one suicide: Lillian Millicent Entwhistle, who threw herself off the H one night in 1932 after RKO studios declined to pick up her option after seeing her first film. From there wander down the horribly crowded Hollywood Boulevard, and you'll pass by famous sights such as Grauman's Chinese

Theatre, where more than 150 of the glitterati have left their handprints on the sidewalk out the front, known as the Walk of Fame.

If that hasn't got you close enough to the stars, every street corner of Hollywood sells maps of the stars' homes in LA. Although they're often out of date and pretty inaccurate, they do give an excuse for nosing around the smarter parts of the city, and you may catch a glimpse of a famous face over the towering hedges and gates. If you're more interested in the legends of the Golden Age, head to the Hollywood Forever Cemetery, where you'll find mausoleums as grand as the houses the occupants once inhabited.

Sunbathing on Santa Monica Beach:
Santa Monica is of the most beautiful stretches of beach on the American continent. It's also one of the most famous, having made countless appearances in movies and TV shows (most, like *Three's Company*, having to do with blonde babes). Located just 13 miles north of downtown LA, this is where the Angelinos come to hang out and show off the body beautiful, making the most of the year-round good weather on this part of the Pacific Coast.

Santa Monica isn't all lounging about on sun-kissed sands. It's all about being seen and being part of the fitness-conscious recreation scene. The emphasis is on action here. Each year up to three million Angelinos and visitors bike, in-line skate, windboard, jog, or simply strut their stuff along the 22 miles of the

South Bay Bicycle Trail, which is 14 feet wide in most places with a smooth asphalt surface and a great view of the Pacific.

The focal point for fun in Santa Monica is the pier, with its shops, bars, and restaurants, as well as the carousels and roller-coasters of Pacific Park. Street performers keep the casual visitor and cafe crowds amused with impromptu performances all day and throughout the evening. Built in 1908, the Santa Monica Pier is the oldest pleasure pier on the West Coast of the United States.

Shopping in Rose Bowl Flea Market:
Dubbed "America's marketplace of unusual items," the Rose Bowl is one of the most famous flea markets in the United States and almost certainly the largest. The second Sunday of each month sees 20,000 shoppers flock to the parking lot of the Rose Bowl Stadium in Pasadena, about a twenty-minute drive from downtown LA, to storm the rows on the lookout for bargains. This is the offline version of eBay; with more than 2,200 vendors turning out for the occasion, you'll find any collectible you've been hankering after and much more besides. There are three main sections to the market: The outside perimeter of the stadium is the territory of craftspeople who spend weekdays fashioning trinkets, jewelry, and creative items and weekends selling them to artsy customers; casual vendors clearing out their attics do a swift trade in household junk and cast-off clothing; and antiques from every era (vintage

clothes and records, art, furniture, ornaments, toys, and knick knacks) are sold by vendors who have been coming from as far afield as Arizona and Utah for the last twenty years. Professional buyers and die-hard collectors come early to bag the best stuff, but as the day wears on, vendors are eager to offload their goods at bargain prices.

Address: Rose Bowl Flea Market, 1001 Rose Bowl Drive, Pasadena, CA 91103, USA

Hours: Second Sunday of the month, 9:00 A.M. to 4:30 P.M. (last ticket entry 3:00 P.M.)

Admission: $7.00 adults, free for those younger than age 12.

Near Palm Springs

The Twin Palms Estate: If you want to relive the high life of the Hollywood glitterati, there's no better way than renting the Twin Palms Estate in Palm Springs, home to legendary singer Frank Sinatra. Following its success as a celebrity hideaway in the 1920s, Palm Springs was remade as the permanent home of the super rich by the likes of Sinatra and Bob Hope. Just around the corner from residences once owned by Al Jolson, Jack Benny, and Cary Grant, Twin Palms was host to some of the valley's most glamorous parties and many of Hollywood's biggest stars, including Joan Crawford, Phil Silvers, and even the reclusive Greta Garbo.

The house itself is a palace of midcentury modernism, designed by the respected architect Stewart Williams for Sinatra and his first wife. The property is full of clean lines and space.

Perhaps its greatest feature is the piano-shaped pool, visible through the massive glass windows of the lounge; when the beams of light from the setting sun pass through the openings of the portico, a shadow is cast on the pool, creating the look of piano keys. The property comes complete with Frank's original state-of-the-art sound system.

Reservations: Phone: +1 (202) 659–7931, or through the Web site: www.timeandplace homes.com

Cost: $6,752 for three nights or $15,000 for the week.

Aerial Tramway Tour Up the San Jacinto Mountains: A must-do activity in Palm Springs is a cable-car trip climbing more than a mile vertically into the lofty San Jacinto Mountains. The brainchild of Francis Crocker, manager of the California Electric Power Company, it opened in 1963 after thirty years of planning and has since transported twelve million riders. The trip takes a mere fourteen minutes to ascend, but you have to stand throughout the journey. On the ascent you'll get wonderful views of the Chino Canyon and San Jacinto Mountains from the front of the car, with the Sonoran Desert below from the rear. It's an amazing experience as you pass through different altitude and terrains: the dusty desert base to the valley station, great for picnics; the mountain station, which has a cafe, cocktail lounge, observation area, and theater showing a film about the history of the tramway; and the San Jacinto

Wilderness State Park, a pine forest at the summit, which you'll need a permit to explore. You can cross-country ski here from December to April, snow levels permitting, or take a mule ride or foot trek on the 54 miles of hiking trails with five campgrounds. It can be more than 30 degrees cooler at the top than the ground, so bring a sweater.

Hours: 10:00 A.M. (8:00 A.M. weekends and holidays) until 8:00 P.M. Ascend until 9:00 P.M. during daylight savings hours. The train closes for maintenance during parts of either August or September.

Admission: $20.80 adults, $13.80 children, $18.80 seniors. Or try a "ride n' dine" buffet deal after 4:00 P.M. for $27.80 adults, $18.80 children.

Desert Tour of Joshua Tree National Park: Situated between Los Angeles and Las Vegas, Joshua Tree National Park is classic California desert territory. It was through this region that Mormon settlers came west, searching for new land. Here you will get a sense of the desolation and aridity of Southern California.

The park encompasses 800,000 square acres, most of which is 4,000 feet above sea level. A desert tour by jeep can be organized from Palm Springs. You'll need your own wheels to access most parts of it, but only by getting out of your four-wheel drive and taking a hike into the hot tundra will you see the amazing plants and wildlife. The vegetation is mostly cactus, some growing more than 20 feet tall,

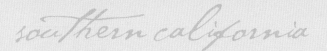

and you'll also find the indigenous *Yucca brevifolia*—the Joshua tree. Not many animals call the salt lakes and dry scrub home, but lizards, gila monsters, and other reptiles survive, as well as the cartoonlike coyote and roadrunner. The most popular hike spot is the Lost Palm Oasis in the Eagle Mountains to the south of the park. Visiting in the summer from June to September, when temperatures can soar to above 100 degrees, is best avoided, particularly as the visitor centers will be closed. Spring is a great time to witness the desert blooms. Whenever you visit, bring plenty of water.

The oddest monument in Joshua Tree is Salvation Mountain, which a local man named Leonard King began building in 1967. Believing he had been directed by God, Leonard began constructing the psychedelic, colorful biblical paintings on the mountain, which can be seen from miles around.

Skiing in Big Bear, San Bernadino Mountains: Big Bear Lake, surrounded by the San Bernardino National Forest, is a superb outdoor vacation destination with lots of family-friendly activities like hiking the Pacific Crest Train, boating and water sports, horse and pony rides, trout fishing, mountain biking (you can take your bike on the chairlift to Snow Summit for $7.00) and night-time entertainment.

Downhill skiing is a specialty on the 8,000-foot ridge on the lake's south side.

The ski season runs from December until the snow melts, usually late March or April, with snowmaking machines pumping extra snow when necessary. Good skiing hours are limited from 9:00 A.M. until midday, when the snows turn to sludge and ice. But what Big Bear lacks in powder, it makes up for with great weather—the town has 300 days of sunshine per year. The main skiing mountains are Snow Summit and Bear Mountain. Bear Mountain is a favorite with locals for its steep upper runs and is also considered to be a place *par excellence* for both beginner and professional snowboarding on the park. Beginner skiers could also try Snow Forest or Snow Valley, a little out of town. Both mountains have a dozen lifts, which cost from $40 a day, with ski and lodge packages starting from $70 a night midweek. Ski equipment can be rented from the base lodge from $10 a day. Also try cross-country skiing through the pines and snowshoeing the backwoods. Children will love the alpine slide, an exhilarating and authentic bobsled ride on two quarter-mile-long tracks.

From April to November you can enjoy golf on the nine-hole Bear Mountain Course, or take the whole family for a eighteen-hole round of miniature golf at the Magic Mountain, complete with breaking greens, water hazards, and attractive landscaping.

INDEX

Abiding Club Golf Society, 136
Abu Dhabi Airport Golf Club, 102
Abu Dhabi Golf and Equestrian Club, 102
Abu Dhabi Golf Club (National and Garden
    Courses), 102
Academia Hills Country Club, 137
Al Ain Golf Club, 102
Al Badia Golf Resort, 102
Appi Kogen, 136
Arabella Golf Club, 66
Arabian Ranches Golf Club, 102
Atsugi Kokusai Country Club, 137

Ballater Golf Course, 26
Belle View Nagao Golf Club, 137
Belleisle Golf Course, 26
Black Gold Golf Club, 174
Blairgowrie Golf Club, 26
Bloemfontein Golf Club, 69
Boat of Garten Golf Club, 26
British Garden Club, 137
Bruntsfield Links Golfing Society, 26

California
    Black Gold Golf Club, 174
    Cypress Ridge Golf Course, 175
    Del Rio Country Club, 175
    Desert Falls Country Club, 175
    Empire Lakes Golf Course, 174
    Indian Palms Country Club, 175
    La Purisima, 175
    Landmark Golf Club, 174
    Links at Riverlakes Ranch, The, 175
    Lost Canyons, 174
    Monarch Beach Golf Links, 175
    Oak Valley Golf Club, 174
    Ocean Trails Golf Club, 174
    Ojai Valley Inn and Spa, 175
    Pelican Hill Golf Club, 174
    PGA West Stadium Course, 164–69

Ranch Course (Alisal Guest Ranch and Resort,
    170–73
Rancho Park, 156–59
Reidy Creek Golf Course, 174
Sandpiper, 160–63
Sherwood Country Club, 175
Torrey Pines, 175
Tournament Course (La Costa Resort and Spa), 175
Westin Mission Hills Resort, 174
Carnegie Club, The, 27
Carnoustie Golf Links, 26
Clovelly Country Club, 66
Crail Golfing Society, 27
Cruden Bay Golf Club, 27
Cypress Ridge Golf Course, 175

Del Rio Country Club, 175
Desert Falls Country Club, 175
Doha Golf Club, 103
Downfield Golf Course, 27
Dubai Country Club, 98–101
Dubai Creek Golf and Yacht Club, 88–91
Durban Country Club, 67

East London Golf Club, 66
Emirates Golf Club, 92–97
Empire Lakes Golf Course, 174
Erinvale Golf Club, 66

Fancourt Hotel and Country Club Estate, 66
Fish River Sun Hotel and Country Club, 67
Fuji Course (Kawana Golf Resort), 128–31

Gary Player Course (Sun City Resort), 54–59
Glendower Golf Club, 69
Gleneagles King's Course, 14–17
Golf House Club Elie, 26
Gotemba Golf Club, 124–27
Gullane Golf Club, 27

Haggs Castle Golf Club, 27
Hans Merensky Estate and Golf Club, 60–65
Houghton Golf Club, 69
Humewood Golf Club, 67
Ichihara Korakuen Golf and Sports, 136
Ichinomiya Country Club, 137
Indian Palms Country Club, 175
Ishioka Golf Club, 122–23

Japan
    Abiding Club Golf Society, 136
    Academia Hills Country Club, 137
    Appi Kogen, 136
    Atsugi Kokusai Country Club, 137
    Belle View Nagao Golf Club, 137
    British Garden Club, 137
    Fuji Course (Kawana Golf Resort), 128–31
    Gotemba Golf Club, 124–27
    Ichihara Korakuen Golf and Sports, 136
    Ichinomiya Country Club, 137
    Ishioka Golf Club, 122–23
    Kago Saka Golf Club, 137
    Kasumigaura Country Club, 137
    Kochi Kuroshiro Country Club, 136
    Mishima Country Club, 137
    Mission Hills Country Club, 137
    Nakasu Golf Club, 137
    Oak Hills Country Club, 136
    Phoenix Country Club Course, 132–35
    Riverside Pheonix Golf Club, 136
    Sun Members Country Club, 136
    Tokuyama Country Club, 136
    Windsor Park, 137
Jebel Ali Golf Resort and Spa, 102

Kago Saka Golf Club, 137
Kasumigaura Country Club, 137
Kimberley Golf Club, 69
Kochi Kuroshiro Country Club, 136

La Purisima, 175
Landmark Golf Club, 174
Leopard Creek Golf Club, 69
Links at Riverlakes Ranch, The, 175
Lost Canyons, 174
Lundin Ladies Golf Club, 24–25

Milnerton Golf Club, 66
Mishima Country Club, 137
Mission Hills Country Club, 137
Monarch Beach Golf Links, 175
Montgomerie Dubai, The, 102
Muirfield Golf Club, 27
Musselburgh Old Course, 22–23

Nad Al Sheba Club, 86–87
Nakasu Golf Club, 137
North Berwick Golf Club, 26

Oak Hills Country Club, 136
Oak Valley Golf Club, 174
Ocean Trails Golf Club, 174
Ojai Valley Inn and Spa, 175

Pearl Valley, 46–49
Pelican Hill Golf Club, 174
PGA West Stadium Course, 164–69
Pheonix Country Club Course, 132–35
Pietersburg Golf Club, 69
Prince's Grant Golf Club, 68

Ranch Course (Alisal Guest Ranch and Resort, 170–73
Rancho Park, 156–59
Reidy Creek Golf Course, 174
Riffa Golf Club, 103
Riverside Phoenix Golf Club, 136
Roxburghe Golf Course, The, 27
Royal Aberdeen Golf Course, 26
Royal Cape Golf Club, 66
Royal Dornoch Golf Club, 10–13
Royal Troon, 27

Sandpiper, 160–63
Scotland
    Ballater Golf Course, 26
    Belleisle Golf Course, 26
    Blairgowrie Golf Club, 26
    Boat of Garten Golf Club, 26
    Bruntsfield Links Golfing Society, 26
    Carnegie Club, The, 27
    Carnoustie Golf Links, 26
    Crail Golfing Society, 27
    Cruden Bay Golf Club, 27
    Downfield Golf Course, 27
    Gleneagles King's Course, 14–17
    Golf House Club Elie, 26
    Gullane Golf Club, 27
    Haggs Castle Golf Club, 27
    Lundin Ladies Golf Club, 24–25
    Muirfield Golf Club, 27
    Musselburgh Old Course, 22–23
    North Berwick Golf Club, 26
    Roxburghe Golf Course, The, 27
    Royal Aberdeen Golf Courses
    Royal Dornoch Golf Club, 10–13
    Royal Troon, 27
    Southerness Golf Club, 27
    St. Andrews Old Course, 18–21
    Westin Turnberry Resort Golf Courses, The, 26
Sherwood Country Club, 175
Sishen Golf Club, 69
South Africa
    Arabella Golf Club, 66
    Bloemfontein Golf Club, 69
    Clovelly Country Club, 66
    Durban Country Club, 67
    East London Golf Club, 66
    Erinvale Golf Club, 66
    Fancourt Hotel and Country Club Estate, 66
    Fish River Sun Hotel and Country Club, 67
    Gary Player Course (Sun City Resort), 54–59
    Glendower Golf Club, 69
    Hans Merensky Estate and Golf Club, 60–65
    Houghton Golf Club, 69
    Humewood Golf Club, 67

Kimberley Golf Club, 69
    Leopard Creek Golf Club, 69
    Milnerton Golf Club, 66
    Pearl Valley, 46–49
    Pietersburg Golf Club, 69
    Prince's Grant Golf Club, 68
    Royal Cape Golf Club, 66
    Sishen Golf Club, 69
    Soweto Country Club, 50–53
    Zimbali Country Club, 68
Southerness Golf Club, 27
Soweto Country Club, 50–53
St. Andrews Old Course, 18–21
Sun Members Country Club, 136

Tokuyama Country Club, 136
Torrey Pines, 175
Tournament Course (La Costa Resort and Spa), 175
Tower Links Golf Club, 103
United Arab Emirates
    Abu Dhabi Airport Golf Club, 102
    Abu Dhabi Golf and Equestrian Club, 102
    Abu Dhabi Golf Club (National and Garden Courses), 102
    Al Ain Golf Club, 102
    Al Badia Golf Resort, 102
    Arabian Ranches Golf Club, 102
    Doha Golf Club, 103
    Dubai Country Club, 98–101
    Dubai Creek Golf and Yacht Club, 88–91
    Emirates Golf Club, 92–97
    Jebel Ali Golf Resort and Spa, 102
    Montgomerie Dubai, The, 102
    Nad Al Sheba Club, 86–87
    Riffa Golf Club, 103
    Tower Links Golf Club, 103

Westin Mission Hills Resort, 174
Westin Turnberry Resort Golf Courses, The, 26
Windsor Park, 137

Zimbali Country Club, 68

ABOUT PILOT PRODUCTIONS

Ian Cross, presenter and golf photographer
Ian Cross is a recent convert to the pleasures of golf; he took up the game in 1994 upon turning forty years old and soon became a keen aficionado of the sport. He believes it's a perfect recreation for men of his age as it's not too strenuous, it's very healthy, and, for the busy executive, it's good for stress-busting—although Ian has discovered that the game comes with its own stresses. He's occasionally lost his composure and taken it out on the greens. While filming for *Adventure Golf* on the King's Course at Gleneagles, he met his downfall at Whaup's Nest, the eighth, where he took eighteen shots to get out of a bunker. Bunkers are his most feared golf hazard.

Ian was born in Melbourne, Australia, and grew up in Canberra, where he was a junior tennis and cricket champ. He began his professional careerthere as a cadet journalist for the *Canberra Times*. Ian's media career in newspapers, radio, and television spans thirty years and three continents: the United States, his native Australia, and the UK, where he now lives with his wife and two children. For three years he was European correspondent for ABC-TV, then in 1988 he produced the *Beyond Tomorrow* science series for the Fox Network in the United States.

When he's not on the course, Ian is the managing director of Pilot Productions, the television company he founded in 1991. Specializing in factual programming—travel in particular—Ian has been the executive producer of more than 250 hours of quality television including eleven series of the multi-award-winning adventure travel series *Globe Trekker*, the most watched travel program in the world; the food and travel series *Planet Food*; and *Adventure Golf*. The company now has offices in Los Angeles, London, and Singapore. After years spent sending film crews and presenters to some of the most exotic and intrepid places in the world, he thought it was about time he joined them on the road.

Ian is a handicap 18 golfer who leads a nomadic-cum-jet-setting golfing life. He has no home club but enjoys playing the game internationally, particularly in northern France and links golf in Scotland and Ireland. During the first season of filming for *Adventure Golf*, Ian experienced some of the greatest golf courses in the world in Scotland, Dubai, Southern California, Japan, South Africa, and Florida. He was bowled over by the high-tech and futuristic golf experience in Japan, in particular the Gotemba Course overlooking Mount Fuji. His dream trip would be to travel the four corners of the world, Phileas Fogg inspired, to play the world's best golf courses and explore the most exotic regions at a leisurely pace, notably Hawaii, Bali, and the little explored courses of Latin America. He enjoys international travel for work and pleasure and regularly jets off to his favorite spots in the Caribbean and the Mediterranean, as well as skiing trips and city breaks in Paris and New York.

Bob Baker, golf author A bank manager for far too long, happily fully recovered and now a director of Pilot Film and Television Productions, Bob has been playing golf for almost forty years. At his home club, Northwood, near London, he plays off a handicap of 16. Having played many championship courses in the UK, Europe, and Africa, he is ideally qualified as an *Adventure Golf* expert. Bob proudly counts himself among the 95 percent of golfers who have totally unorthodox swings and can't putt to save their lives—but he knows what makes golf fun to play and why the hackers always come back for more.

Bennett Galloway, golf author, Japan
Bennett Galloway is the director of golf for Gotemba Golf Club in Japan and a teaching professional. Originally from Victoria, Canada, he has worked on eight golf courses in Japan over fifteen years and has dedicated himself to promoting the Japanese golf industry to the world. "Golf is like an old friend who kicks you when you're down, smiles with you when you're up, upon whom you can always rely."

Peter Wisdom, playing technique expert
Peter Wisdom is the director of the *Adventure Golf* television series. Born in Deal, Kent, he started playing golf in the 1970s on the links courses of Deal (Royal Cinque Ports) and Sandwich (Royal St. George's). Peter now lives in London, and his home course is Woodcote Park in Surrey.

Peter started work in television making the tea at the BBC in 1976 and has been directing travel and entertainment shows since 1989. He has directed *This Is Your Life*, the travel series *Wish You Were Here*, an advertisement for American Express, and pop promos for George Harrison. As a freelance director, Peter says, "The only chance I have to lower my handicap is when there is no work around. That is why it is still 14!"

Kate Griffiths, Nigel Hildrich, Richard Cooke, and Susi O'Neill for providing additional travel and golf course texts. Edited and managed for Pilot Productions by Susi O'Neill.

Pilot Film and Television Productions
Since 1991, Pilot Film and Television Productions has produced documentary series for broadcasters in more than forty countries and won more than thirty international awards.

shows, multimedia and community features, and an online shop.

Golf photography by Ian Cross. Selected images of Dubai Creek Golf Course courtesy of Christopher May, Dubai Creek Golf & Yacht Club. Selected images of Gotemba Golf Course courtesy of Bennett Galloway. Selected photographs of Dubai copyright Steve Davey 2004. All other photography and graphics and

The Adventure Golf *crew,* South Africa

Steve Davey, photographer, United Arab Emirates Steve Davey is an international photographer, travel writer, and a founding partner of travel publisher La Belle Aurore. His work has been published in newspapers and magazines around the world. He is the author/photographer of *Unforgettable Places to See Before You Die*, published in 2003 by BBC books. www.stevedavey.com

Contributing authors
Special thanks to Dave Lowe, Electra Gilles,

Pilot has released the highly acclaimed travel series *Globe Trekker* (which airs in some countries as *Pilot Guides*) on home video and DVD, and the original music from the series on seven CDs. Based in London, with offices in Los Angeles and Singapore, Pilot Productions is developing, producing, and distributing a diverse range of new programming of history, leisure, and food-based series. The company's popular adventure travel portal www.pilot guides.com provides off-the-beaten-track travel guides, further information on its travel

all text copyright Pilot Film and Television Productions Ltd. 2005.

Contact information: Publications Manager, Pilot Film and Television Productions Ltd., The Old Studio, 18 Middle Row, London W10 5AT, UK.
E-mail: info@pilot.co.uk
Official Web site: www.adventuregolftv.com

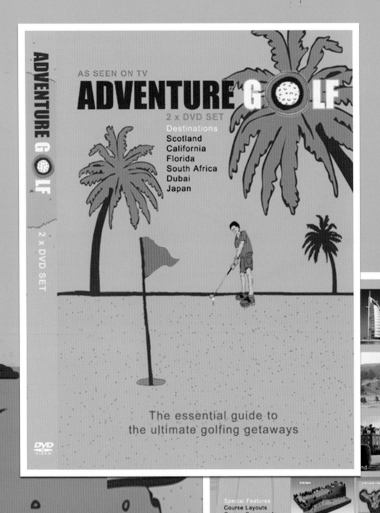